Dee Dee Glass was born in Chicago in 1948. She has been making films and television programmes in Britain since 1973, when she produced and directed a documentary about residents of the UK's first refuge for battered women. Since then she has made documentaries, current affairs programmes, dramas and factual series for the BBC, ITV and Channel 4. Many have focused on sexual violence, prostitution, child abuse, women's personal safety and the policing of domestic violence. She has worked as an adviser to leading academics and women's organisations dealing with sexual violence, and has participated in the training of the police and other professional and statutory agencies. The question everyone asks is – Why don't women leave? *'All My Fault'* is her answer.

D0532583

'All My Fault'

Why women don't leave abusive men

Dee Dee Glass

Published by VIRAGO PRESS Limited April 1995
20 Vauxhall Bridge Road, London SW1V 2SA

A CIP catalogue record for this book is available from the British Library

Typeset by
Keystroke, Jacaranda Lodge, Wolverhampton

Printed and bound in Great Britain by
Cox & Wyman Ltd, Reading Berkshire

'*All My Fault*' is dedicated to:
my mother, Lorraine Sampson Soudek,
who showed me by her brave example, many years ago,
that it is, after all, possible to leave an abusive man.

the memory of Kathleen Locke,
who inspired everyone she knew with her wisdom
and her unstinting love.

Jean Irvine,
one of the participant interviewees, who died while it
was being written. For her courage in speaking out
about all the abuse she experienced, I hope this
book will serve as a permanent tribute.

Contents

Acknowledgements

So many women gave me so much help – their time, ideas, advice, newspaper cuttings, books, contacts and friendship. I was never short of offers of support. Every woman I spoke to seemed to take a personal interest in the book.

Thanks must begin with Norma Moriceau, the first person I told about wanting to write this book, who instantly gave me her blessing, the title and her support ever since.

My profound admiration goes to my agent, Elaine Steel, who always showed tenacity and cool under fire.

My gratitude to the experts who never lose sight of their roots: the Child and Woman Abuse Studies Unit of North London University for always responding to my impossible requests with help; Robyn Holder for her unfailing generosity and her library; the Women's Aid Federations of England (WAFE) (especially Caroline McKinlay) and Scotland, as well as all the Women's Aid refuges and social service departments who kept me in touch with work on the frontline; Linda Macleod in Ottawa, Canada, who didn't know me from Eve when I rang her on WAFE's advice, but who gave me the benefit of her wide knowledge and plugged me into her formidable network – especially to Sharon Swann; to Professor Rebecca Dobash and Dr Russell Dobash for always finding the time, as well as for being a beacon of sanity and good humour.

I am grateful to the National Association of Local Government Women's Committees, Solicitors' Family Law Association and Victim Support for allowing me to attend their conferences and to ask awkward questions.

For over twenty years I have relied on the silent support of policewomen and others in the criminal justice system whose need to remain anonymous speaks volumes about how far we have yet to go in making it safe for them to talk openly about domestic violence.

My heartfelt thanks to those who helped find participants: Leslie Brown in Aberdeen and everyone at Surrey Women's Aid whom I never met, but who went out of their way to help; Southall Black Sisters for setting an example of unwavering dedication; and to my friends Wilma Bulmer, Sonia Joseph and Maxine Schultze who made it possible for such a wide range of voices to be heard.

For their patience, friendship and critical support, sincere thanks to Nicolette Bolgar, Kathy Hobdell (who also helped find participants and made an invaluable contribution to the advice section at the end of the book), Donatella Moores, Hayley Murt and Stephen Oxley.

I will always be grateful to Dr Reva Berstock for her wisdom and insight.

I owe the most enormous, unrepayable debt to Dr Susan Blake, Catherine Doran (who also helped find participants), Jane Mills, Nancy Platt, Dr Betsy Stanko, Joan Vis and Amrit Wilson who were always there – day and night – with their love, support, expertise and, most importantly, constructive criticism when the right words failed me.

But my greatest thanks go to the twenty-two participant interviewees for giving so completely and unselfishly of themselves that we might all lead lives free from abuse.

Participants

Alabee is mixed-race Asian, in her mid thirties, and lives in London where she works in a Women's Aid refuge. She is working class, the mother of one child, and is heterosexual.

Anne is middle class and white. She is in her late forties, is heterosexual and has three children. Anne lives in rural England and works with horses.

Anita lives in London, has no children, is heterosexual and works in residential housing management. She is in her mid forties, middle class and white.

Barbara is working class and white. She is in her late thirties, lives in Aberdeen, has two children, is bisexual and has a job as a community centre worker.

Candace is African–Caribbean in her mid thirties. She lives in London, has three children, is heterosexual, working class and is employed in a Women's Aid refuge.

Carmina is middle class and in her early forties. She is heterosexual, African–Caribbean, lives in Aberdeen, has two children and is a community worker.

Christine lives in Lancashire and has five children. She is working class, white and in her early fifties. Christine has a job in a women's refuge and is heterosexual.

Daksha is middle class and Asian. She is in her late thirties, lives in London, has two children, is heterosexual and is a volunteer worker at Southall Black Sisters, a black women's advice centre.

Eleanor works in a women's refuge in Lancashire where she lives. She is working class, white, in her late forties, has seven children, and is heterosexual.

Elizabeth is middle class and white. She is in her late thirties, lives in London, and has two children. Elizabeth is a lesbian and works in an advice centre.

Elsa lives in London where she works as a nurse. She is working class, African–Caribbean and in her mid fifties. Elsa has three children and is heterosexual.

Jackie is a working-class, white heterosexual. She is in her late thirties and lives in Manchester where she is an unemployed care worker.

Janie has three children and is a heterosexual African–Caribbean. She is in her mid thirties, is working class and lives in Manchester where she is a mature student.

Jean died while this book was being written. She was working class, white, in her late forties and lived in Aberdeen where she worked as a cleaner. Jean had no children and was a lesbian.

Kiranjit Ahluwalia was imprisoned for murdering her husband. She became well known as a result of the successful campaign on her behalf led by Southall Black Sisters. Kiranjit is in her late thirties, is middle class and Asian. She lives in London, has two children, is heterosexual and volunteers at Southall Black Sisters' advice centre.

Mary is working class and white. She is in her mid thirties, lives in London, has one child, is heterosexual and works in a Women's Aid refuge.

Marian works as a primary school teacher and is in her mid forties. She is upper working class, lives in London, has one child, is heterosexual and white.

Molly is white and in her early thirties. She lives in the Home Counties, has one child, is working class, heterosexual and has a job in office administration.

Saroj is heterosexual and working class. She is Asian, in her late twenties, lives in London, has no children and is a volunteer worker at Southall Black Sisters' advice centre.

Sally has one child, is middle class and white. She is in her early forties, lives in London, is heterosexual and works as a university lecturer.

Samantha is a police sergeant and lives in a southern English market town. She is lower middle class, in her mid thirties and white. Samantha has no children and is bisexual.

Tessa is working class and African–Caribbean. She is in her early sixties, lives in Manchester, has seven children, is heterosexual and works as a professional foster parent.

'All My Fault'

Why this book?

I had declared myself a feminist some years before I made my first film, *Women Without Homes*, in 1973. It was about a group of women who'd left the apparent security of homes they shared with violent men. Most moved out empty-handed, often with children in tow, for the uncertainty and some-times squalid conditions of Britain's first women's refuge. The majority of these women had no other choice, having been denied the state benefit that would have enabled them to get places of their own. They were considered to have made them-selves intentionally homeless. They got practically no support, apart from the embryonic Women's Movement. Yet those women clung tenaciously to the right to be free from abuse.

Their courage moved me beyond words. It was the first time I had experienced women's potential for such bravery.

Since then I have made several dozen films, many of which have dealt directly or indirectly with violence against women. Even though there is now much greater public awareness about such issues, all services for those affected by domestic violence suffer from chronic shortages of state support. And I am still overwhelmed by women's capacity to triumph in the face of male abuse and public neglect.

But gradually I began to feel uneasy. I spent much of 1988 in the first domestic violence unit in a British police station. No one could fail to feel the pain of the battered women it served. Yet there was another kind of distress that I hadn't expected to experience: that of the two female police officers, Annette and Colette, as they watched helplessly when women returned time and again to abusive men. The policewomen's frustration and anger did not lessen their commitment to the job nor their sympathy for the women. Nevertheless, on top of all the other pressures of this kind of work, the battered women's recidivism undoubtedly contributed to the need of both police officers to change departments. They had suffered emotional burnout.

Though neither Annette nor Colette saw it that way, I worried that women who don't leave abusive men see themselves and are seen by others as failures. And I began to wonder how different such women really are from someone like me who put up with an emotionally abusive father for over forty years. So many women I know have been unable to break away from an abusive brother, uncle, male cousin, in-law, family friend, colleague or partner. Though lots of women claim not to understand why battered women don't leave, perhaps if we all looked deeper into our hearts, we'd discover yet another way in which we are sisters under the skin.

What this book is

Too many of us have known at least one woman we liked a lot who has driven us crazy by being unable to leave a man who abuses her.

We have cried with her, hugged her and tended her wounds. In between the midnight phone calls, journeys to hospital, cups of tea, brandy and cigarettes, we've gotten her the names and phone numbers of solicitors, women's refuges, shrinks and the police. Yet even though the beatings get worse each time she still doesn't leave him.

It looks as if nothing we do ever helps. We are tempted to give up out of the exhausted confusion of seeing someone who, no matter what we do or say, seems to go back for more. And why doesn't she leave? How could anyone keep putting up with that?

We begin to wonder if maybe she really likes it, wants it, asks for it.

Experts of all kinds are always eager to join the latest theoretical bandwagon so they can pontificate about why women do (or don't do) whatever it is we do. Rarely are the women actually involved asked for an opinion, certainly never in any depth nor in a way that might help family, friends and sympathetic professionals give practical and effective support.

When women do leave for good it is usually only after repeated and long-term abuse. Every time I've asked a woman why she didn't do it before, her reply has nearly always been: because I thought it was 'all my fault'.

This book explains that response largely through the voices of women who have been imprisoned by male abuse. They reveal it to be a particularly impregnable fortress where the family is often the cell bars and the state is always the gaoler. To break up (out of) the family is the worst sin a woman can commit, for the family is the cornerstone of civilisation. In separating from her violent husband, father, brother, lover, a woman is tearing up the very moral fabric of society. 'All My Fault' looks at women's lives from cradle to grave – from the most intimate personal relations to the whole range of statutory agencies whose operations try to determine our options and impose their own limitations.

All too often a woman knows she will be pursued by the enraged man aided and abetted by his financial superiority and the sympathy of his friends. The women who participated in this book describe how they suffered harassment and deprivation as a result of the powers that religious, social, cultural and government organisations use to punish women who dare to leave. Considering all this, the real question we should be asking is: how on earth *do* some women manage to leave?

Why do we never ask that question? Why do we always throw up (our hands) in horror when a woman we care about seems to keep going back for more abuse? Isn't *our* failure to challenge it only compounding her agony?

I believe that women are controlled by the threat and reality of the whole continuum of male violence. This ranges from everyday harassment openly committed in public, through the less reported abuses in semi-private places like schools and at work, to the secrecy of the greatly under-reported rapes of adult women, child sexual abuse and domestic violence. The hiding, covering up and denial of abuse are themselves often the biggest obstacles to breaking that control.

And while some people will no doubt accuse me of a kind of philosophically jack-booted feminism in my analysis of the agencies of women's imprisonment, I hope you will also recognise my determination to reflect the infinite variety of women's experiences in suggesting practical solutions. Our differences are as important as our similarities. For it is in recognising that each woman must define her own situation that friends, family and sympathetic professionals will find ways to be truly supportive.

One thing, however, has always seemed perfectly clear to me. Male violence is men's responsibility, completely, totally and utterly without reservation. Women never ask for it nor can women be blamed in any way for what men do. No matter what, no one has the right to use physical violence except in self-defence.

This is not a book about the roots of male violence nor about why men do what they do. Though clearly women's responses to male abuse have a strong basis in our relative positions in societies and cultures, 'All My Fault' is only interested in those inequalities of power in so far as they relate to women's survival of male violence. Ultimately, we should all like inequalities to disappear. But this book takes that as read.

There is a popular misconception that being hit is worse than being shouted at; that being raped is worse than constant threats of brutality. My view is that there is no hierarchy of pain. Different women are affected in different ways by what appear to be the same or similar experiences. The same women are even affected differently by the same or similar experiences at different times. One day being flashed at might seem just very irritating. Another day it feels like a devastatingly intimate intrusion. Many women have said that after months and even years of constant verbal, psychological, emotional and mental abuse, a single act of physical violence – especially if afterwards they know there will be a respite from all abuse – seems less horrible.

I define sexual violence in this context as anything that is experienced as fearful, controlling and threatening when used by those with power (almost invariably men) against those without (mainly women and children). If a women is scared and feels controlled by the behaviour of a man she lives with, has lived with, or has had an intimate relationship with, if she thinks it's domestic violence, as far as I'm concerned it is. I can't imagine anyone reading this book doubting that every woman who participated was subjected to serious abuse. When I put my definition of domestic violence to all of them, they agreed with it. Because of this, you will see that I use the words 'abuse' and 'violence' almost interchangeably.

'Battered women' is a term that has been used for many years to describe women who have been subjected to domestic violence. However, there is a growing body of opinion that believes it implies a too rigid and overly narrow definition of what women experience and that it characterises women as mere punchbags. The word 'abused' is increasingly preferred to 'battered'. Similarly, there is some objection to referring to women as 'fleeing' or even 'escaping from' domestic violence. However, because I believe this book is being published during a transitionary phase in their usage, I have used 'battered' sometimes, but mainly opted for 'abused', and tried to avoid 'escaping' and 'fleeing' as much as possible.

What this book isn't

I am suspicious of those psychological and criminological theories that make sweeping generalisations about domestic violence, yet are based on no scientifically recognised or statistically sound research. They either come from theoreticians' clinical observations of highly selected groups of individual 'patients' or through the administration of narrowly focused psychological tests and questionnaires to equally unrepresentative samples. Though I believe none of these theories has anything to offer, they are often the only explanations of domestic violence many people have ever heard. So I think it is important to know what assumptions lie behind them and, even more importantly, to look at why they exist.

Almost all of these theories concentrate solely on the

individual(s) – either on the man or woman alone, or on them together as a couple. Most portray the 'problem' as that of each person, as overwhelmingly some deviation from a so-called social norm, or an immaturity, or a lack of development. The majority suggest that domestic violence is a disorder manifested in psychological/personality defects or sociopathic behaviour caused by an organic or an environmental illness. Treatment is seen as the central solution: it varies from the surgical/medical through the psychological to the institutional, in combinations or on their own. In order to 'treat' people they must be 'sick' or 'diseased' in some way – that is not normal, but marginal(ised).

Many theories about male sexual violence blame mothers – far more than ever suggest it's connected with fathers (except where male deviance is associated with missing fathers – their absence often said to be the mothers' fault). Almost all theories about why women stay with abusive men either blame the women themselves for being under-developed, weak, masochistic, 'asking for it', or turn the women into helpless, withdrawn victims, child-like in their inability to be responsible for their actions. Such theories imprison women by infantilising them, a process very similar, in fact, to the way male abusers undermine and control women by making them feel stupid, useless and utterly helpless without the constant intervention/subvention/supervision of the abuser. This subjugation perpetuates the position of women as second-class emotional citizens.

Some psychological theories depict sexual violence as a kind of equal dynamic – that male abuse could not exist without either the willingness or neediness of the woman (or the child, in extreme versions). In this way, the woman is rationalised as readily offering herself, wanting, desiring (and this definitely becomes sexualised in most theories), asking for it. Women (and sometimes even children) are said to be addicted to violence. Men, women and children are supposed to be imprisoned in a 'cycle of abuse': that those who witness violence as children inevitably grow up either to be abusers or to seek out abuse. Studies of the 'cycle of abuse' show that this is not the case (a number are summarised by Kaufman and Zigler in 'The Intergenerational Transmission of Child Abuse',[1] which shows that 65 to 85 per cent of adults who were abused as children did not grow up to abuse their children;

Kelly in *Surviving Sexual Violence*,[2] who found that few battered women in her study had experience of domestic violence in childhood; and, amongst others, Hotaling and Sugarman in 'An Analysis of Risk Markers in Husband to Wife Violence: the State of the Knowledge',[3] who found a range of significant influences on whether men abused or not). Indeed, it has often been observed that those who witness abuse as children exhibit inclinations to heal, rather than abuse.

'Learned helplessness' and 'battered women's syndrome' are two other theories designed to show that women become universally and singularly lobotomised by abuse. Yet, again, research does not support either of these theories.[4] Experience and research continue to show quite the reverse in fact – that women subjected to domestic violence are highly resourceful and engage in the most remarkable help-seeking activity.[5]

Criminological theories are often socio-pathological, suggesting that poverty, unemployment and social class are important factors in causing abuse (yet no studies have ever shown major differences between abusers according to their economic status), or that it only happens in 'dysfunctional' families, defined as those where communication between its members has broken down, where children can't mature, and which do not function as a unit, therefore scapegoating individual members who develop 'personality disorders', like anorexia in children. 'Dysfunctional' families are also said to be ones without the traditional, gender-based parental role models, not following the nuclear family doctrine of women as primary carers and men as breadwinners. Yet observation and research has shown that as many abusers seem to live in apparently 'functional' families as not. There is also the theory that drink and drugs play a significant part (statistically disproved: even studies of violators who had drink or drug problems showed that those same men frequently abused when sober).

I believe these are all ways of 'othering' domestic violence, that is pushing it away from 'us', pretending it only happens to 'other' people. By denying its existence amongst 'us' (the norm), we marginalise domestic violence, playing into the hands of those who see the individual treatment of damaged people as the solution.

Those who invent theories about domestic violence based on the aberrant individual almost always study people only as discrete entities, separate from the rest of society: highly selected people who have either been sent to them as 'suffering' from some psychological illness or who have already been classified as deviant. Not surprisingly, these theoreticians often develop very narrow, skewed views of human behaviour and, consequently, the whole range of sexual violence. They become blinkered and rarely contextualise any of their work within the expectations that society as a whole places upon women and men. It has been left largely to feminist and Marxist theoreticians to place such 'private' behaviour within the sphere of general political, economic, cultural and social constructs.

In their book *Women, Violence and Social Change*,[6] which is well worth reading, R. Emerson Dobash and Russell P. Dobash have a whole, wise chapter called 'The therapeutic society constructs battered women and violent men'. In it they distinguish individualistic, hierarchical therapeutic practice from the cooperative stance of activists whose work focuses on autonomy for those who have experienced domestic and other sexual violence.

Though I would never be proscriptive (nor, I believe, would they) about any form of *practical* support a woman thought was useful – indeed, personally I have found psychoanalysis to be of great benefit – their criticism of the therapeutic approach as a *theoretical* model is eloquent:

> Whatever the therapy, the relationship between client and professional is usually hierarchical, with one-sided forms of communication in which the person seeking help is transformed into the objectified condition of the client ... As taught in most therapeutic interventions, the relationship between the therapist and the client is crucial to reformation, and the therapist provides a model of the healthy functioning adult. Growth or development is seen as a purely personal matter with little connection to the wider social and especially the political world ... The individualized approach of the therapeutic society makes political perceptions and wider social action in the public forums unlikely, if not impossible. Given this, all we can change is ourselves.

> Therapeutic relationships are the antithesis of the visions of activists seeking social change. Instead of normalizing tendencies associated with middle-class conceptions based on the therapist as a model, there is a recognition that success and development must be assessed relative to the circumstances and possibilities associated with the concrete position of women.

Indeed, I believe that, though they may not set out to do so, traditional/non-feminist therapies, when practised in isolation, risk making (reinforcing) women think(ing) it's all our fault. It is, therefore, within the wider context that the Dobashes describe that I seek to place this book.

What's behind this book?

'History' often carries with it the presumption that things change: that somehow time elapsing in and of itself will bring improvements, because economic, social or political conditions may have altered in favour of some women.

The present UK legislation governing marriage originated in Ecclesiastical Law, reflecting the influence of the Church in a number of ways: subjugating the wife to the authority of the husband; limiting divorce; emphasising the seriousness of adultery. The legal existence of a woman was suspended during marriage. Until the late nineteenth century, she couldn't keep the property she brought to the marriage nor hold any other property herself. Before 1949, a married woman had no right to have a say in where the couple lived. During the 1960s, the law officially stopped regarding women as men's property, but until 1973, wives had a duty to provide 'reasonable services': cooking, washing and sex. It is only since the late 1980s that the possibility that rape within marriage is unlawful has been recognised.

Yet despite such apparent improvements, the core notion that men own women and children and have certain inalienable rights to exert their authority over them (from access to children they have been convicted of abusing or kidnapping through to murdering uppity women) is unchanged, and is daily reflected in the news and in our own experiences.

How many times have you ignored a woman's screams because you thought her assailant was her boyfriend, husband, father, uncle or brother (as though, presumably, such men have a right to violate women)? You didn't want to intrude on a private matter? Tried to tell yourself it was just an argument? Convinced yourself that all those stories about how the only result would be that she'd turn on you were true? I hope this book will help all of us to challenge such behaviour.

What's in this book?

Twenty-two women participated in this book by giving in-depth interviews about their lives, focusing on the difficulties of leaving abusive men. All the participants were given the opportunity to preview the edited versions of their contributions. The women's details, given in the text and at the beginning of the book, were correct at the time all the interviews took.place in 1993. Each woman then chose whether or not to use her real name (and where not she picked another, limited only by not being allowed any other woman's real name or someone else's already chosen alias), defined her own social class, race, occupation and sexuality and gave information about her age and children.

Clearly with such a small sample, I make no claims for quantitative or qualitative results that are scientifically sound. However, I have compared many of the shared experiences of the participants with all the research, large- and small-scale, that I could find from Britain, Canada, Australia, New Zealand and the US. Though I believe this book is unique in the way it draws together first-hand experiences with historical analysis and practical advice, what the participants describe in 'All My Fault' is reflected over and over in every study I came across.

Notwithstanding the size of my 'sample', the demographics of the participants – the ranges of age, class, race, geography, whether they have children or not, occupation and sexuality – cover a reasonably wide area. The most glaring omission is that there are no participants who defined themselves as disabled. Indeed, despite my wide network of contacts, no disabled woman who felt she could be interviewed, even in total anonymity, came forward. I believe this is because of the ways disabled women are often isolated and put into positions of extreme disadvantage by non-disabled people.

Nevertheless, I hope that disabled women and their supporters will find this book of use. Furthermore, I hope that soon disabled women themselves will write a book like this, sharing their experiences of domestic violence and exposing the complicity of non-disabled society.

How to use this book

'*All My Fault*' is for family, friends, statutory and voluntary agencies, those who work in frontline services like education, housing, social services, fire and health, the civil and criminal justice systems, activists, academics, and researchers.

Nearly every chapter begins with a personal anecdote about me, to let you know where I fit into the story. I am forty-six, white, middle class, Jewish, heterosexual, have a half-brother, no children and was born in Chicago. The abuse I experienced was from my father, not my ex-husband.

The participants' experiences structure and fill most of the rest of each chapter. Occasional additional information is provided by the details of studies or research on the particular subject of the chapter. I draw together conclusions and offer my own analysis from time to time.

You can read '*All My Fault*' from cover to cover. Or if you're interested in a particular subject, you can go directly to that chapter. At the end of the book is a practical advice section for everyone: family, friends and sympathetic professionals. There is also a summary of guidelines on being a supporter, together with organisations that will give advice and help. For those who are interested, I have included some ideas for campaigning as well as longer-term actions that I feel need to be taken by us as individuals, by the government and by society generally. Finally, the selected further reading section suggests books and other materials that either go into greater detail, give historical background about specific issues or provide research and statistical back-up for findings about domestic violence described in the book.

More than anything, I hope '*All My Fault*' will be a positive and practical guide to finding ways of offering your own right kind of support and understanding. With so much increasingly stacked up against women who don't leave abusive men, such help is more important than ever. But no one ever seems to be there to tell you how to do it. Now, for the first time, the voices of women who have stayed and finally left will guide you . . .

1
Making little women

In America in the early 1950s, it was fashionable for little girls like me to be dressed in underpants so stiff with ruffles that our skirts stuck straight out. I can remember the pride in believing that my own pants were frillier than anyone else's. And I can still hear the scratchy sounds every time I moved and feel the starched ruffles scoring the tops of my legs. Most powerful of all, though, is my belief in my family's stories that I regularly and spontaneously bent over in public, flashing my frilly bottom. I'm even convinced that I've seen a photograph of it. Yet whenever I've asked, no one can produce the picture.

For me, my performing underpants weren't just a form of attention-seeking. For as long as I can remember, I have had a sense that I don't exist without other people's reactions. Most especially, that no one will love me for just being, that I have to do something to be loved.

Maybe because the frilly underpants themselves are such a powerful childhood memory or maybe because I am stuck with too many feminist delusions, I began thinking about this chapter as one about the roots of femininity in a very outward way: girls dressed in girly dresses, playing with dolls, dreaming only of being wives and mothers. Sometime fairly early in the interview process, I realised that, though my underpants were the key in understanding my own reality, it was how I related to them, rather than the fact of them, that was important in understanding the part they played in my feminisation. Not that I think such extraordinary garments are without intrinsic meaning. I believe they do send a clear message to those who wear, buy and see them being worn, that an important element in femininising little girls is turning us into elaborately fragile-looking display objects – rather like Dresden dolls or ornamental china dogs. Nevertheless, each woman needs to understand the process of feminisation through her own unique lens, with its personal, cultural and social filters, to discover how she has internalised its message.

The route to understanding is different for every woman, yet for most of us the search is filled with anxiety and curiosity. It often feels as though the past is something we are desperate both to know and to deny. No wonder we regularly question ourselves and others about whether a childhood reminiscence really happened.

Such is the power and complexity of memory. What's true isn't so much what we can prove to be real, but what we each feel, deep inside – our emotional truth – that is our reality. My frilly underpants symbolise a powerful mixed message for me: that I was supposed to be a perfectly passive little Jewish princess doll and, at the same time, that I could not expect anyone to take any notice of me unless I actively pursued their attentions. In trying to be both, I only succeeded in being either inappropriately aggressive or hopelessly passive. I endeared myself to no one and angered – and depressed – myself. The impossibility of living up to such contradictions is reflected and refracted in the experiences of the women who participated in this book.

The quality of our lives is shaped by the ways in which these individual realities affect our expectations and match up to our experiences. Our ability to look after ourselves and to feel in control of our own destiny is firmly rooted in that sense of ourselves embedded in each of our own earliest emotional truths.

Roots

Candace is African–Caribbean and was born in 1957 in London where she still lives. She works at a refuge for battered women.

> I was brought up in a boarding school when I was young. Because my mum and dad worked very hard, they put me in it for a couple of years. I was the only black child there, surrounded by white girls.
>
> Oh yes, the white girls with blonde hair – it was really in me. I used to read fairy stories and always used to have fantasies. I would play behind the settee and dress up as a beautiful princess, have a white towel on my head as my hair. And because at the time I was an only child, I had to imagine everything. I imagined I was in a beautiful castle that was in a forest. I was left there and I had to fend for myself until my prince came and found me. And I always used to be married to him and we'd live happily ever after.

Candace's experience vividly describes how the perfection that, one way or another, all girls learn can never be achieved becomes uniquely mutated for a young, black child.

Alabee also works at a refuge for battered women. She is mixed-race Asian and was born in 1956 in London which is still her home. When she was small, her mother's health was poor and her parents had money problems, so they sent Alabee to live with more prosperous relatives.

> I was brought up basically by an aunt and uncle for the first eight years of my life. My aunt was a dressmaker, so she had this whole wardrobe full of dresses that I hated. They were all the same to me. They were all with under-petticoats and frills and bows. And you used to put them on and you felt like you'd been starched. You had to sit in the same positions; if you moved they itched, scratched under your armpits or they felt like they were going to split, because they always fitted into the waist and then came out full, round, and flowing.

So you were dressed up like a little princess, with your hair just so, a little bow in the back. It was awful. Terrible.

My life looked idyllic. I used to have lots of clothes, lots of toys, and it looked like I was a really happy little girl. But I used to get beaten brutally. And that went on for the whole eight years, as far back as I can remember it was going on. So it was horrendous.

Alabee believes that to have enjoyed such prosperity in the austere post-war years, particularly against the odds of endemic racism, was a sign to girls like her that they were meant to feel especially grateful. And knowing she was meant to be grateful, when she was so miserable, acted as a powerful device to silence her telling anyone that she was being terrorised by her benefactors' abuse.

Anne is a horse breeder living in rural England. She is white and was born in California in 1946.

My father was a total disciplinarian and was very, very strict, very undemonstrative. My mother's the complete opposite, a social butterfly, in the nicest sense of the word, and a very warm person.

My father expected to be obeyed. He was a cruel, rather arrogant man. If you questioned or crossed my father in any way, you found you got the silent treatment and that things became unpleasant. He wasn't a physically violent man, but very stony, very steely and you were just frozen out.

We were expected to conform rigidly. Our grades were studied and if they ever fell below a 'B' average, personally, my horses were taken away, as well as television. This was a strong incentive to get the grades back up because I was a very horsey, doggy child – a very lonely child – and animals were my best friends.

My mother wanted us all to be a jolly family, so she would say things like, 'You must never do that, it would kill your father.' If I heard that once, I've heard it a thousand times. I was truant from school once and you would have thought I robbed a bank. Anything was family honour, everything was absolutely, totally constrained by that. One must never bring dishonour. Particularly from my father, there was an emphasis on the family name – from the time I was five onwards. As time went on, it was, 'What would the neighbours think? What would his friends think?'

Interviewing Anne was a watershed for me. Her affluent background was as superficially different from many of the other women in this book as you could imagine. Yet just under the surface were striking similarities. She was never encouraged to have a mind of her own. In her case, as with some of the other participants, it was her father's will that ruled her early life. She feared she would never be good enough and would fail to live up to his expectations. And being presented with such contrasting parental role models created anxiety and confusion. Anne was desperate to please her mother, terrified of displeasing her father.

Barbara was born in Edinburgh in 1954 and now lives in Aberdeen. She is white and works in a community centre.

Both my mother and father came from working-class backgrounds and from families who were very involved in politics and trades unions and that kind of scene. When I was about ten, my mother was beginning to get involved in the women's movement, but she still seemed to run round my father. My mother went out to work. I mean she would come home from the school meal service at three o'clock, clean the fire and put the meal on. So that by the time he came in at five o'clock the meal was ready and the table was set. I remember that he often used to get his meal by the coal fire because he had been outside working all day, whereas the rest of the family would sit at the table. But my mother would never sit down at the table with us. She cooked the meal – she served the first course, the second course – but she never sat down at the table with us.

At about that same time, in the mid sixties, when I was eleven or twelve, I can remember sitting in the audience in the big, main hall in town, and my mother on the platform talking about how sanitary towels should be on the National Health Service. I felt extremely embarrassed at that age.

So there was like this contradiction going on. My father would talk about the oppression of women and how it was wrong, and that the oppression of anybody, black or women or disabled or whatever, was not on because it didn't fit in with his communist politics. But in practice it was quite different.

The particular hypocrisy between what Barbara saw as her parents' public stance and their private behaviour must have been especially confusing. After all, wasn't her mother a woman? If the oppression of 'women' was wrong, why was her mother doing at least twice as much work as her father? And if there was confusion about whether or not her mother was a woman, what did that make Barbara?

Growing up

Molly works as an office administrator. She is white and was born in 1956 in the suburban Home Counties where she still lives.

I was still going on family holidays when I was fifteen, sixteen. I don't think I would have been allowed to stay at home on my own, I think that would have been disapproved of. It was a case of we do everything together.

I was never terribly ambitious. Some little girls want to be this, that and the other, I wasn't like that. I'd say I was more of a tomboy. I had dolls and I used to play dolls and dolls' houses and things like that. But having an older brother, I found I could climb trees with him and do stuff like that. But I never had a fixed ambition as to what I wanted to be.

I knew I always wanted to get married. There are two sides to me. There was the one bit that was very conventional, and very much get married, settle down, have your 2.4 kids, whatever it is, a dog, live in suburbia – there was that bit I really wanted. There was another bit of me that just wanted to break free of all of that. But deep down there was still that bit that I wanted to get married and have children.

Molly now sees that her conflicting desires created perhaps less of a problem for her than never being encouraged to believe in herself: to believe that she had the right to make decisions about her future.

Barbara felt her future was clearly mapped out for her by her mother.

I think I realised that the expectation, certainly from my mother, was that I would be clever in terms of education, academic. That I would get some kind of career that would pull me, a woman, out of the whole working-class struggle. And also that I would be attractive in the usual sense of like heterosexual terms and what constitutes a woman being attractive. And I was expected to behave impeccably as a female.

For example, just sitting at the table. If I was drinking milk with my meal and if I kind of gulped the milk, then I would get a telling off for that. If my brother did it, it wasn't quite as terrible.

I would create and jump up and down. I can remember when I was very young sometimes having temper tantrums and being told this is not behaviour which is acceptable, because it was allowing yourself to get out of control.

I think she tried to say that not having table manners was not acceptable – that was not part of her idea of what feminism was about. She's very much, I would probably put her in the kind of category of like it was about work and it was about sexual harassment and it was about rape. But it was not about saying, 'Fuck you lot. I'm going to be me and if you don't like it, tough.'

I was raised to put other people's feelings before my own, very much so. In my mind it is connected with my parents' communist politics, which is for the greater all, then that's what counts. The individual is important, but must give way to what's best for the majority, for all.

Barbara believes her parents openly proscribed her feelings and behaviour. For other women, the impression that what they wanted didn't count was imposed less overtly.

Mary is white and works in a refuge for battered women. She was born in 1958 in London where she still lives.

When I was little, I spent a lot of time with my father. My mother had me at, I think, forty, and I don't think she was quite prepared for that. My father was an alcoholic and I think she really had a hard time. I think she had two near nervous breakdowns. I can't really recall any times spent with my mother, like doing things. I used to go out with my father, walking and stuff like that.

I'm not too sure whether I identified with any role models. It would have been sportspeople I think. But no one in particular. I think most of them might have been men and not women role models really. I think I was very much a tomboy. I was always with the boys, though I was clear there was an imbalance. It felt like boys got a better deal. I didn't make a conscious choice and I had to make an effort to fit in with the boys. I just didn't feel like a girl and so I never really played with girls. I was quite upset if I was given girls' toys and stuff like that. I think I was probably androgynous – I used to get mistaken for a boy a lot. So it just became easier to be a tomboy.

I think some of the confusion came from the mixed messages I got from my mother. She wanted me in pretty little bows and frocks and things. She made all my dresses. But they were pinafores with a dropped waist – I was never allowed to have my real waist. I was always encouraged to be shapeless. One day she'd put bows in my long hair, then the next she'd put a pudding basin on my head and cut it all off. I remember she seemed to get very angry at me because I didn't change into the kind of pretty thing she wanted. When she did dress me up, things were always coming unripped and she was always quite disappointed. It's taken me till I was thirty-six till I could buy clothes with a waist.

Christine still lives in Lancashire where she was born in 1940. She is white and works in a refuge for battered women.

Even as a child, doing baby-sitting and baby-minding and things like that, I was always taught to consider other people's feelings, and to respect other people's feelings and not to transgress on other people's territory or feelings.

Something else I was taught as a child was that looks were important. How you looked was very important. It's only in the last few years that I've been able to relax and wear jeans and sweaters. My mother has a fit when I turn up with a pair of jeans on. 'Jeans at your age! Trainers!' I mean, she has a fit. It's made me think. Growing up believing that how you looked and what people thought about you is very important, whereas it's really, I know now, it's what's inside.

I was always the leader of the pack, I was a tomboy. It was always Christine and the shadows when I was a teenager. I was always the one to the fore. I was a Brown Owl, I was Sunday school teacher, the chairman of the youth club. I was always popular. I was lucky as a child. I always had holidays and days out.

Choices

Very early on, Christine, Mary, Molly and Barbara worked out that boys got a better deal in life than girls, so of course that's what they wanted to be. And because, like most children, they probably didn't question the reason why such 'deals' exist – it just seemed natural – perhaps they also felt that boys were somehow inherently better and so, of course, deserved more.

Alabee, Anne, Barbara, Molly and Christine all got the message that they weren't allowed to have their own opinions, to make their own choices, whether it was about their behaviour, their wishes or their ambitions. Everyone else's feelings came first and, in any case, other people – especially parents – always knew better. Some version of this message was received by every participant in this book. Indeed most women I have ever asked, irrespective of age, class, race or culture, remember growing up with the belief that when and if their feelings counted at all, they came last and that, more often than not, other people knew what was best for them, better than they did. Not only does this have the potential to undermine any woman's self-confidence, but it can make her feel as if she doesn't exist.

If we are brought up without a sense of our self-worth or individual identity, and without the skills or the confidence to make decisions for ourselves, we are all too often left without the means to stand up for ourselves.

Christine reflects on the effect of such strictures.

> I was brought up to be seen and not heard, and that children have their place. If I'd been allowed to have opinions, to say how I felt – maybe children are given too much today, but at least they can stand up for themselves. If I'd been able to just stand up once and voice my inner feelings about what I felt, then I might have been able to stand up to him.

Elizabeth is white and was born in Scotland in 1954. She now lives in London where she works in an advice centre for young people.

> I wasn't aware that I had any feelings or had any rights to have any feelings. I was such a good child, I never did anything wrong. I was always perfect, consciously so, as my sisters were more rebellious and would get into trouble a lot, whereas I was always frantic to be OK and not to upset

anybody. So that didn't come up very much, my parents saying, 'Oh, you've got to be like this.' Because I was already doing it.

I found it very difficult to imagine myself grown up. I used to feel quite frightened at the thought of leaving home, because my parents were so protective, that outside was dangerous, inside was safe.

Sally works in London as a university lecturer. She is white and was born in 1952 in the north of England.

The relationship that I saw between my mother and father was aggressive and quite violent. I think there was a lot of tension and anger in the home. It was a very isolated home because it was on a remote farm. Not many people came to the home and we didn't go out of the home very much. So it was a very kind of enmeshed, isolated situation. My role was, I think, to be the good girl, and to be the quiet girl and to be the sweet girl who wasn't any trouble.

There were a lot of children in our family and I was responsible for the cooking from being very young. I think from being nine or ten I was responsible for all the cooking. I've thought about that quite a lot. And I think the result – I know the feeling that I had as a teenager and in my early and late twenties even, was the feeling I didn't exist. That there was nothing inside me.

Both Sally and Elizabeth hoped that by trying to live up to other people's expectations of them, by always giving way to everyone else's feelings and wishes, by being perfect, they would be safe. Elizabeth even tried to extend that sense of safety to her less well-behaved sisters. It is striking to me that they both strove for a kind of perfection so resonant of many self-denying religious women throughout the world and throughout history. By their modesty and silent goodness, never troubling anyone for anything, they and others under their protection might transcend the terrible things that other women experience (in order to avoid men sexually, religious women sometimes actually physically disfigured themselves by tearing out their eyes or cutting off their breasts). And while safety may have eluded them, they did achieve transcendence through emotional self-mutilation: Elizabeth in her lost feelings and Sally in her non-existence, her emptiness inside. For religious women this loss of self (sometimes an erotic submission and merging) strengthens their bonds to the (inevitable) patriarchal god. Both Sally and Elizabeth believe that this childhood self-abasement was a key factor in binding them to abusive men when they grew up.

Marian was born in Cheltenham in 1948. She is white and now lives in London where she works as a primary school teacher.

> My family background is upper working class. Very secure. No violence at all in my childhood, which is, I think, why it was such a shock to me. Because I never encountered anything like it before. It was quite a secure, close-knit family in terms of cousins and aunts and uncles. But, in the last ten, fifteen years I've realised it was very stifling. They're very controlling and they think I'm odd because I don't have a Volvo.
>
> I would say nearly right through the whole of my school life I was very well behaved. I didn't get my little pink dresses dirty, didn't like playing in the mud, always did as I was told. I didn't feel there was anything wrong with that. I was quite happy with being a good little girl.
>
> I'm not sure that I had any real strong ideas of my own. I think I was influenced by my mother always saying, 'Teaching's a good job, because you can still have children and be a teacher.' Then, when I got to the age of about sixteen or seventeen, I started, I think, from their point of view, to become just a little bit too clever for them. So I then rejected the idea of being a teacher and I was going to be a probation officer, and they all thought this was a joke.

Marian's happy memories of being a good little girl in her nice frocks are a reminder of the importance of context. I am convinced that dressing anyone – especially girls and women – in clothes that are so utterly restrictive is a way of exerting power over them, by those who wouldn't dream of wearing such things themselves. But I also believe that it's the overall control that each girl or woman feels in her own life that makes a crucial difference to the way we experience that restriction.

Alabee reflects on the context of her own rebellion.

> Everybody tried to make me into this nice little girl that sat down quietly. As soon as their backs were turned, I was up getting dirty. So I was always rebellious. I was a little bit of a tomboy, I suppose.
>
> I didn't think that being a wife and mother was really what I wanted to do. I thought it looked quite boring, actually. I don't think, initially, I wanted to be a mother or play with dolls for a lot of reasons. One of the reasons being, as I've got older and I've found out, was a feeling of rejection. Out of the five children, I was the only one that was taken care of by my aunt and uncle. The other four stayed at home with my mum. And I felt slightly, well, quite a lot rejected by that. And I had to deal with that.
>
> Then shortly after I did go home, my mother died, so that was another rejection for me to handle. I think a lot of rebelliousness came out, as far as my dad's concerned, was because I needed somebody to blame for that situation, and he got all the blame.
>
> In my early teen years, I felt quite guilty from time to time because of my dad's background, being Muslim and women having a certain place in his culture. It was very distressing for him, and I could see it was distressing for him, but I couldn't seem to change the way I was going.
>
> As far as wanting to be a mother, I can't remember wanting to be a mother until I actually got pregnant. I never had any real passion towards it.
>
> I wanted to go into the Navy. I've got a real passion – it sounds really weird, considering I now work for Women's

Aid – but I've got a real passion for, like, old war films, submarines and all that. I've watched them since I was a kid. I think it's my brothers' influences, mind you. I felt like I had to watch them when I was little and it's just gone through. I always wanted to be a radar operator, so as I'm growing up, that's what I wanted to be. I wanted to go in the Navy and play with little machines. The only reason I think I didn't do it was because I had my daughter.

Sally's ambitions were a reaction to her early home life on an isolated farm where she felt controlled by her father's violence.

Thinking about the images of women that I had when I was a child, I think my image, my idea about what I would like to be like is what I *am* like. I think I thought, 'I won't get married, I won't have children, I'll be independent and have a career.' That was always very strong. My mother always made that very clear, that we had to have a career and be independent. I thought, 'I won't put up with nonsense. I'm not going to have a man treat me like my father treated my mother.' I mean that was my main feeling when I was growing up. 'This isn't OK and I'm not going to have it. I'm not going to wait on a man.' So though I did the cooking, though I waited on my father very much, I was very resentful about it.

Coping

Samantha is a police sergeant in a southern English market town. She is white and was born in 1960 in Dorset.

I think I was quite assertive and also had quite a strong value system. Very early on I gave away Christianity and chose to be an atheist – I can remember at about twelve saying 'I am an atheist'. So at the age of ten, eleven, twelve questioning things. I couldn't stand any form of abuse or violence towards animals, children or anybody else. I couldn't bear injustice in any way, shape or form.

I wasn't a meek and mild little girl. I used to ask why. 'Why do you want me to do that? If you give me a good reason, I'll do it, but if not, then, no, I don't want to do that.'

Any form of argument or going against my father particularly resulted in violence. It wasn't on, but I still tried and I think I continued to do it. As I got older, I got a bit more freedom to get out of the house and get away. My love was horses and so I would go away to the stables for long periods of time. If I was with the horses that was fine and that was my escape. So by removing myself from the situation, that solved things to a certain extent.

Learning to manage (and be protected from) male violence is a skill that many children teach themselves at an early age. Strategies vary from child to child. Some try to be perfect and invisible, like Sally and Elizabeth. Others, like Samantha and Anne, escape with their horses.

There is a vast range of evasive and confrontational techniques that many of us – male and female – probably don't even realise we used to protect ourselves when we were young. A number of possibilities exist as to why such techniques have probably always been so widespread and yet remain unacknowledged. Though threats and abuse occur as part of, rather than separate from, our normal activities, this is rarely recognised, even nowadays when the prevalence of sexual violence is more openly discussed. Most of us still see it as something apart from, as 'other' than, our banal, ordinary routine. Maybe it's too scary to admit that abuse happens at home, at school, at work, at play – as a part of family life – overwhelmingly perpetrated by those we know, often very well, and sometimes love.

Children, in particular, are made more vulnerable to abuse by adult attempts to control them in the guise of protecting their innocence. This is done by denying children information about their world – especially in areas like sex education and personal safety – which might threaten parents' and other adults' power over them. But for whatever reasons, the very commonplace of something as unmentionable as abuse means it remains for so many children something they keep secret. And when children do disclose abuse, very often they're not believed. They have been imprisoned in the idea that they cannot tell the difference between right and wrong, truth and lies, that they are sneaky, manipulative sub-human little creatures. Too many of us accept that children are unreliable and that only adults can interpret their experiences for them.

Children's reactions to abuse are complex, varying as widely as do the circumstances of their lives. The results of experiencing violence, like other traumatic events, are not predictable.

Saroj lives in London where she volunteers at Southall Black Sisters, an advice centre for black women. She was born in 1965 in Fiji of Indian descent.

> When I was one year old, my mum tried to kill herself. My dad treated my mum very badly. He used to punch her, he used to kick her, throw things at her. My mum worked all the time cooking and selling sweets. And whatever she earned, my dad used to take away. I've got three brothers and five sisters and he used to hit us all the time.

> When I was a little girl, at that time I was not thinking of what I wanted to be when I grew up. Not job-wise. I was thinking that I wished to get married to a nice person and have a nice home and stay at home. That was my hope from childhood.

Anita is white and was born in 1947 in London where she still lives. She works in residential housing management.

> Looking back now, in hindsight, I can see that although it looks as if everything's nice – I was well cushioned and fed well, nice clothes, looked after, amused, taken out – I did not get what I needed from my parents. I did not get my emotional needs dealt with by my parents.

> My mother came from a working-class family. My father was more middle class, although his father had actually been working class, but worked his way up, and he'd married someone from a middle-class family. My parents were

highly respectable, et cetera. It was, how I perceive it now, as if when I was born, my mother felt this duty that I had to be good enough for my father who she held in very high esteem. Really most of her life revolved around my father.

I wasn't allowed to be naughty, 'cause that would upset my father and, therefore, she hadn't produced a good enough child for him. She was a very cold person, not able to give emotionally – cuddles, hugs and things like that were very difficult.

No, no I never had any ambitions and my mother never had any ambition. What I thought was, I was going to get married and have children, though I didn't particularly want to get married, but I thought that's how things were going to be. I never really – no future was ever discussed between me and my parents. They sent me off to school, and felt that school would take care of that sort of thing.

Daksha was born in 1953 in rural Gujarat, India. She is Asian and now lives in London where she volunteers at Southall Black Sisters.

When I was seven my mum died and I grew up with my sister-in-law and my brother. I was the second youngest. I had a big family with four sisters and two brothers. When I was little I was very innocent and never thought about what I wanted to do, what I was going to do with my life. Because we were brought up in a very strict family.

But when I was seventeen, I wanted to go to college. I had to ask my father. If he gave me permission I could go, otherwise I couldn't. It was very strict. My father didn't want to send me to college, but I forced him, saying, 'I want to study, let me do it.' My older brother agreed with me, because he is free-minded and he told my father, 'Let her go, she wants to study.'

I studied for my BA in Gujarati, Hindi, Sanskrit, economics, psychology, English and logic. I only went to college for one year. In my second year, my father thought I was

with a boyfriend, that I was going with men. My father
wanted to marry me to a high caste Patel. He believed in the
importance of high caste. I didn't want to marry this high
caste Patel, but it's what my father wanted.

In some cultures, there is pressure to marry within the same
caste, in others it's social class that matters. Though the
differences between caste and class systems reflect the societies
from which they spring, both ensure their respective social
orders are preserved and economic disparities between people
are maintained.

Kiranjit Ahluwalia is Asian and lives in London. She was born in
1956 in a small village in Punjab, India. In the 1980s, Kiranjit was
imprisoned for murdering her abusive husband. She was released
as a result of a successful campaign led by Southall Black Sisters.
Kiranjit now works as a volunteer in their advice centre.

My father died when I was so young, I have never even seen
a photograph of him. My mother died when I was sixteen, so
I went to live with one of my brothers and my sister-in-law.
They are great and brought me up just like a princess.
Whatever I needed, my brother and sister-in-law always
provided for me. Even before then, in so many senses, I was
a spoilt baby. Unlike almost all other Indian girls, I never had
to do any cooking or cleaning. I couldn't cook any curries.

Before my mother died, I still lived in the village. The
people there were very narrow-minded. Even after doing
all the cooking and cleaning, they thought girls shouldn't
be allowed to go out. We were just meant to show respect:
we shouldn't talk too much, shouldn't play with boys or do
any job.

But I wanted to do something with my life. I wanted a
career. I used to think if I was a boy – I used to curse myself,
'Why am I a girl? I should be a boy.' I saw my nephew and
my brothers go out in the evening to the cinema. I wasn't
allowed to go. Boys could go. I must be kept pure for my
future husband.

I didn't want to get married because I wanted to do a job and live my own, happy life. But I knew one day I'd have to get married. I couldn't defy my brothers, they brought me up.

I passed my Bachelor of Law degree in India. But then I was twenty-one, that's considered to be the right age for Indian girls to get married. I wanted to continue studying, but my brother said, 'If you finish your course, you're not going to get a job and earn money. Whatever you need, ask us.' So going against my brother would have been very difficult.

I had refused men before I met my husband. But I knew eventually I had to get married. By the time I met him, I couldn't find any excuse to say no.

Tessa was born in Blackpool in 1933. She is African–Caribbean and lives in Manchester where she works as a professional foster parent.

I come from a stable background of Mum and Dad. In the early years, Dad was away at sea a lot, but Mum was the core of the family. We had a normal working-class upbringing which was quite strict. We were allowed to have our play freedom, but not allowed to wear make-up. No walking around the house like you see with young girls now. We were brought up narrowly where we weren't allowed to be flighty. I was the rebel where I would try to break away.

Mum couldn't just send me to the shop, I had to wander. There wasn't a corner in Blackpool that I didn't know, wasn't a street or back street that I didn't know. I would purposely go out and know I wasn't coming back for four or five hours. I knew what I would get when I got home. We weren't allowed to do this, but I'd do it because I wanted to do it, but I knew I was in trouble when I got home.

I wanted to be a singer or a dancer. I didn't even want to be a shop assistant, because I knew I'd have to write things down. I didn't want to do anything where there was a pen or pencil.

I wanted to be a mother, I think that's one of the reasons I wanted to have a baby, maybe I thought that was security.

As a teenager in the 1940s, becoming a parent represented the kind of stability Tessa had had as a child. For Mary, growing up with an alcoholic father and a mother who couldn't cope seeded a kind of dislocation she felt throughout her childhood.

There wasn't this loving harmonious kind of family thing. I was very much isolated into a much older family. My brother was eleven years older than me, my sister twenty-one years older. So I was this little thing in this family of large people that now seem to me to have been communicating in a very strange way with each other. I was there kind of looking up thinking, 'This is all really bizarre what's going on.' They were looking down at me thinking *I* was rather bizarre, because I didn't fit into what they wanted.

It just seemed like I was in the wrong place at the wrong time. It felt like I wasn't supposed to be there, and that I was kind of in the way. So the more I blended into the background was easiest. I think they were also quite concerned about me. They thought I was a bit of a strange child, because I had quite a vivid imagination. I'd be standing on my own, talking to myself.

Christine also remembers when she was small and feeling that things weren't right at home.

I became aware, as a child, that there was no demonstrative love in our house. I remember being on holiday and taking a picture of my parents and forcing them to stand together and saying, 'Go on, put your arm around her.' But my father didn't put his arm around her. I remember another time, running home and saying that I saw my friend's father kissing her mother. Then another time, I remember seeing a friend running home from school, her mother picking her up and swinging her around. And I ran all the way home, and I was going to throw my arms around my mum. And when I got to the front door, I just didn't. You didn't do that in our house.

I was very aware of the rows that there used to be in the house. There were always rows. I remember my dad trying to chop the furniture, the radio and an alarm clock in half. My mother had said half of everything was hers, so he said, 'She can have her half.'

My mother used to say she was leaving. But she used to go out and walk round the block, saying she was leaving and then come back. I asked her this: didn't she realise that we didn't know she was only standing outside the back door. She used to come up to my room at night and say she was sorry. I can remember once when my dad tried to strangle my mother.

Because my father had wanted a son, a younger sister was brought up as a son. She'd do all the gardens and all the things like that with my dad. Whereas I was sitting in the house cooking and dressmaking and things like that. My father used to cover up all the time for my sister when it was her turn to wash the dishes. He would wash the dishes while she just stood there. And there'd be a row if my mother found out.

Unlike Christine, who sensed something was wrong when she was young, Samantha has only recently found herself re-evaluating her childhood.

I think my childhood was what I would now call abusive. My father being brought up by a single mum in a strict family background and being in the army resulted in him being very strict with his two children.

Originally my parents wanted a boy child, but they got me instead, after a miscarriage. Then my younger brother came along who was like a white sheep and I was the black lamb.

So I was subjected to a lot of very strict, austere violence – lots of swagger sticks over the bottom if I did something wrong. Or locking away in the cellar. I can remember being locked away in the cellar when I was a kid.

What I would look on now and say was quite a violent and abusive childhood but really then didn't strike me as such. I was very much at the age of nineteen or twenty saying, 'Here I am a fine upstanding member of the police service. I got a beating when I was a kid but it didn't do me any harm.' And now that's changed.

A number of participants described feeling like they didn't fit in when they were children, and some were conscious of wanting to rebel. One myth about domestic violence is that it only happens to those women who resist – by word or deed – male authority. But other participants described how perfectly behaved they were, always trying to please. Fictions that blame us if we are abused also reinforce our feeling that there is something inherently wrong with us. For some it's our bodies – we are too fat/thin/tall/short, etc. – or we should have been born male. For others there is a sense of being psychologically removed from other people, always feeling slightly outside the group we're with – never being let in on the secret. For still others it varies from physical to mental unease. Sometimes we experience both at once. I believe this anxiety is the alienation caused by instilling the belief in all growing girls that we are 'other' – that is always different and separate from the norm, which is men.

So, like Anita and Mary, we never feel good enough, we don't fit in. Or, like Samantha and Christine, we'll never transcend our parents' disappointment that we're not boys. I also believe that some of our ambivalence about marriage is rooted in this abiding 'other'-ness.

Saroj saw her parents' relationship as one of her father abusing and her mother suffering, yet she looked forward to finding love and security in her own marriage. Both Daksha and Kiranjit came from happy homes, but though they were clear that marriage would end their independence and hopes for a career, nevertheless they believed it was an inevitability they could not avoid. And Tessa, whose childhood was also secure, saw motherhood as an escape from her strict family. It seems to me that Saroj and Tessa tried to make the fantasy of having a man one that would enable them to fit into 'normal' life. And even though Daksha and Kiranjit said they knew that marriage would diminish them, they also knew that they couldn't resist the process that would 'normalise' them through it. In both buying into and resisting the power of marriage, we acknowledge that with it we are seen as more normal and that without it we are seen by others and ourselves as more 'other'.

These experiences of 'normality', 'other'-ness and self-blame cut across cultures and social classes. And whether you have suffered domestic violence or not, if you're a woman you've probably been inculcated with two imperatives: that you must always put other people ('s feelings/opinions/interests/wishes) first and that it is your responsibility for making everything all right.

Growing up with no choice in their lives and a lack of entitlement to having an opinion was echoed again and again by the participants in this book. It's something that most women and some men will recognise from their own experiences. If you haven't been abused and can't imagine how and why women don't leave abusers, perhaps thinking about those imperatives will help. Maybe the difference between you and an abused woman is just the luck of the draw.

For many women this means either never feeling separate from her family or having no identity of her own – sometimes both. A process that doesn't just produce no self-confidence – it often results in making little women with no sense of ourselves at all.

2
The first time

My earliest memories of family life are of my father shouting and my mother crying. Or me crying. Or both of us crying. My father was not one of those closet abusers. Everyone felt the rough edge of his tongue at harrowing and unpredictable intervals. Like many bullies, he was particularly vicious to those who could least stand up for themselves: people closest to him – me, my mother, my grandmother and my uncle; his employees; waiters and chambermaids, as well as others dependent on his tips for their livelihood.

But he was also abusive to his friends, business associates, and even to people he might need, or authority figures like the police. His public performances were often before audiences of bewildered strangers and cringingly embarrassed family members.

My father's behaviour alternated between charm – even acts of generosity and kindness – and sudden, unpredictable verbal attacks. He was like a Jekyll and Hyde. Though usually mistaken for a purely drug-induced phenomenon, I believe my father's changes were as calculating as those of the original character in Robert Louis Stevenson's nineteenth-century novel. Respectable Dr Jekyll intentionally created Mr Hyde to act out all his wildest fantasies – the drug was merely a vehicle. In the book, the resulting power struggle was, crucially, *inside* Jekyll who always stayed in control – just like my father.

And like the fictional Victorian's victims, my father's never knew who or what he would be next. It appeared that my 'Dr Jekyll' father could be set off by the most innocuous conversation, the most innocent remark, or by nothing. And every time it was a sickening shock. The pit of my stomach would knot and a wave of nausea would sweep over me. And then I would go curiously numb – trying to block out the pain and the shame. Trying to pretend it wasn't really happening. Nobody who said he loved me, least of all my father, could behave like that.

As I got older, whenever I was forced to witness my father abusing someone who couldn't fight back or who might conceivably do us harm in return, I always felt compelled to try to repair the damage. I'd apologise, make excuses for him, offer some sort of compensation. This damage limitation was, I think, also necessary to convince myself that what he'd done wasn't really so bad and that his behaviour was not out of (my) control.

Because my father's emotional and psychological abuse is my earliest memory, I cannot remember the first time it happened, except to say that my whole childhood seems like the first time. But I can still identify with women who describe the shock of the first time that someone you love, who is supposed to love you, is abusive. Like most of those who experience abuse, I lived in a state of more or less permanent anxiety – especially when my father was actually there.

Had I done something to make him angry? Of course it was inadvertent, but he didn't know that. I'd rack my brain and fix on anything, swearing I wouldn't repeat it. I'd do better next time. It would never happen again. And I'd make myself believe that he would finally turn into the steady, reliable, emotionally stable and protective father that everyone is supposed to have. After all, if I wasn't getting the emotional security I needed, it must be my fault.

Being constantly fearful and controlled by my father's abuse increased my self-doubt and insecurity. Such reactions to the whole range of sexual and personal violences are all too common.

These feelings permeate the participants' descriptions of their first experiences of domestic violence; Jekyll and Hyde are terms that many used themselves to describe the men's behaviour.

Jekyll and Hyde

Alabee had wanted to join the Navy before she became a mother. Her first experience of domestic violence happened when her daughter was small.

> I really didn't know this person was like that, because he was so caring and gentle – or I felt he was at the time. What I realise now, looking back, is he was quite manipulative, but I wasn't aware of those type of things at that time. And then it came to a head.
>
> We'd had an argument because he was quite into other women. He liked to go with other women from time to time. I'd found out about his last escapade and I'd given him an ultimatum, if he didn't stop it: 'I'm going to go out as well.' And I did. Because he didn't stop.
>
> Then we had this big row and I marched out of his house and went home. But the next day, I got this phone call saying, 'I'm really sorry, let's talk about it. Come round and we'll chat and what have you and make up.' I went round his house and he locked me in his bedroom, threw the key on top of the wardrobe. I heard the thing go, the catch, and I can remember turning round and the next thing I was being punched all over the place.
>
> Then I was stripped off. I was told to strip, take my clothes off. I was very shy then, and for me that was one of the most humiliating moments of my life, I think. I don't think I'll ever live a more humiliating moment. Because I wasn't that type of person where I would take off my clothes. I was quite plump and I was shy about the size of my body.
>
> Then I saw him go behind the wardrobe and he pulled out this cricket bat and proceeded to beat me all over the place

with it. Then it went from that to him sitting down, getting a knife, running it across my skin so that it just let a little bit of blood come to the surface. It was like, 'This is what I'm going to do to you all over your body. But I'm really going to cut you.' That is what he was inferring, 'This is how it's going to feel.'

Then he raped me after that. He was quite brutal in it, the sexual attack, he damaged me quite badly inside, I found out after.

Then he continued to beat me on and off for the next two and a half hours. Halfway through the beating, there's a woman upstairs that came down and said, 'Everything all right in there?' There's me screaming at the top of my voice, 'No' and 'Help.' And his saying, 'No, we're just having a row, it's OK, go away.' And she went away.

A little while before I actually did get out of there, he went like a Jekyll and Hyde. He said to me, 'Would you like a cup of coffee?' His kitchen led off his bedroom. And I was, 'No.' But he brought me back this boiling hot cup of coffee. It was like he took great pleasure in seeing me try to drink it, knowing damn well I couldn't, because my lips were swollen and I had cuts in them. And I couldn't. It was just coming right out of my mouth again and dripping down my face.

I knew why *he* thought he was doing it. Because he was telling me while he was doing it. In between each punch or kick or whatever he was doing to me, he was telling me he was doing it because he loved me. But that to me made no sense at all, so I wasn't listening to that. But he also told me that he'd put me so far on this pedestal that he'd made me out to be somebody, basically, untouchable. And that it was because I was supposed to have been better than everybody else and that he was going to spend the rest of his life with me, and I'd shattered all his dreams. So I knew why *he* thought he was doing it. *I* thought he was doing it because he thought he was able to do it; that somewhere along the line I felt I must have given him the impression that he could do that to me if he wanted to; that I was his property to just bandy about, either punch or kick or abuse in any way he liked.

I kept thinking to myself, 'Get up and do something.' I'd not been brought up in the type of family where you actually stood back and let anybody hit you. I had three big brothers that had always shown me how to fight or defend myself. I know I've never understood it to this day, why I actually stood there and actually did nothing. I can't even remember trying to push him away. I can remember holding my arms up across my face to protect myself. But I can't actually remember trying to push him away. I actually thought I was going to die. I didn't think there was any way out.

Mary felt isolated as a child in a much older family and retreated into herself. She remembers reacting to the first time in a similar way.

I was about eighteen, married about a year, the very first time. He told me in front of someone that he was going to take a load of sleeping tablets. I didn't think he was actually going to take an overdose, he was just being dramatic about the subject and that wasn't his normal way. That wasn't his sort of thing, I'd never heard him say anything like that before.

And I turned around and said, 'There you are then, go on if you're going to do this.' And I got kicked.

He got me right on the chin and all. I was quite shocked. I was like stunned. It just, now I can see it, triggered off all this stuff I had repressed about my brother who'd physically abused me.

I was absolutely in awe of this person. You're not in awe exactly, but like fearful of their Jekyll and Hyde kind of personality, which this person was, very. One minute very smooth.

I remember reverting in. That kind of shocked me right back inside myself at that point. I think I stayed in there for quite a long time. Our communication between the two of us just completely broke down.

Marian's happy childhood, full of memories of being a good little girl in her nice frocks, left her unprepared for her partner's apparently two-sided character.

He was definitely a Jekyll and Hyde. I mean, he is a charmer. He can be extremely charming, and I think a lot of people found it quite hard to think of him behaving in the way he was behaving towards me. I think it took a lot of our friends a very, very long time to actually recognise it.

Carmina is African-Caribbean and was born in Hermitage, West Indies in 1953. Soon after, she moved to London where she grew up. Carmina now lives in Aberdeen where she is a community worker. She didn't find it difficult to leave when her first partner hit her. But when the next one abused her, it was different.

The very first time he hit me, he says, 'I promise it won't happen again. It looks like you're scared of men and I'm a different sort of guy. I'm not that kind of person and I will help you.'

I did believe him. Put it this way, I wanted to believe it. 'Cause it was like I wanted his company, I was scared of being on my own. 'Cause I've always had company, I was brought up in a big family and I always liked company.

I wanted to be, on one side, I wanted to be on my own. But I didn't know whether I could manage. But saying that now, I think I could have managed, 'cause I'm pretty strong. But the weakness was the enticement that he could be like the father figure for me and my son. That's maybe what I was looking for, like a father figure.

As a child on a remote farm in the north of England, Sally tried to be perfect and quiet in order to minimise abuse. She believed that if she had a career she would avoid being trapped like her mother. But it didn't help Sally the first time her husband was violent.

> I can remember the first time and I do remember it quite clearly. We'd moved down to London from the north of England where we'd both been studying. I'd got a job as a teacher and he decided to do further studying. We were staying with his mother for six months before we got somewhere to live. His mother was in the bathroom and he wanted to use the bathroom. So he went and shouted at his mother to get out, because he wanted to use the bathroom.

> Then he came back into the bedroom and he started twisting my arm right behind my back, shouting at me, 'You're a fucking bitch.' It felt devastating. I felt hurt, very hurt. And shocked. It felt like this unprovoked attack which was to do with pure hatred, really.

> Although I was probably twenty-two by then, I was completely unprepared somehow for living in the world. I didn't know how to look after myself – and because I couldn't distinguish between me and somebody else, I had no way of dealing with somebody else's violence and couldn't understand what was happening.

Marian, too, remembers the first time clearly.

> I know that when he hit me the first time, that had nothing to do with anything I'd done. That was because he was drunk. He'd been rejected by a very old friend of his. For some reason, years before, they'd had an argument and he tried to patch it up and this friend rejected him. He then smashed up my car. When he came home and told me this had happened, I was angry that he'd smashed up my car. I just showed some anger and he punched me in the face. That was the first time he actually hit me.

> Then, because he was so drunk, he collapsed on the bed. And I was not only physically dazed, I was completely

shocked by this behaviour. I got up and got dressed and I went out. It was after midnight. I went to a friend and spent the night with her. She reacted in an extremely sympathetic way.

But what I don't understand is why the next morning I eventually went back. Before I went back, I was still in pain. I thought he'd done something to my front teeth and I went to casualty to check them out. I said I'd been punched. They didn't seem very interested in the whys and wherefores.

I think I went back because I wanted him to see what he had done. I wanted to show him what a dreadful thing he'd done. My lip was very swollen. He was so remorseful, so incredibly sorry. I think I must have felt sorry for him because his friend rejected him. I knew that he was drunk. So I made excuses in my head. I didn't think it would happen again.

Drink and drugs are common excuses for all kinds of otherwise unacceptable behaviour. In fact, the majority of studies show that while some men are abusive while intoxicated, most do it stone-cold sober. Even those who are apparently chronic drug or alcohol users have been known to be violent without taking anything. Still, these remain the most popular (self-)justifications for abuse.

So is it surprising that, like Marian, many women make excuses and don't think it will happen again? How reasonable is it to expect anyone to end a relationship after just one bad incident? When, like the majority of women, we are brought up to believe that it is our responsibility to make everything all right, wouldn't we be accused (and accuse ourselves) of bailing out at the first sign of trouble?

Most women invest a great deal of emotional and physical energy in creating the world that they share with their men. To 'destroy' it just like that is very difficult. There is an overwhelming tendency to hope for the best after anything shocking like the first incident of domestic violence.

That need to believe it will never happen again is so powerful it will almost always stifle any feelings of uncertainty. It is hard for anyone to face the fact that someone who professes love could inflict pain. Therefore, that person must have made a mistake. Or it wasn't really that bad. Or they were drunk. Or upset. Or they were pushed into doing it. In desperation to convince herself that it will never happen again, a woman may believe that it was within her power to prevent it: that somehow it was all her fault.

Denial

Though part of Molly grew up wanting to get married and have children – as she sees it, to be conventional – and part of her was a tomboy and a rebel, she feels that it was never being allowed to have any real ambition that had a greater influence on what she became. Molly now believes that how she reacted to her first experience of domestic violence was a reflection of what she then saw as her strengths and weaknesses.

> He had a bit of a reputation for being a womaniser, and I was warned after I started going out with him, because he's very good-looking and he's very charming and all the rest of it. I used to think, 'Why me? If he's had all these different women, and he hasn't had a serious relationship for four or five years, why me, I'm a single parent?' I'm not putting myself down for being one, but I mean there are restrictions that go with being a single parent. But he carried on seeing me.
>
> He was very considerate, initially a real gentleman. There was no physical contact between us for a good six weeks of our relationship, which I found quite surprising. He was just wonderful to begin with.
>
> I can't remember when it all started to go wrong. But the first time he did hit me, he'd been drinking, and I think he'd been taking drugs. So I put it all down to that – it was really me wanting to excuse his behaviour. 'Cause I didn't

want to face up to what he'd done. I was shocked, but I really felt like I could control it. You see, I thought, 'I'm quite a strong person.' I thought, 'I can calm him down, I can cope with this.' And he eventually calmed down himself.

All I wanted him to do afterwards was to say, 'I am really sorry.' I had a massive bruise on my leg and the next day I was limping and he couldn't believe what he'd done. 'Did I do that to you?' I said, 'Yes you did.' And he said, 'I promise I'll never hit you like that again.' I said, 'Never mind about hitting me like this, you won't hit me at all.' But he did. I couldn't tell you all the different instances. But as far as I can remember, that was the only time in all the times he's assaulted me that he actually said he was sorry. I wanted to believe it would never happen again.

For some women, like Molly, the first assault seems to happen out of the blue. But for most women, like policewoman Samantha, the first physical violence occurs after a period of gradually increasing verbal, emotional and psychological abuse.

I married in January '81 and there was a six-month honeymoon period where we were both very much hearts and flowers. I was baking my own bread and hoovering daily. It didn't matter what shift I was on, I was out there doing the wifey bit. And things were OK. He would come home and devour the cakes, the biscuits and the bread and look at the floor and not say anything and it was OK.

We were both highly ambitious and within six months it was patently obvious that our careers were going in different directions in different departments. I was going all out for promotion and so was he, but I wanted to stay in uniform and he wanted to become a detective.

The abuse really started with the odd what I would call barbed comment. It was more mental or emotional abuse. 'These biscuits are soft', or something like that. It was just tiny things, 'You haven't ironed my shirts right.' And

I would think, 'Why don't you iron them yourself?' But then I would just iron them again. So there was no real power in my life at all. I was desperately trying to hold on to this, 'We can be equal, we can do this together and this is a shared thing.' It was all going down the toilet and I didn't realise it.

The odd barbed comment at home became barbed comments in front of colleagues, friends at social dos. He would be critical of my appearance, my behaviour. He would get stroppy if I danced with other men or if I went away from his side, if I wasn't a fashion accessory on his arm. If I went off and started speaking to friends of mine on my shift [group of police officers who work together], he got pretty arsey. It would be like, 'You're supposed to be with me. Your shift didn't invite you here today.' Or, 'Do you want a lift home or do you want to walk?' We would go to a Christmas function and he wouldn't speak to me and I would feel so totally humiliated. He would say, 'I'm going to go now.' So it was a removal of any form of affection and niceness. It was that distancing, that coldness. But it was also those very patriarchal comments being made, quite poisonous, that started to get me down.

It then escalated into rows where I would try to put my point of view forward. It just didn't work and sometimes he didn't come home at all, so there was no point in having a row with him. So we could go three or four days without even seeing each other and then he would come home and act as though nothing happened. So it was just left. By then he had become a detective and was drinking quite heavily, so it started to go really bad.

The rows were starting to get pretty horrific – screaming and shouting. The first time he was physically violent was when he slapped me where I burst into tears. It was another row, it would have been over something minimal like my saying, 'Why can't you do some ironing as well as me? You're working nine to five, you have every weekend off. I'm working shifts and I only have one weekend off every month. Why can't you put some effort into the relationship?' I burst into tears, got very upset with him and he slapped me.

I was incredibly surprised. 'How come this guy who's supposed to love and cherish me has suddenly done something quite abusive?' That almost unhinged me. It certainly put me off the rails a bit and I sat there agonising over what I could do to draw him back.

Whether the abuse is sudden or gradual, like Samantha and Molly, most women are aware of the pressure to fix whatever it is that has become, apparently, temporarily unhinged. This is because we are brought up to believe that women are the centre of the family and that in nearly all cultures it's women's responsibility to keep the family unit together. Not trying or failing to do so isn't only a sign of failure as a woman, but has the effect of 'unwomaning' – removing both her female essence and substance – and therefore rendering such a woman non-existent.

Wedded bliss

Tessa's conventional working-class upbringing in Blackpool in the 1930s and 1940s did not prepare her for the first time.

I decided when I was fifteen and a half that I couldn't put up with my parents' strictness much longer. So I met this guy and I got married at sixteen. I blackmailed my parents 'cause in those days to get pregnant was a bad thing. So it was moral blackmail and it was either you let me get married or I'm gonna get myself pregnant. I daren't come out and say things like that, but in a roundabout way I did it like that. Now I married this man that was eight years older than me. I was madly in love with him. I thought the sun shone out of his backside.

He was mentally cruel to me. He made me feel very inferior. He used to tell people, 'She can't read, she can't write, she's stupid.' My younger sister hated him for it and she used to say, 'You're daft, Tessa, and he's making out you're stupid.' I think she was glad when I left him. But at the time I thought, 'She's interfering.' Growing up, she and I were so close, but we used to fight a lot, argue. And I just thought, 'She's trying to take my life over and she's interfering.' Because she was much brighter than I was. I resented it and I wanted to find my own self. This was my way of doing it. But I didn't.

I think he hit me a couple of times, not to say a bad beating, but I got slapped. But it was mental cruelty with him. Also being young, coming from the narrowness that I'd come from, I just laid back and took it.

I think I thought, 'This is the way marriage is and women have got to be subservient.' Even though my mother wasn't a subservient woman, in my eyes, 'cause she stood up to me dad. I didn't know that women have orgasms. I mean I'd left my first husband before I even knew. I didn't know what it was, the first time I thought I was having a heart attack actually.

My first husband did buggery on me and that's why I left him. I went to Hull. Then I came back to Manchester, to my parents. My dad said, 'Look, you're a married woman.' I'd never told anybody what happened to me. My dad said, 'You must patch your marriage up.' Mum said, 'No you shouldn't.' But it was my dad's house and I thought, 'I will.' I was willing to make a try.

And my husband said, 'I'll take you back, but not because I love you, but because I pity you.' I think that opened my eyes.

Barbara left home, and her politically active parents, to get married. The effects of psychological and emotional abuse were her earliest and most powerful memories of domestic violence.

I think that when my husband and I got married (I was seventeen and I was pregnant), I compared him to my father. Because my husband was nineteen and knew how to handle alcohol and he didn't make a scene of any kind in public, whether that was singing at the top of his voice or shouting abuse at somebody at the other side of the street or whatever – he didn't do that kind of thing. He seemed to somehow, for what was important on my agenda at that age, not do things my father did. It was a comparison. It was, 'He's better than my father.' In my mind, according to this criteria, therefore he'll do.

I suppose it was when my son was about four months old was the first time my husband was physically violent. At that time we had no transport and we were in a small, isolated cottage with an outside loo, no hot water, no bath. Two rooms, basically, with a sink you couldn't fit your standard basin into at the window. Really the worst thing of all, before he was physically violent, was that the way he was abusive, I think, was causing my loneliness.

He would go out on a Friday night. He would come in maybe three o'clock in the morning (we lived outside the town, so he would've walked). He would get up on a Saturday morning and, again, not come back until Sunday morning about three o'clock. He would get up on Sunday morning and go out hunting and come in about six at night. Then he would go to bed at about nine o'clock on a Sunday night. So weekends were very lonely, I was there on my own with our child.

I didn't have any friends as such, because all my friends were still going out to discos. We lived in an area which was very clannish and we were very much outsiders. I can remember on one occasion where he promised me faithfully that he would be home on Saturday night by six o'clock. He had been working as a building labourer, but had suddenly packed it in. So in terms of poverty it became really bad. Nevertheless, I had spent more than I had budgeted for, for a meal, so that when he came in it would be a nice meal and all the rest of it.

I had put the baby in the pram and had gone out about four o'clock in the afternoon for a walk with him

I came back and it was starting to get late and I knew by looking at my cottage that if the light was still out, my husband wasn't in. I kind of made this pact with myself that I would not go in the house until he was back, till the light was on. I walked around till about ten o'clock at night. I kept going back and going back and he wasn't in. Eventually, because the child was getting so cold, I was forced to go in. I think around about that time, I suppose, I kind of went into a depression.

It cannot be said too often that domestic violence cuts across cultures and social classes. But the material conditions that different women experience by virtue of their race, class, age, ability, sexuality, etc., mean that the effects of domestic violence and the possibilities of managing it do vary, sometimes markedly, between women. For Barbara, poverty played a key role in entrapping her.

Eleanor is white and was born in 1944 in Liverpool. She now lives in Lancashire where she works in a refuge for women escaping from domestic violence. The way she was brought up, Eleanor believes, left her unprepared for dealing with abuse.

About a week or so before the wedding we were arguing. I don't know what we were arguing over. And he slapped me across the face. I knew I didn't want to marry him. I remember telling my mum the night before I was getting married, I said, 'Do you know, not for this baby, I wouldn't marry him.'

But I didn't tell her or anyone else that he slapped me. Probably because I thought it was my fault. I was nagging him, he had pressures from the wedding. I don't know. It didn't occur to me, I don't think, to tell anyone.

Anne went back home to New York as a single parent, having divorced her first husband. She felt pressured by her father into returning to England and marrying again, because she was pregnant. She had only slept once with the man who was to become her second husband. He was inundating her with phone calls, letters and flowers. His relentless pursuit of her, from across the Atlantic, culminated in him showing up in America, where they got married.

I was fond of him. I've only ever been intimate with two men in my life and I've married both of the buggers. I felt cornered into marrying my second husband. I had grave misgivings.

It started mostly as insults and mean remarks: 'Can't you get it right?' And things like that. Then I remember him saying, 'It's probably not my kid, after all, and you just married me for my money.'

He's a great one for weeping and crying. 'It'll be all right, we'll be all right.' When you're a matter of ten days off having a child, you think, 'Just keep yourself calm. Just keep calm. One day at a time.' He fluctuated from being weepy to being sarcastic and verbally abusive.

It would have been something as simple as not enough milk in his coffee. He's also the kind of person that a fingerprint on doors or paintwork, anything could set him off. I remember being so astounded. 'I've just married this man. I'm due to have his child any minute. I've just gone through this tremendous upheaval and he's bitching at me about enough milk in his coffee.'

He simmered down a bit in public. In private he switched from being attentive and affectionate to being rude, scathing and sneering. If we went somewhere, he would just walk away and leave me. In a matter of weeks it was such an abrupt turnaround that most of the time I stood there with my jaw hanging open.

You feel rotten, you feel lousy. You feel grotesque and very, very pregnant. I thought, 'I don't believe it, what have I done? What do I do?' I felt that my judgement had been weak, that I had ignored all the alarm bells. I was probably, 'I planted myself in this mess.'

Kiranjit left her home in India to get married, because she wanted to please the family members who brought her up when her parents died. She sees the first time in the context of the combined pressures of the wedding and the dislocation of her new married life in Britain.

> My brother came from India for my wedding. We all stayed in London with my sister the first week of my marriage, because my whole family was here. Then my husband and I went to *his* family's house on the Sunday night. On Monday, he went to work and in the evening he came back and he slapped me badly. I consider that this was the first day of my marriage because it was in his house.
>
> My husband went to work Monday morning and he told me he's coming back about seven o'clock. My mother-in-law and father-in-law used to work the night shift. Because I was too shy to talk with other people in my husband's family, I spent all day in my room waiting for him. I had a cup of tea or coffee and looked at the wall thinking, 'Oh, he's coming so we can talk, I can laugh. He can take me out.' 'Cause he told me he would take me out for an evening walk, he hadn't got a car then.
>
> At seven o'clock he came home and I was in our room, a small box room. First thing he went straight in the kitchen to see what kind of curry he was going to have. After that he came straight upstairs and asked me, 'How are you?' I said, 'Fine.' And he said, 'Who made the curry?' I said, 'I don't know, maybe your elder sister or maybe your mother.' He said, 'No, you're lying to me.' I said, 'What should I lie for?' Then I said, 'I don't know.' He said, 'Look, my mother makes curry out of melted butter – ghee – and today I can smell oil. This curry is made in oil today.' I said, 'Honestly, I don't know. I swear upon God I don't know. I didn't make any curry today.' Suddenly he said, 'Oh yeah, you're lying to me.' So he slapped me. I never knew that he could get so angry, he had a different personality as well.
>
> It was a shock. He was really angry. He started shouting and screaming and I started crying. He pulled my hand saying,

'Let's go downstairs.' He was pulling me downstairs. And I was frightened of falling down because I was wearing an Indian dress, I couldn't walk very well I was so used to trousers then. And he dragged me downstairs.

He took the saucepans and threw them on the floor saying, 'Look at this.' I was in shock. I was crying so hard I couldn't see. He was screaming. His family was there, but nobody stopped him.

I was crying like a baby. It was a shock. None of my family ever hit me, never shouted at me, never pulled me like this. Then suddenly he grabbed my hand again and he was pulling me upstairs. I was so scared he was going to beat me there. I was asking him, 'Please don't.' But nobody came to stop him. Then he picked me up, he was big, and took me upstairs and put me on the bed. He slammed and kicked the door very hard. Everyone was in shock, standing downstairs. Five or seven of his family, none of them said a word.

As a child, Elizabeth was frantic to be the best little girl in the world. She grew up frightened at the thought of leaving home, unprepared for the outside world, because her parents were so protective. She remembers her first experience of domestic violence.

I was already pregnant the first time he hit me. I must have been about four months pregnant, I suppose. I had no idea, no inkling at all that he was violent. We'd had an argument, walking home one evening, because he'd invited round a man that I really didn't want to see. He was a previous boyfriend and he'd treated me very badly. And I said, 'Look, I really don't want him in the house.' And he was saying, 'But he's a friend of mine.' And I was saying, 'But this man was a bastard to me.' And he said, 'Tough, it's my decision.' And I walked off ahead and walked into the house and shut the door and went upstairs.

He kicked the front door in, came upstairs and assaulted me, which was very shocking. I certainly wasn't expecting it, I certainly wasn't expecting him, the father of my child, to beat me. There was a house full of people, nobody did anything. Nobody said anything. Nobody said to him, 'I don't think you should be doing that.'

There was bruising all over my back because I'd curled up to protect my belly. It was more shock than anything else. Just complete, 'Oh my God.'

I felt I shouldn't have annoyed him. I thought, 'I'll be more careful in future and I must try really hard to get his affection back.' That was the most primary objective – to get his love back. Then that was going to protect me – if he loved me, he wouldn't hit me. That was what I was thinking. I wasn't thinking, 'He was wrong, he shouldn't do that.' I was thinking, 'Oh, oh, I shouldn't have shut the door like that. I'll be more careful in future.'

The amount of milk in a cup of coffee, fingermarks on the paintwork, who prepared the food, the way a door is closed, how a shirt is ironed, impatience to use the bathroom, drink . . . all may seem like utterly ludicrous reasons to assault anyone. But these are the sorts of excuses for abuse that women have been reporting for years and the stories that frontline workers find themselves hearing daily. The hopelessly banal activities of everyday life are inextricably linked with the apparently unimaginable horrors of abuse. And that's the point, really. Domestic violence, like child abuse, rape, sexual harassment and every other kind of personal violence, doesn't happen in extraordinary circumstances. It doesn't just happen to those with drink or drug problems, to the unemployed, to the 'mentally' ill, to 'dysfunctional' families: so called because they are non-nuclear or are judged by others not to be communicating properly; that don't function as a unit, thus scapegoating individual members and supposedly preventing children from maturing; or where women and men fail to conform to male and female stereotypes. Domestic violence happens in everyday life to every-day people.

We need to ask ourselves who among us has ever lived in an entirely functional family? Is there such a thing? Do you know of any family without some element that would be considered 'dysfunctional'? Who decides what is 'dysfunctional'? Where does the notion come from and what is it really for? Like many pseudo-scientific psychological theories, it's often used to police troublesome members of society by giving them the label 'dysfunctional'. But it seems to me that one of its most insidious effects is to let men off the hook for their abuse, by pointing the finger at everyone else.

Evidence from all over the world suggests that domestic violence is far more widespread than most people suspect or will admit. Yet the word that recurs time and again throughout all accounts of the first time is 'shock'. This shock is often linked to the powerful and universal belief that marriage or partnership with a man is the ultimate goal for all women. The taboo against admitting failure to reach it is so strong that it renders the possibility of domestic violence invisible. Tessa and Eleanor both describe their reactions to the first time: it just didn't occur to them to tell anyone.

Women, despite propaganda to the contrary, are terrifically good at keeping secrets, at hiding the truth from ourselves and from everyone else. And for good reason. Many women and children are not only silenced by the fear and threat of further violence, but because they know that the penalty for failing, if they can't even manage to keep their men happy, might be the loss of support from family and friends. So we all hope that the first time is the last.

3
It ain't me babe

Since I began making films in 1973, most of them have been about women's struggles for better lives. Like many film-makers, I am conscious that my own history has a large part to play in my choice of subject matter. Because I identify so closely and so personally with women's issues, the process of making the films often transforms not just my ideas about that particular subject but deep-seated feelings about myself.

When working on women and food, I could not escape my own eating hangups: cycles of dieting, comfort eating, self-loathing and dieting. By the time I'd finished the second film on the subject, I felt much better about food, my body and me.

For over twenty years, the area in which I have made most films is sexual violence: child abuse, domestic violence, women's personal safety and prostitution. Yet until I was forty, I could not admit to myself that I had had an abusive father.

I complained about his rude, unpredictable and vicious behaviour towards everyone. I feared his visits, knowing that whatever he'd asked me to organise would fail to meet his requirements and that he would scream at me and whoever else he held responsible. I especially hated the way he treated my grandmother and the woman who lived with him – not only brooking no disagreement with his opinions, but dictating their every thought and deed including what they wore and ate. I felt controlled by his anger, but powerless to stand up to him.

Though I sometimes argued with my father, in the face of his rage I usually either remained submissively silent or scurried around trying to repair the damage. In the end I always gave in.

The one thing I absolutely could not do was name what he was doing – and what I was being subjected to. I was able to say that my mother had divorced my father when I was seven because all he ever did was shout at her. But somehow or other I couldn't admit to myself that my father was an abuser.

There is often shame attached to being subjected to any form of violence, especially if it's sexual. Victims of rape and child sexual abuse are regularly told by the police, barristers, judges and the media that they are partly, if not entirely, to blame for what happens to them. It seems to me that all over the world victims of sexual violence have always been considered soiled by the very crimes committed against them. And, of course, we all internalise this sense of blame and will go to extraordinary lengths not to identify ourselves as victims – somehow believing that by not naming it, it hasn't really happened.

By admitting my father's abuse, I would be including myself in that vilified and pitied group – abused women. The stigma of failure as a woman is hard for any of us to bear. I simply couldn't stand to be dirty and 'unwomaned'.

Of course what *has* happened is that by not naming our abuse we suffer doubly – sometimes trebly. The abuse has happened no matter what we admit. We go through terrible agonies to keep the truth from ourselves and from others who might help. And finally, our silence allows the abuser to continue abusing – if not us, others.

For some of us, the fear of naming also includes the fear that we will have to do something about the abuse once we admit it's happening. I do not remember being conscious of this, but I suspect it was there. Contemplating any kind of change can be frightening. It is especially so when we are surrounded by a hostile world that mainly holds us responsible and blames us for being abused, and is likely to punish us if we try to leave the abuser or seek redress for the abuse.

Naming

When Eleanor's husband slapped her, just before they got married, she told her mother that if it wasn't for the fact that she was pregnant she wouldn't be marrying him at all. Yet afterwards, Eleanor remembers making excuses for his violence.

> I've used every excuse in the book: I fell downstairs; I walked into doors; the baby hit me over the head with a bottle.
>
> Then he started leaving marks. The black eyes and the thick lips were coming in then – the broken nose. I ended up with a hairline fracture of the jaw.
>
> I started to hear about battered wives. But I still didn't consider myself a battered wife, 'cause I didn't have broken arms and broken legs. I used to say to him, 'I'm becoming a battered wife.' He'd say, 'You're not a battered wife. Do you want me to show you what a battered wife looks like?' And you back down then.

The first time Molly was assaulted by her partner, he claimed he couldn't believe he was to blame for the massive bruise on her leg that made her limp. It was also the only time he said he was sorry. She wanted to believe that the first time would be the last, but it wasn't. Molly's partner always denied he'd caused her injuries. Her experience of her partner's denial was similar to Eleanor's.

> He said, 'Oh, you think you've been battered. I'll take you to a battered wife's hostel and I'll show you what it's really like.' And there were warning bells going on through my head all the time, thinking, 'I shouldn't really have anything more to do with him.' But I could not break that tie, it really would have been difficult. So I would say for the first six weeks or so, he would do anything to make me happy. He was bending over backwards, he was giving up his Friday nights with the lads to be with me. He was taking me out to dinner, he was buying me things.

While all this was going on, I was really depressed. At one point I felt really suicidal and I hated myself for having him back. All the time I was feeling very vulnerable and emotional, he felt very confident.

Some of his friends do it to their girlfriends. Perhaps not to the degree that he's done it to me. One night we went out and this friend of mine said, 'Oh, your mascara's smudged.' Then she realised it was a bruise. Even then, you see, I didn't want her to question me. I didn't want her to say, 'What's been going on? You tell me what he's done to you.' So I defused the situation by saying to her, 'Oh we had a row and I provoked him.'

I'd never wanted to face up to it before, 'cause I've always had this picture of wanting to maintain certain standards and expectations of myself. I have high standards and I don't want to fail in anything. So I didn't want to have to admit to anybody that that's what he was doing. Because then I would have to face it myself and I didn't want to.

Christine believes her inability to name her husband's abuse came from growing up in a family without love and because her father always favoured her sister over her. Like Molly and Eleanor, Christine's husband reacted with disbelief when she went into a refuge.

He couldn't understand why I was in a refuge. 'You're not a battered wife,' he said. I said, 'But you don't have to beat me up every week.' I said, 'Look at the times I've had ruptured kidneys and perforated ear drums.' I said, 'That's not right, you know, you're not supposed to hit women.'

Since they were both working police officers, Samantha sought equality with her husband. Her demands met with physical violence after months of emotional abuse. Samantha recalls how her miscarriage, caused by her husband's violence, prompted her to reassess her situation.

Shortly after the miscarriage, I thought, 'There ain't something too good here.' But I wouldn't actually put the label on it, I think I fought shy of that label for a long time. I've talked to other policewomen who've had husbands who've been violent or partners who have been violent. All of us have laughed about the fact that battered women are *other* women.

There was a lot of resistance about putting any form of label like that: battered woman, battered wife; my husband's domestically violent, he is a violent person; he's abusing me, he's misusing his power; and all the rest of it, all those sorts of labels. There was a tremendous resistance to putting that label on me because I didn't want to wear it.

Also it seemed false because when you were at work, you were up, together and one hundred per cent and OK. So it was like you were a part-time battered wife. You were doing it in job share. It was that sort of mentality. That part of you was a battered wife and the other part was like this OK person.

It's a common thing that we've all been quite resistant to that label. When you actually realise it, even then you just say, 'OK, now I'm a battered wife, how can I change him? So don't tell me what I am, let me push this label out of the way. What can I do to change him?'

Janie is African-Caribbean and was born in 1960 in Manchester where she still lives. She is a mature student.

It was when I realised that I didn't have a life that I admitted to myself that I was a battered wife. Everything I did, he had to be involved with. It was as though he was frightened that I was going to go out and tell everybody what he was doing to me. And that's when I realised that I was as trapped as I thought.

Tessa's mother made her welcome when she left her first husband for good in the early 1950s, after he said he'd take her back not because he loved her but because he pitied her. Fifteen years later her mother had died and, without that kind of support, Tessa was unable to a face up to being a battered woman, again.

I had nowhere to go. I mean when you've got six kids – five were at home. Where were you gonna go with five kids in those days? And I'd seen worse cases than mine. I said to myself, 'You've put yourself in this, you get yourself out.' In any situation I get into, I *always* think, 'You've put yourself in it, you get yourself out.'

At that time he wasn't abusive in the sense that he didn't beat me up. I didn't have black eyes, I wasn't black and blue half the time. And a nagging husband is part of the norm at any rate.

Another thing he used to do. He knew when I was frightened. 'Cause he knew I could stand up for myself. It takes a lot to get it out of me, but when it comes, you know it. To quieten me down – he knew I was frightened of anything sharp. I've always had a phobia about sharp things. My knives are never sharp. He used to leave his docker's hook next to the bed, so I wouldn't answer him back. Regardless of what he said, how he carried on.

He could carry on from eleven o'clock at night until six o'clock in the morning. I'd just lay there and not say a word.

I think it was that kind of fear that was getting me down, intimidating me. I used to blank it out. I used to think, 'It's not so bad.' Because where we lived, I've seen women that were treated terribly. So I used to think, 'My life's not that bad. Put up and shut up. What if you were her down the road that was getting kicked every night and sent out on the street?' Or the woman that lived next door to me who had an alcoholic husband? He used to bounce her off the wall and I used to have to run in and get her and the kids out. So my life was a piece of cake towards theirs.

I used to go and get them and drag them in my house and he'd try to get in my house. And I'd say, 'Oh, no. The day you put your foot over there is the day you're going to jail.' But you see as soon as he'd calmed down, she'd go back in. You'd do it a few times and you'd get fed up in the end. I wouldn't be like that now, I'm more understanding. But then I'd say, 'She must love it. She must enjoy it, otherwise she wouldn't keep going back for more.' I suppose that's the way my older sister looked at me. 'Cause she used to say I was a masochist.

Then when I self-analysed myself later in life, I realised I was a person that walked into things and took it for quite a bit before I'd break down. And to me I wasn't as bad as some women that stuck it and stuck it and stuck it. I still can't understand those women that stick it for twenty-odd years.

Anne blamed herself for getting pregnant by an abusive husband. She also thought she had no choice, that she was stuck with him – as an isolated American in rural Britain. Not surprisingly, Anne had difficulty in naming herself as battered.

You had to recognise that you were. That you'd been ignoring it, to the extent that when my mother would send me pamphlets or books, I refused to read them. There's a book called something like Men Who Hate Women and The Women Who Love Them or the other way around. I refused to read that. Maybe one day I will read it. I couldn't bear to look at it in the face and to see in print stereotypes of what I was married to.

I felt it was my pride really that wouldn't allow me to think of myself as abused, 'cause I'm not the cowering type. Every time that he was abusive to me, when I had strength – I'm a fighter when I have the strength – I had to blast back and be seen to be fighting back.

To me, then, the person who admitted to being abused is the person that stands there and says, 'I'm stressed, I'm abused.' I couldn't think of myself that way. I'd think, 'All right. I know he's abusive. I know he's a pig, but I'll fight him every yard of the way.'

Elsa is African-Caribbean and was born in Barbados in 1936. She now lives in London where she works as a nurse. She didn't name her situation until years after the abuse.

> I didn't think of myself as a battered woman at the time. Long afterwards, I remember one night we were watching a film about battered women and my daughter, she said, 'Mum, what you went through, I'll never go through.'

> And because sometimes she talks about things I don't even remember, I said, 'I never knew you would remember that.' She says, 'Mum, what you went through I will never go through.'

Sally was unprepared for her husband's violence when he suddenly lashed out after he couldn't get into his mother's bathroom. She remembers her sense of helplessness.

> It wasn't that I didn't recognise aggression and violence. It was that I didn't have any sense of judgement. I didn't have any ability to be critical of other people or judge them. All my relationships with other people were about what would they think of me and how would they judge me, rather than what kind of people are they, are they nice people, are they people I can trust or are they people I can feel safe with?

> So I feel like I had no ability to do that in any way at all. I didn't trust my own feelings. I didn't have any feelings. The only feelings I had were feelings of intense kind of pain or depression. I did have quite long periods of depression. Actually depression is not a feeling. It is a denial of feeling.

Being unable to name what we're experiencing also includes denying anything's happening at all. By moving the boundaries (and the severity) of what we would call abuse just that bit further away from us, we can avoid acknowledging it altogether.

Jackie was born in Liverpool in 1955. She is an unemployed care worker and now lives in Manchester. She remembers, in 1973, how she felt about herself.

When it was happening to me, I thought battered women were those you see with big black eyes every day, broken noses. When I saw them I'd think, 'Oh God. Isn't he a bastard.' I'd had a few black eyes, but not a broken nose. I never really thought or said, 'It's happened to me.'

Samantha describes how denial grows.

At first I thought it was my fault that he was angry with me, but it wasn't my fault he hit me. But then that very quickly went and everything was my fault. The more abusive and the more distant he became, the more I actually internalised that and made it my fault.

So it was my fault if the dinner wasn't ready. It was my fault if something went wrong. It was my fault that he had assaulted me. It was my fault that I'd upset him. It was my fault for nagging. I was continually told I was a nag. This withdrawal of affection and me wanting to be tactile ended up with our home life and everything suffering, including our sexual life.

Then there were taunts of me being frigid. And I was saying, 'Hey, how can I be loving and warm with somebody who's not loving and warm to me?' I was trying absolutely everything to try and keep the relationship going. And it was dying in a big way.

It's this wonderful 'if only' question that women who are in a domestic violence situation need to forget quickly. This, 'If only he stops drinking he will be fine.' Oh I thought I could change him. I thought I could stop him drinking. How I was supposed to do that, I don't know. I bought a book from Al Anon and I read that. I thought that then I'd be able to know the secret and I would just slip in the magic word and then he would be cured. I was so naive.

It's almost a desperation as well. I thought it was all down to me – it was all my fault – so obviously it was my responsibility to fix it. I had to change him and I was sure

I could. I was sure that if he got that one particular thing, he would be better. Then there was always something else that was going to happen that would make it better. The reality is it never does and that nobody can change anybody except the person themselves.

I phoned the Samaritans and I phoned Relate. I didn't actually go and see Relate, but I got some books of theirs. And I looked at these relationship books that were starting to burgeon in the shops in the late 1980s – *How to Survive Your Relationship* and all that jazz. I would sit there and say, 'OK, don't get angry with him, don't raise your voice. But just sit down, try and be reasonable with him.' And I would try and be reasonable and he would just scream and shout or he would walk out.

Sally's denial took a different form.

Switching off, I think. I think I didn't 'think'. I think I pretended it wasn't happening. I'd disappear. I'd become, I suppose, what I'd learnt to do as a child. My survival mechanism there was the same one that I used. I didn't exist.

Once it was happening, I would cry. I would never fight back. I would cry. Then afterwards, until it happened again, I'd cut off all feeling really. I think what it is, is that you separate out and there's this denial going on. And, yes, I think that the person that I was was battered, but it doesn't feel like me. You somehow split off.

The cutting off, blanking out, depressed withdrawal that Tessa and Sally describe are common reactions in many women. Such behaviour may appear to others as a lack of emotion or indifference and is often misinterpreted as women not being particularly bothered or not caring. In fact, these are very powerful defence mechanisms – protecting the person from acknowledging what's going on and being devastated by pain.

After her first experience of domestic violence, which happened when she was pregnant, Elizabeth believed that the most important thing was to be more careful and to try to win back her partner's affection. Elizabeth feels she had no other choice because she was never encouraged to be anything but passive.

> I remember this argument very well. We were living with his parents by then. He'd never work, because he was an artist, he didn't need to work. He completely flipped out and managed to dislocate my shoulder.
>
> Now his parents were in the other room and they came tearing in and said to him, 'What's going on?' But nobody said anything to me. I was eighteen years old and nobody said to me, 'Oh this is awful, Elizabeth, are you all right? What's happening to you?'
>
> His parents just told him not to make so much noise. Which is exactly what my mother used to say – 'Don't make so much noise, the neighbours will hear' – to me, not to my father. So again, it sort of reinforced the guilt. It's my fault.

Because no one ever told Elizabeth that what her father and her partner did was unacceptable, she was unable to name either's behaviour as abuse. For Elsa, denial was a matter of degree.

> I don't know exactly when I saw the change in him. At the time, I could remember thinking he was the type of person who couldn't do anything wrong. I used to maybe put him up on a pedestal. Even when things were going wrong, I used to say, 'No he wouldn't do this, he wouldn't do that. He didn't mean to do this.' I used to make excuses for him.
>
> Even sometimes people would come in and say they'd seen him in certain places and knew he was having affairs. And I would think, 'No, he wouldn't do that.' Or I would say, 'One thing with him, he's very truthful.' Things like that I would say. It wasn't an excuse to me. Looking back, I thought it was true. So I used to say, 'No, he wouldn't do that.'
>
> After he started to become more physically violent, it was a different story. It started in the seventies, when I went to

work. Things really got bad. Really got bad and it was terrible. I just couldn't take it any more.

Denial, as Elsa suggests, is also about *what* she chose to accept he would do. Because her partner had been drunk and rejected by an old friend, Marian wanted to believe that after the first time it would never happen again. She also thinks that for her, it was *who* she believed he was.

Somehow, there was a part of me that believed that it's not really him that's being horrible to me. It's some deranged evil bit of him, but it's not really him. The real him is thoughtful and generous and charming.

For Christine, the key to denial was justification.

The way I put up with it over sixteen years – I was with him for sixteen years – is by analysing everything he'd do. Once I'd worked out why he acted like he did, I could put it aside and cope with it.

I never thought about leaving him. I thought about throwing him out many times. And he did leave me a number of times. He would leave to go to another woman. He had many, many other women. I thought he would change. When I married him, I thought it would stop. Because I was his.

But – it sounds so stupid saying it now, because I know it was wrong and he was unfaithful – at the time I reasoned that it's the way his life had always been, the way he'd grown up. And they were only one night stands. They were always the same type of woman. And he always came home. I was his wife, and the other women were unimportant.

Anne found herself making different kinds of excuses.

Wife number two, before they parted company, came and said to me something that made me think she liked rough

sex. I thought, 'Hey? How peculiar.' Because believe me,
I don't like being knocked about. And that was lodged in
the back of my mind. If a man is provoked, and she freely
admitted that she liked 'the boys', and if someone likes a bit
of slap beforehand . . . You find yourself making all sorts of
excuses. And all tied up with this attitude, you think, 'If he's
treated decently . . .' I didn't think, 'Change.' I thought,
'Bring the best out.'

And, worse luck, I'd never looked at another man. Too
bloody tired.

I've gotten over a large part of the self-disgust that I felt
for years: that I disappointed my family, my friends; that
I hadn't left him the minute he started his behaviour.

I don't feel sorry for him any more. I went through years
trying to think, 'Why is this man acting like this? He's had
an unhappy upbringing.'

For years I've dealt with large animals professionally. Quite
often you find that there's never truly, very rarely, truly,
a bad one – they will come round. And I thought, 'Right.
Wife number one and wife number two, he had a hard time
and they liked the boys.' I thought, 'If he's treated decently,
surely he'll come round.' Now that's the way my logic
worked. For years I dealt with problem animals, and rarely
do they not come round.

Tessa thought that if she created perfection in their home, that
would change her abusive husband.

I was the type of woman that as you walk through the door,
the dinner was taken out of the oven and put in front of you.
You never had to go into the drawers and say, 'Where's my
clean shirt?' They were all hung up in the wardrobe. Your
underwear and socks were put in your drawer. Everything
was laid out for you. The only thing I would never do is set
your bath. I wouldn't get down to that level. But otherwise,
everything.

Say if he was working Saturday morning and we were going out Saturday night. I'd have the bedroom all nice and tidy. His suit would be ready, out of the wardrobe.

But I stopped going out, 'cause I thought if we don't go out then we can't argue. He wasn't so bad when we weren't going out. It was possessiveness, jealousy. He'd boast to people what a good housewife I was and how I could knit and sew and cook. He'd say to his mates, 'Come round to my house, my wife always cooks a little bit of extra dinner.' He was very proud of that side of me, actually. But he was a nagger and he knew my weaknesses.

Because of, or perhaps despite, her abusive father, since she was a child Saroj has wanted nothing more than to live happily ever after with a husband, home and children. She feels this explains her deeply rooted desire and need to change her abusive husband.

I thought probably I could change him. Then I think about my mum. My mum used to say, 'I can change him.' Which she never did. Like up to now, my dad is living with some-one else and my mum is living with all the kids to look after. So that's why I think it's good I didn't have kids.

Now I feel when I see a boyfriend and girlfriend or a happily married couple, I always pray to God, 'Let them live like that.' I wish I had a lovely marriage.

Like Samantha, Anne, Tessa and Saroj, Eleanor was convinced that it was her responsibility to change her husband.

When I was going through the difficult times in my marriage, I still thought I could change him. I can remember actually making excuses up to my parents, saying it was my fault. Deep down I still thought I could change him. I think I thought if I loved him enough, I could change him.

Women always think they can change a man. I thought I could change him. Women don't like to be classed as failures. And the way I looked at it – to go and tell my mum and dad and my family and everybody that he was beating me – I thought I'd failed in the marriage.

Telling

Naming abuse has two sides: admitting it to one's self and telling others. Hearing the words spoken out loud sometimes feels so irrevocable, so out in the open and susceptible to the judgement of others, that keeping it secret seems like the only option. Even now, Sally finds talking difficult.

> I notice the book's called '*All My Fault*'. I think it's true. I mean what you say about self-esteem, I think it's absolutely central, low self-esteem. I don't think I felt I didn't deserve it. That's not the same thing.

> I don't know if it's exactly the same thing. I don't think it is quite. I don't think I thought it was my fault. I think I could clearly see that I wasn't doing anything to bring on those attacks. But I think that somewhere deep inside me I felt that I deserved it.

> I never talk about it. This is why I was quite interested in talking to you. Because I haven't talked about it.

Janie describes how not telling is one of a number of factors that contribute to not leaving.

> A lot of women who get beaten won't tell anybody because they feel ashamed that they could let somebody else do that to them. That's how I felt. I felt ashamed that I was letting him do things to me that I wouldn't let anybody else do.

> I didn't want anyone to think that I'd failed. It was something in me, the way I felt, that I didn't want them to think I'm a failure.

> People used to say to me, 'Why don't you leave him?' I just wasn't brave enough to leave him. I didn't want to be on my

own. I think I stayed with him for the fact of just staying with somebody. I didn't have the courage.

It was worse after I had the boys. I thought, 'What would I do on my own with three kids?'

Who we tell and when we tell them are complex decisions. They vary not only from woman to woman, but within each one of us at different times, depending on the particular circumstances of our lives. Whereas participating in this book, after her marriage ended, felt to Sally like the right time to talk about what had happened to her, Tessa chose to tell one of her oldest friends while the abuse was still going on.

He wasn't abusive to me in front of other people. But she could see something was wrong when I popped into her house one day after work. It was only a part-time job, two hours a day, because he used to think you should be home when the children were at home. I said, 'Just let me do this little twelve till two – only a dinner lady for school dinners, helping to serve the dinners.'

And one day I was walking home from work and life was really getting me down. Now she and I have known each other since she was seven. I got into her house and I started to cry and she had never seen me cry before and she said, 'What's the matter?'

But I've always been a person who never actually shows what's inside of me. Even to this day, I can have the biggest worry in the world and nobody will know. Even my own daughters, I don't tell them.

I cried and I said, 'I've had enough. He's getting on my nerves. I can't do anything.' I said, 'Yes, he gives me money and I've got everything in the house. I've got nice furniture, nice home, nice three-piece suite. Nothing bought on the weekly.' It had to be cash, so to me that was a stable man. That was our way of looking at a stable man in those days. I tried to hang on to it till I couldn't take any more.

She never really commented on it. She still doesn't really.
She never takes sides. A shoulder to cry on, that was it.

Kiranjit felt isolated in Britain, first living with her husband's
family who did nothing to prevent his violence, and then just with
him. She describes what prevented her from telling and how
widely reactions varied when she did.

I just gave up. The first thing in my mind was that I have
to go by my family system. I have to please them, I always
wanted to please my family, my in-laws and then my
husband. I had to please all these people. My choices and
wishes meant nothing. I was the last person who should
think about myself. My life wasn't mine. I was the property
of my husband, my in-laws, then again, my family.

I told no one in the family for about three years. During
that time I worked and was saving money for my husband
and I to visit my family in India. I made a couple of friends.
After I got my first injunction, I told one of them how
I was suffering, because she first told me how much she
had suffered from her husband. I showed her my damaged
finger and said, 'He beats me.' But I asked her to promise
me not to tell anyone. But people from the outside found
out I was suffering.

To my surprise, they said that all of them were suffering,
but they didn't want it to come out. It was the same story.

It was very hard for me. I couldn't tell my family because I
felt that Asian culture was running in my blood, 'Oh he's
my husband, it doesn't matter.'

I used to cry for a few days after every beating. But he used
to apologise. And he used to help me. If I went to the
kitchen, he used to help me. He'd take me out for the weekend to see my family. If not the family, he used to take me
out for lunch, to town for shopping. If we did any shopping,
he used to carry it. He would make tea – we both liked tea
very much. And sometimes he used to make my favourite
things like English food: sausage and beans.

But I couldn't tell my family. They couldn't do anything and I used to feel embarrassed, ashamed. I thought my family would laugh at me – that other people would laugh at me.

The day after the first time he beat me, my hand was cold. I said to my mother-in-law, 'I'm freezing.' I was so cold. It was shock. He hit me without any reason and I felt like my body was getting frozen, motionless. My mother-in-law took me into her bedroom – my father-in-law was there. I was crying. When they asked my husband, he acted like nothing happened. He was having fun. My mother-in-law shouted at him, 'You bastard. Her brother came from India, he's still here and you started beating her. This is your second week of marriage, what are you up to?' And he was going 'snap' with a camera and there I was crying. In front of my father-in-law, as a daughter-in-law I was feeling embarrassed that I was crying. But I was hurt mentally and physically.

I thought that if I told my brother then my husband would get angry. He had a split personality: one minute he is laughing and the other minute he is just an animal.

I eventually saved up for two tickets to go to India. My brother and sister met us at the airport. They were over the moon. 'Look at her, he is really handsome.' Both of us looked really nice – a good-looking couple. Inside they didn't know what was happening. I was so happy when I saw my brother, nephew and nieces.

My husband was very calm, quiet. After a couple of days, I burst into tears. Then my eldest brother, who brought me up, asked me what's wrong. 'Are you happy with him?' And I said, 'He beats me.' And my brother lost his temper and shouted at my husband, shaking him.

My brother told me not to go back to England with him and I nearly went for a divorce. I said, 'That's it, our marriage is over.' I told him my plan and that now he couldn't do anything, if he hit me again, that's it, the end of our marriage. That night he apologised and cried before every member of my family – even my nephew. And promised he won't touch me again. Because if his family found out that I'd left him, that would be worse for him. He'd be a failure as a man.

So he apologised and promised. But still I told my brother, 'I don't want to go back to England. That's a shit country.' I spent six months in India. After six weeks my husband left, but he rang me every day. I told him I'm not coming back.

But what made me come back was my father-in-law was very seriously ill and he died. I loved my father-in-law a lot. I respected him and still do. So my husband said, 'You must come back. His funeral is on such and such a day. Please do come back.' He was very upset and I believed his promises and I came back.

For Anne, being an American living with her abusive, British husband in rural England played a large part in her not telling.

By virtue of being a foreigner and terribly proud, for years I never said anything. I never thought that there was anyone that I could trust. I was kept quite alienated for years. Anyone that befriended me was denigrated and you get embarrassed for people coming and being insulted. It was always his friends, his this, his that, which kept me very isolated.

I had no family here, my parents are elderly – I'm not the sort to wear my heart on my sleeve. I'm bloody-minded, I'm proud. Also my son was just over a year old in 1984, the first time my husband beat me severely – he broke my leg.

I was sitting on the settee. He walked into the room and went into a rage. He dragged me off the settee and he started to slap me. I swung back. He threw me back on to the settee and went to kick at me. There were some heavy glass ashtrays there and of course I flung one at him and I only grazed his eyebrow, damn it!

That enraged him. And he picked me up, slapped me, punched me, spat in my face, threw me in a chair, picked up this table, swung it, smashed my leg, dragged me into the hall (it's quite a big house) and he kicked me and punched me. He kicked me in the stomach and in the crotch and slammed me up against the wall. And I knew straight away my leg was broken.

You lose track of time. But it was probably no more than five to eight minutes, I guess. Of course it woke my little boy. I wasn't having to crawl then, 'cause adrenalin keeps you high. I've been smashed up by horses over the years and you just carry on till it hurts so bad, you can't.

It wasn't till teatime that I found I couldn't walk. I had to crawl. Then there were his floods of tears, and this and that, until about three in the morning. I would rarely let him see me cry, rarely. And we were lying there on the bed and I was watching him sobbing – which he often did over the years, sobbing at the side of the bed. You think, 'Oh God, he's such a screwed-up bugger.'

I was sort of smuggled into casualty the day after he smashed my leg. I tried to drive myself and the bones were crunching and I could just about depress the clutch. Only then, because you can imagine he had these pangs of guilt, did he actually drive me to casualty himself. It was twenty-four hours after.

I told them straight, 'He hit me with a table. He's built like a blacksmith and picked up a large coffee table.' They didn't phone the police. It was considered just domestic violence.

I was six weeks in plaster. No one came to help me. No one phoned.

My husband was a big fish in a little pond. I discovered how utterly alone I was. No one from the church, not the vicar, not the doctor – no one came.

After that he was positively treacly for maybe a month, six weeks. Then the verbal abuse started again.

He also knocked the farm secretary about and no one ever pressed charges. No one ever did anything. It was always swept under the carpet.

Everything had a blind eye turned to it. 'Cause his attitude was, 'They all need me for something. I have the grain dryer, I have the storage bins. The local church is in the middle of the farm and they've got to be nice to me so that I will provide them with these things.'

He's a very good farmer, very clued up, has his fingers in many pies.

The first person I let on to was my mother. Three years before I left him. She was on a flying visit from America. In a moment of weakness, I remember sitting there, and all I said was, 'I want to die.' I never said suicidal or anything. And she got on the phone to my oldest friend in England who was a very strong personality – who didn't get on with my husband at all.

Then I bumped into this same friend at some horse show or sale and she caught hold of me by the shoulders and shook me until my teeth rattled, quite literally. In her words I was a beaten dog and she was so enraged at the state I was in, it was more or less, 'Don't you dare think of committing suicide. What about your kids?'

Of course, the kids were always on my mind. 'How could I make it tidy? What could cause them as little upheaval as possible?' She really got angry with me. 'He's not worth it. He is not worth it.'

Maybe I was just waiting to have somebody say something like that. 'Cause I lived in such isolation and I thought there was no way out.

I had *got* to be able to deal with it, I told myself. It was the old thing, you couldn't see the light at the end of the tunnel. I went through days and mentally I don't think I could have looked at the view out of the window. I closed down so much that I just saw a black hole. I suppose this old friend provided a pin-point and one just kept plodding on toward that. It wasn't 'going to', it was 'got to, I've got to, I've got to'. I mean for years one kept the smile in the jar by the door, put on a good face. Finally, I thought, 'Sod it, we go for it.'

I thought, admittedly with the spurring on of good friends, 'You might as well.' It felt like standing in the middle of the street, after all those years, and screaming, 'Help me.' Before pride wouldn't let me and I thought no one was there to listen anyway. But there is no point smiling and saying, 'I'm fine.'

Mary's tendency to revert into herself may be why she relied on the kindness of strangers.

The first person I told would have been a woman along the balcony in the next block. I think she sussed because she was in a violent relationship herself. On a few occasions, when I went to stay with people, I remember the kind of response was very much, 'You're in there now. Either get on with it or get out.'

But I never really talked to a lot of people about it because you know what all the answers are, but you can't do anything about it. It was kind of like I talked myself around it in my head.

I even started talking to people at bus stops. It's very bizarre. I didn't like talking to people I knew. But with strangers, it was like you're talking out the situation. You're talking it out, until you can actually move out of that pattern. It's like a purging of your soul.

You keep talking about it. I ended up talking to different people that I didn't know. I think in the end, my network of people that were supportive closed the door. Because they didn't like him and his behaviour was very bizarre to everybody else. It was, 'You've made your bed, lie in it.'

Samantha believes that isolation prevented her from telling.

> Nobody at work knew. After we'd been married six years, there were rumours that we weren't getting on too well. By that stage he'd been doing a lot of heavy drinking in the bar late at night. People knew that he wasn't going home, which is not what husbands normally do.

> I didn't speak much to the neighbours either. I had a retired police officer on one side and a couple of old ladies living the other side. There wasn't really anybody to talk to.

> My husband was seen as the all-round good egg and snappy dresser. He was a very popular, very charismatic guy who is very, very highly regarded. It was, therefore, going to be lumped straight at my doorstep that it was my fault that the relationship had broken down.

> There were one or two people who I started to be a bit open about the violence with and started to say things about how we hadn't been getting on for a while. Then it got to where I'd be sitting there thinking, 'When are you going to let it out and get rid of it and talk it out.'

> By that stage, I'd done some training in counselling and active listening so I was aware that talking things through is actually very, very positive and was the first step to healing and recovery. So I was actually using that and I said to the shift that I was supervising, 'I don't care if I bore you rigid, but I'm no good at the moment and I need to talk this out.' So I would talk about how I felt, whether I was happy or sad; what was going on for me; what I'd done. Slowly bits would come out as and when I felt comfortable.

> I think one of the big watershed points for me was when we went to a violent domestic where a woman had been assaulted quite badly: she'd had her jaw broken. And I took hold of her and said, 'Why don't you leave?' And she said, 'I can't.' And I said, 'That's what I said.'

> It was the first time I'd said anything to anybody I didn't know about being a survivor. She looked at me and her jaw

was hanging open anyway – but it just dropped to the floor. And I said, 'Please believe me.' And I wrote down my name and number on a piece of paper and gave it to her and said, 'Just phone me.' And she did. She did subsequently leave and she's OK now.

I can remember that I went home and I felt really proud of myself. Not, 'You have achieved something.' But, 'You've actually been honest and open and you've actually told somebody you don't know, "I'm a survivor".'

Elizabeth describes how telling helped her to realise it was not all her fault.

The first person I told believed me completely. She, at the time, was doing a community course and was working in a women's centre. So she knew about listening to women who'd been abused.

Not until I said it to her, not until I actually said it out loud to her, did I decide I was a battered woman.

I realised it was wrong and it shouldn't have happened. It didn't matter what I had done, nobody had the right to dislocate my shoulder or beat me or verbally abuse me.

I think that those women who can't say to themselves that they were battered women just haven't worked it through yet. They haven't come to terms with it. They are probably still, on some level, thinking it was their fault. I don't think it was my fault at all.

Escalation

It takes most women a long time to believe that someone they've chosen to love could turn out to be abusive. Usually the hope is that the man's behaviour is just a one- or two-off and will stop. But in over twenty years of experience in the field, every abused woman, frontline worker, academic, activist and expert I've met agrees that not only do men never stop, but the violence always gets worse. Kiranjit describes her experience of escalating abuse.

> The injuries got worse because I started to answer him back a little bit. He had never used a knife before, but he started pushing me into a corner, pressing the point of a knife under the skin of my neck, hurting my veins. Before that he used to scream and shout and throw things at me.

> He broke my shoulder and fractured my finger. One day he pushed me so badly I fell and my wedding ring stuck. My fingers got so swollen that I had to go to the hospital to have the ring taken off. On another occasion he hit me with his bracelet and nearly blinded me.

Having been an isolated only child with no sense of ambition, Anita felt particularly affected by the escalation of her boyfriend's controlling behaviour.

> He gradually started grinding me down, taking everything that was me. He didn't approve of my business, because I was making money. He criticised my friends, he criticised my family. He was nit-picky about my clothes. He would try and dress me how he wanted. He tried to take everything of me away.

> It was very difficult because of this whole thing about the shame involved in it. You think, 'God, I've really made a very bad mistake here.'

> The other thing was that he'd blow me up like I was the most wonderful person. So he was very clever.

> I tried really hard. I sometimes planned to go somewhere for a weekend. Maybe he was doing something and he would cause a scene to stop me from going. This began to be a pattern. Those were my problems: that he could actually be sweet, could be really nice natured; and then he could really be an absolute monster.

Anne experienced a combination of isolation, escalation and extreme mood swings.

> You never knew exactly what would happen. His rages could be twice a day, they could be once a day. Anything could set them off. Me, the kids, anything. If he was crossed, if you had a different opinion. Everyone would freeze as he would come in the house. And you would wait to see what kind of a mood he was in.
>
> There weren't very many major physical attacks, but the verbal abuse was constant. The rages were constant. There were things like suddenly smashing me on the back of my head in the middle of the night. Those kind of attacks were so frequent I lost count. That could be a weekly occurrence. It could be a couple of times a week up until I moved out of the bedroom, three years before I left for good. You can only survive so long on two hours sleep a night.
>
> That enraged him: 'I'm not having that.' I said, 'Then put two single beds in there.' He said, 'I'm not having that.'
>
> You never knew when the attacks were going to come. At night he would get frustrated and randy. Never would he be calming and soothing. If one wasn't ready to do the business, he would attack you. Usually he was careful not to mark me – hence the attacks on the back of the head along with his tirades until three in the morning. And it's the screaming that would, of course, waken the children. And you would think, 'Just for the sake of the kids, peace and quiet.'
>
> But I didn't leave, oh good heavens no, I had nowhere to go. And I was constantly taunted that I had nowhere to go. He utterly isolated me.

For Samantha, the escalation of the physical and emotional abuse happened in tandem, after the miscarriage caused by her husband's violence.

After the slapping came a gradual, very slow progression from slapping to kicking. He would kick me out of the bed on to the floor and say, 'I don't want to sleep with you. Go and sleep somewhere else.' Or he would shove me into a wall and as soon as I broke down in tears, he would look at me with contempt and walk away.

He was never abusive for no reason at all. There would always be an apparent reason as far as he was concerned – or a perceived reason. Something had happened that was making him angry. But the distancing was the most distressing part for me. The physical violence was almost something I could deal with, but the other I couldn't handle.

Mary felt submerged and surrounded by her partner's abuse.

I would say it was near-on constant. If the person didn't get what they wanted, it was just violence. In any way. Like, if the house wasn't cleaned, the food wasn't cooked, he just exploded, it just escalated.

Then it was like, bringing other women into the house. Every kind of way that he could get a reaction from me. I think I must have gone totally in. I kind of really escaped inside. It was for safety and a hiding place.

'Eggshells' is a word that many women use when they describe managing men's violence. Carmina believes that, in looking for a father figure for herself and her son, coping with her partner's abuse was part of a test he put her through.

You're sitting there on eggshells. I was really nervous. I used to just shake, 'cause I didn't know what to do. I would be perfect. I'd have the meal ready at the time he wanted. Anything, I jumped and I did it, sort of, 'Yes, Bill, no Bill, sorry Bill.'

Even things that I thought I wasn't doing wrong. 'Cause he always said things like, 'If you really loved me, you'd do this.

If you really loved me you would do that.' And I tried to do it and you'd think to yourself, 'I'm trying to show you love, but every time I show you, you keep rejecting it. The harder and harder I try.'

Anita tried to balance her needs alongside dealing with her partner's abuse.

Then you realise you were treading on eggshells. You couldn't actually be totally you, because the fact was that I was still having to do all the shopping and most of the cooking and cleaning. So I wasn't happy with that, I was very unhappy with that. And he would go off a lot and do his own thing.

There were these ambiguities too. He seemed to really like the home life, but then he liked to go out clubbing and take drugs as well. He loved coming home, the comfort of home and me being there.

If I went out with my friends, he would get difficult about it. If I came back, it may not be that day, maybe the next day, I'd get flak for it.

He wanted to control me, he actually said as much, he wanted to control me.

Sally's experience echoes Anita's.

His control was that if I wasn't the person he wanted me to be or if I didn't do what he wanted me to do for him, then he'd be aggressive.

But it wasn't an explicit threat. It was more an implicit threat – that that's what *would* have happened. So I felt like I was tiptoeing around on eggshells all the time. I had to be careful.

Kiranjit and Anne describe how they connect the escalation of violence with their own resistance. For Mary and Carmina, as for most women I have met, passivity – like the constant attempts to be the perfect wife and mother – increased abuse. Many women have also said that resistance can *reduce* violence. But there are no absolutes. Each woman becomes an expert through her own experience of trying to manage the man's violence.

It has been suggested that men's violence arises out of their power and women's resistance to it. I have never seen any proof for this assertion. As well as women's submissiveness over time appearing to intensify men's abuse, my observations and those of frontline workers I know is that women's *initial* reaction to men's violence has no predictable response. And to me, such notions also smack of woman-blaming. While it may well be that male fantasies about women's resistance are connected with men's abuse, the fact that these fantasies may be projected on to women remains something that I believe is only within the control of the men themselves.

Women overwhelmingly act to minimise and manage the results of male violence, for self-protection and to ensure the safety of children. But stopping abuse must finally be acknowledged as something only men can do.

Barbara began married life in the poverty of rural isolation. She found vigilance, and the extent to which she was expected to act on her own, necessary to managing her husband's violence.

> One of the things he could do when there wasn't an antago-nistic situation going on between us was he could make me laugh. He was witty, but there were certain things he could do which were cruel.

> I can remember on one occasion we were lying in front of an electric fire and I had slippers on. Now this cottage didn't have any earthing in it. When you put on the cold tap, if my ring went near the cold tap, then I would get an electric shock.

> We were lying in front of the fire. It was like one of these romantic situations and we were laughing and being quite good humoured with each other. He said to me, 'If you touch that electric fire with metal on it, you would get an electric shock. But if you touch it with the sole of your

slipper, you won't.' And I did, because he coaxed me to and I got an electric shock. But because he was touching me, he also got an electric shock.

He found this very funny. He found my trusting of him something to be laughed at. Whereas I experienced it as something that was very cruel to do to somebody, because I had really believed that the sole of my slipper was rubber. It wasn't, it was plastic.

I think there were a lot of incidents like that, where I would be either physically or emotionally hurt and he would think that it was funny. I think he in his mind, though he never said it, felt I was almost too naive to believe.

The violence was escalating in that I would say to him, 'You've done all these things and now you're being violent. What it really is all about is your trying to control me. You're not going to control me, I'm going to be my own person.'

I can remember saying these words, not in terms of a feminist ideology, it was not an intellectual response. It was very much an emotional response, 'There's lots you've been doing, but there's nothing left that you can do to me. So if you want to keep money from me, if you want to hit me, if you want to leave me on my own, if you want to gamble the money away, it's water off a duck's back.'

I think he began to realise that I wasn't going to allow his violence to control me. On one occasion we were at one of his brothers' house and his brother's wife had just put down the supper to us. He suddenly decided he wanted to go home. I said, 'No, I'm not going to be rude, I'm going to stay here. I'm going to eat my supper.' There was a scene and eventually he punched me twice or three times. I fell down. He kicked me up and down their hallway.

His brother pulled him off and his brother's wife locked us all in the house and went for the police. She came back, but by this time I was in the bedroom with the two children who had witnessed the violence. I overheard him and his brother talking about when the police arrive. His brother was saying, 'They're not going to get you out of this house.' So I knew there was going to be further violence between my husband, his brother and the police.

I was still in the bedroom and I can remember going to stand with my face right up to the wall to control myself. I think it must have been something physical. It was solid, this wall, and that meant that in my line of vision, the wall was all I could see. This was my world – to let me suppress the emotion. 'Cause I was getting very distressed, so I felt I had to get myself under control.

His brother's wife came back and the police came to the door; they asked to see me. I went to the door. The policeman said, 'Do you want to press charges? You've got witnesses.' And I said, 'No.' And he said, 'Are you sure you're all right?' And I said, 'I can cope with this situation. It's something that's got out of hand. If I need you, I'll phone you.' And they went away.

I went directly back into the bedroom and he came through full of apologies: 'I don't know what happened. It just got out of hand, I shouldn't have done it. I'm really sorry.' He started to cry, the whole bit. And I said to him, 'I'm not coming home with you tonight.'

Then I sneaked out of his brother's house, went downstairs and hid in the dustbin recess. He came down the stairs and I heard him go to the front of the close, looking around, and he couldn't see me. He went back up the stairs again and I thought, 'Now this time he might come round the back.' So I got inside a bin and pulled the lid over my head and basically sat there and waited and waited. It seemed like an age.

I got out of the bin, listened at his brother's door and couldn't hear anything. The next-door neighbour opened the door and said to me, 'What are you doing?' and started to laugh. I said to her, 'What are you laughing at?' And she said, 'What are you doing, where have you been?' And

I said to her, 'What do you mean?' She said, 'I think you better come in.'

She took me into her house and I was sitting there shaking and she said, 'Come on, what's been going on?' And I kind of told her. And she said, 'You've got a teabag hanging from your hair.' This is what she had been laughing at.

She said, 'I'll go next door and I'll knock on the door and I'll try to find out whether he's still there or not. If he's still there then I'll come back and let you know.' I don't know what she thought was going to happen after that, but she certainly wasn't going to tell him that I was in her house.

As it turned out, he wasn't there and I went back into his brother's house. And his brother and his wife were saying, 'This is not acceptable, it's not on, and why didn't you charge him, you had the opportunity there.' By this time they kind of knew that he'd been violent in the past. I think I must have told them at some point. At least I had told the brother's wife. But for his brother, it was the first time he'd actually witnessed any kind of violence and thought it was not on.

However, he also said to me, 'I couldn't watch my brother being lifted out of my house.'

It is significant that though her in-laws protected Barbara and fetched the police, they blamed her for not bringing charges, when the brother-in-law himself was not even willing to see his brother arrested. It is as though there are no limits to what women are meant to endure.

Anne was worn down and isolated by her husband's emotional abuse.

He, many a time, said to me, 'You just don't know how to handle me.' I'm pretty fiery, but for many years he told me that I'm mad, I'm old, I'm ugly, that I can't get it right, that I'm a bad mother – all that stuff that deep down helps you keep your sanity. You know they're not spouting unique sentiments. It's almost as if they've read the book.

Prior to the first severe beating, he'd grab hold of me and shake me. Or he would walk past and knock me out of the way. It was degradation all the time. And I remember when my son was a week old, he said, 'Take your brat and get out of here.' And then, two weeks later, I did book my passage, got everything sorted, took my son to the American Embassy, got his passport. And I was going. Then my husband had all the hysterics and the tears and the this and that. And these terrible fluctuations, which there again are not unique. But I thought, 'He's highly unstable.' And he'd say, 'Oh, I've had a hard life, you must feel sorry for me.' And this and that.

They always go for the jugular, they always find the weak spot. Underlined with, 'Where on earth are you going to go with my baby? And how are you going to survive? You're not eligible for any benefits.'

'Cause until you actually go and find out what you can do and can't do – which I only did just before I left, I went to the DSS with passports from over the years – you don't know where you stand. I had to know before I left. It had been a struggle with one child, but how was I going to manage with two? How could I feed them, how could I look after them?

I expected them to say that I was eligible for nothing. To my relief they cleared it with the Home Office and said, 'Yeah, you're eligible for everything.'

But I'd been frightened to death for years to make any move, to give any sign I was going to bolt. 'Cause by this time, I had some nice bloodstock that I'd gathered around and they'd been doing nicely in the show ring. Every time I stepped out of line, he would threaten the horses. Before that it had been my son from my first marriage. It was always whatever was closest to my heart that was always the lever.

He said, 'You just don't walk out the door. And you certainly don't walk out and leave with your children. You don't walk out and leave with your horses.' Though my horses don't come first – he always included everything. So I knew that everything had to be planned carefully. Somehow I had to stay sane, stable, upright. 'Cause I did nothing but think about suicide for the last two years.

I spiralled into depression and I lost a block of two years. When I went to the solicitor and I said 'I'm forty-five', the friend who went with me said, 'Anne, you're not forty-five any more, you're forty-seven.' I obviously had gone through the motions of the kids and so forth. But people would say, 'Oh you remember such and such.' And I don't.

Those two years, as far as events, I obviously walked and talked. But I've lost huge blocks of time where I'd find myself sitting and I wouldn't know how long for.

As a foreigner, Anne is fortunate that she and her British-born children were entitled to state benefits. Though being white, middle class and American may have been in her favour, the climate of suspicion surrounding all non-Britons who seek government assistance is growing. In the last twenty years, I have noticed that increasing official xenophobia actively prevents more and more foreigners from receiving any help from the state.

For years, many Asian and African-Caribbean women have found that applying or even inquiring about benefits and rights results in their immigration status and nationality being investigated. If a woman has come to Britain to marry and her husband keeps her passport, trying to get away from his abuse is further complicated by being unable to prove her right to be here. Countless women are threatened with deportation if their marriages break up or appear to break up, for whatever reason. And the probability that a woman of colour will face a racist response from officialdom may be used by her abusive husband to persuade her to stay. Resisting and surviving such racism is inextricably linked with struggling against abuse.

Isolation and shame, combined with the certain knowledge that women who leave often face hostility from their family and friends, as well as lack of sympathy and resources from the outside world, are major factors in preventing women from naming abuse.

Helping women to name abuse enables many to begin to take (back) control. As long as it is being denied, abuse will persist unchecked. It is not easy to risk classifying oneself as part of a despised group. But naming brings the possibility of beginning the process of change. And there is also the chance of getting the support that being part of a group can bring. The start of self-definition can help bring an end to isolation.

4

The good mother and the bad mother

When I was a teenager, my mother used to say that the point of any incident I described, every story I ever told, was that no matter what it was actually about inevitably it was always the mother's fault. Though I can remember being annoyed when she repeated herself over and over in what seemed to me a dull litany, I can also remember thinking she was right. I *did* think it was all the (my) mother's fault. She didn't protect me from my abusive father. She didn't train me to be a sparkling, self-confident young woman, drawing girlfriends and boyfriends to me like a desirable social magnet. She didn't equip me with the right clothes, the right artistic or intellectual skills to succeed. I was surly, gawky, self-conscious and depressed. I was a failure and it was all my mother's fault.

It's no consolation to mine or any other mother that I was far from alone in blaming her for everything. Crime, poverty and unemployment are only the tip of an eternal iceberg of social, political and personal crimes blamed on mothers. Whatever happens to anyone in their families or whatever anyone in their families ever does, if it's bad it's the mother's fault.

It should be easy for most people to see that mothers aren't really to blame for all society's ills. Yet few women can feel quite as forgiving of their own mothers. We hold emotional grudges against what we know intellectually cannot possibly be the all-powerful mothers of our fantasies. And no matter how clear we might be about the failings of our fathers, most of us are far harsher in judging our mothers. We grow up learning to blame our mothers and, by extension, all women, and ourselves, for whatever goes wrong in our lives.

I have no doubt now that my father bears total responsibility for his emotional, psychological and verbal violence. Yet not only did I hold my mother responsible for not making me into a perfect woman, I have also come to realise that, in blaming her for not protecting me from my father's wrath, I was saying that part of his abuse of me was, in effect, her fault. Though I am now proud of my mother's bravery in leaving my father in the 1950s, when divorce was still heavily stigmatised, I can see that before then, as a small child, I might even have thought that his violence towards her was also somehow *her* fault.

On the whole I believe that most of us have been brought up to have a clear idea of what our fathers are supposed to do. Though we may also hope for apparently impossible things from them, such expectations are strangely finite and quantifiable. It's quite possible to list their failings neatly against their strengths: disappointments on one side, achievements on the other. Our mothers, on the other hand, are supposed to be and deliver everything (else) we can ever think we want – continually, infinitely, hopelessly unattainably. So mothers can only ever disappoint and never satisfy. Whatever they do, we always want it more and better.

Does this mean that the good mother will forever be just a fantasy? Why have we women allowed mother-blaming to go on for so long and be so pervasive across societies all over the world?

As a result of the Women's Movement of the late 1960s, my mother and I have come to understand, accept and appreciate each other. I've always loved my mother, but in the mid sixties we had hit such a low point of vicious rows, me running away from home, coming back, only for her to eventually throwing me out, that we had nowhere to go but up.

We are now able to respect our differences. I am no longer desperately embarrassed when my mother voices an opinion I don't like. I believe I am able to love her especially for what she is, not for what would change her into me. And I feel confident that she loves me for who I am. Feminism has provided us both with the context to reach this point. For me, it was also through psychoanalysis that I have been able to see that my mother did the best she could – she has become, in the language of that therapeutic process, the good enough mother. That is, I have reached harmony with her within me.

But for many women, the social and statutory construction of motherhood denies them the possibility of being good enough mothers in the eyes of the world. If a woman is being abused, it may be physically as well as psychologically impossible for her to provide for all the material and emotional needs of her children. Domestic violence often involves sexual coercion and rape. The additional stresses on women who are forced to go through unwanted pregnancies or give birth as a result of being raped make the achievement of ideal motherhood even more impossible.

It is, in any case, inevitable that for nearly all mothers there will be rough and smooth patches. But most women feel guilty when they have any ambivalence at all towards their kids. This is especially true if they have always lived in isolating nuclear families without any previous experience of raising children.

Mother-blaming pervades much applied psychology, promoting spurious notions which suggest that by not fulfilling our 'womanly' roles properly (whatever *that* might mean) we are deviant. One theory says that it's the fault of bad mothers if their children are abused and that they 'make' their male children become abusers. This is a particularly pernicious brand of misogyny that gives woman-hating, and therefore mother-blaming, academic, intellectual and, most frighteningly, judicial and medical status. Another, companion, concept is female masochism – the idea that women seek and derive sexual pleasure from being abused and are therefore to blame for their mistreatment. In both theories abused women are said to be too assertive and too submissive; too warm and too cold; too strict with children and too lenient; too independent and too dependent. Whatever we are is wrong and therefore bad. Whatever is right (and good) is what we aren't. And, most definitely, whatever bad things happens to us (and, if we have them, to our children) are our fault.

Most of the women who participated in this book reckoned they had had good enough mothers, though a few are still angry at the way they were mothered, both when they were small and as women experiencing domestic violence. Studies always show that the most likely person a battered woman goes to for support is her mother. All the participants felt that how they dealt with abuse as adults depended less on whether their mothers had experienced domestic violence or if they had been abused as children, than on the support and care they received from everyone when they needed it.

Being mothered

Tessa had been able to help a neighbour who was being abused more easily than she could help herself when she was living with the violent father of her youngest daughter. Years before, she'd had no such difficulty in leaving her first husband and going back to her parents, despite discovering she was pregnant. Tessa describes how her mother reacted.

> My dad was a bit annoyed, but my mother said, 'You're not the first and you won't be the last. One more mouth in the family to feed makes no difference. Because I didn't want you to marry him in the first place. So don't go back with him, don't live a life of misery.' She thought I was too young and they never really liked him. I suppose they could see more than I could see. She must have seen the arrogance in him that I didn't see.

> I got divorced. As much as everybody sees me as a very outgoing person now, in those days I wasn't. I was very insecure. No self-esteem, not one little bit, because I was dyslexic and I couldn't understand. I knew I had a brain, but I couldn't understand why I couldn't express myself on paper.

Candace, who as the only black child in her school fantasised about being white, describes her mother.

My mum is a very independent woman. She's always been independent. I mean she married my father, but the reason why she stayed with him is because of us, the children. But my mum's always been very independent. She's always been for me someone to look up to. But she's never stood for any bullshit.

My mum thinks I'm stupid because I now let my sons' father, who used to beat me, come here to see them. My mum said to me, 'Why do you have that man coming round to your house after what he's done to you?'

Barbara once hid in a dustbin to get away from her husband. How she coped with domestic violence is connected to the complexity of her relationship with her mother, and is a reflection of both their reactions to abuse.

I would never tell my mother about being sexually abused by my brother. Because basically I don't want to lay it on her. She's much older, she's coming up for seventy, she doesn't keep terribly well. I don't see any point in putting her through that kind of mill.

She hasn't had a very good life. As far as I'm concerned, she still doesn't have a very good life with my father. She has said ever since she married him that she's going to leave him. She has attempted to on various occasions, but never quite manages to stay away.

Even when she knows that my father is being abusive – either by his behaviour, although he's not physically violent, but certainly in other ways he's abusive – that although she knows it's wrong and she knows intellectually all the reasons for it being wrong – and if she was an advocate for any other woman, she would fight very, very strongly on that woman's behalf – when it comes to herself, it's like, 'I'll phole [bear] it.'

I think I tried to emulate my mother and that was because I feel that somewhere it had been implanted in my mind that my father never quite made the grade (and my mother had, of course) and so it would be better to be like her than my father.

For instance, one night after my husband had beaten me, I escaped to his brother's house. The next day, I agreed to go to the pub with my husband. By this time, I had a black eye and a split lip and, I remember, I had a bit out of my chin. And I was aching from head to toe. He took me to the pub, bought me a few drinks and said, 'Please come home.' I said, 'No, I'm not going home with you. I'll tell you what to do. Go and get my mother. Bring my mother to your brother's house and we'll take it from there.'

So my mother arrived and she came into the house and she said, 'Come on, Barbara, you need to go to your own house.' I just went downstairs, went into the car, went home. I knew when we drove into my street that I had made a big mistake.

I went into the house, the ceiling light was on, and I turned around and she looked at me. Then she looked at my husband and she said, 'You didn't tell me when you spoke to me earlier on this evening that her face was in that kind of state. You're not on. This is not going to be tolerated in this family.' That was really the first time my mother was aware of how severe the problem was.

She stayed the night and I think she was waiting to see what I would do. Because I did nothing, she went away. I think what she was saying to me was, 'You are fully aware of your situation. You have got to make the choice. You've got to make the decision. I cannot make it for you.' Also I think there is part of my mother which was going along with what I was thinking, although I never ever said it, which was, 'We have a good house in a good area. The kids are at a good school.'

I think, by that point, there was one part of me that felt, 'This is it. This is life. This is the way it's going to be.' Another part of me was fighting back: I had managed to get my daughter into nursery and my son was at school and

I was studying for an O level in English, behind my husband's back.

He found out about it and there was a big scene about that. He threw my books that didn't even belong to me in the fire. He could hardly write and he could just about read.

When it came to filling in forms for social security or anything like that, it was me that did that. When it came to fighting to make sure that the children went to a particular school, it was me who went and did all the arguing and all the rest of it.

Really, once the community learned that I eventually ended up in a women's refuge, they couldn't believe it, because I seemed so tough, confident, competent and organised.

Sally was never able to name herself as a battered woman. She felt controlled by both the reality and the implicit threat of her husband's violence, which seemed to happen if she wasn't who he wanted her to be or if she didn't do what he wanted. Sally believes that the way she coped with her husband's abuse was partly a reaction to the way she was mothered.

I feel angry with my mother for not protecting me from my father, but not about my husband, no. Because she lives in the north of England and I live down here in London. She really doesn't know what goes on in my life, because I don't actually tell her.

She stayed in an abusive relationship. She made the decision that the best thing for her and her children was to stay in an abusive relationship. I think when you've made that decision for yourself, it's like if you then say to your daughter, 'You shouldn't stay in an abusive relationship' it's almost like saying, 'I made a mistake, staying in an abusive relationship.' It's a big thing to accept though isn't it? It's like saying your whole life's a mistake. Especially as she's still with my father.

My mother's very controlling, that's how I see it. I think she felt that it was not quite OK that she had seven children. Because of that she was absolutely determined that we'd all be perfect. So my kind of image of going out, on the rare occasion that we did go out as a family, is like this little crocodile of perfectly behaved, perfectly dressed children.

I don't think I would've left my husband if I hadn't had a child. Not at the point I did, anyway. I think my strongest feeling was, 'I'm not going to bring my daughter up in this situation.'

Sally has never told anyone in her family that her husband abused her during their twelve-year relationship. She felt it would be wrong to burden her younger brothers and sisters with her problems. Clearly she also felt that she was unlikely to get any support from her mother. Long after Sally left her husband, she heard through a friend that her mother had said it was a great shame Sally's marriage had broken up.

Elizabeth believes that the key to her leaving for good was being instantly believed by the first person she told. She compares this response to the ways both she and her mother dealt with her father's abuse.

My father was always a man of great temper. Very little things would flare him up, just shouting and yelling. He thought it was perfectly all right to physically punish us – myself and my sisters.

When I was about fourteen, it got a lot worse and he would completely lose control and he'd really, really beat us. It went on for about a year. So it was my fourteenth year when he was being very violent. I could cope with it for myself. When he was hitting me it was like, 'Just get through it. Keep your mouth shut. Just get through it.'

But I couldn't bear to hear my sisters being hit. It was terrible. I actually stopped him doing it. Because I was listening to him beat one of my sisters who must have been five or six at the time. I went to the bedroom and opened the door and said, 'You're not allowed to do that. If you do it again, I'm going to call the police.' I can remember him turning round and looking at me and me thinking, 'My God, I'm dead. He's going to murder me.' But he didn't. And I walked back to my room and he went downstairs and he stopped hitting us after that.

But my mother's role in this was she always made you feel like it was your fault. If only you were a good girl, it wouldn't happen. But I wasn't doing anything and he would just come in, pick on some minor thing like a sweet paper on the floor, something stupid and ridiculous. As a child you think, 'It's me. It's just the way it is. Just my existence is enough to set him off.'

I found out after, round about the time I was leaving my partner, my mother talked a bit about her experience with my father. And she said, 'Yes, he used to hit me in the early days of my marriage. But, of course, I was so hysterical I needed it.'

My mother believes that women need a man to keep them under control by being physically violent towards them. She still believes that. She still lives with my father. He hasn't hit her since the early days. He verbally assaults her a lot, but he doesn't physically hit her. She thinks she deserves to be verbally assaulted. She puts him at the head of the family. What he says goes. She can't make a decision on her own at all. It's very painful to be around.

When I finally decided to leave my partner, I had a huge row with my mother. I rang my mother up and said, 'I'm going to stay with a friend.' I'd never told her before that he was violent. I rang her up and said, 'I'm going to stay with a friend because he has been very violent towards me and it's been going on for a long time.'

I didn't actually want to say that he'd raped me. I found it difficult to say it, especially to my mother who doesn't want to talk about sex at all. What she said was, 'What did you do, Elizabeth? What did you do to antagonise him? I know what you're like.' And I felt sick. I know what I'm like.

I said, 'He did about the worst thing a man can do to a woman. What do you think that is, Mother?' And she was silent. Then she said, 'Oh, oh, how long are you going to stay at your friend's?' Though she never talked to me about what had happened in the years I lived with him, when I actually told her what had happened and I said, 'I'm going to leave and I'm going to go to London', she never said, 'Don't do it.' She said, 'If it feels right, we'll support you.' So although she couldn't talk about it, she kind of acknowledged that the situation I was living in was so awful that I had to get out.

Anne's husband taunted her by claiming she had nowhere to go. In coping with his abuse, she lost two years in her conscious memory. It was her mother who finally got Anne to admit to herself that she was a battered woman.

She came over just to spend Christmas. Reading between the lines, and seeing the state I was in – and my husband was on his best behaviour – she still went up the wall. 'How can he talk to you and treat you like that?' 'Cause she would see him – if the plates weren't hot enough at Sunday lunch, he would stand there. I mean I'd been ignoring that for years, because compared to the other stuff that's nothing. I said, 'Mother, leave it. Let's have a quiet time.'

She made a diary while she was here of things he said to the children and the way he treated me. Because I had long since – if you rose to everything, you would have been a gibbering wreck. So you get to ignore a lot of it. She kept hammering away: 'I will not see you abused like this.'

She's dealt with violence to women and child abuse. She said, 'To see this happening to my own daughter. Why didn't you tell me?' I said, 'Mother, you're such a volatile character I didn't want you jumping on the next plane which, in the event, you've done anyway.' 'Cause she came back again. She'd only been home a few weeks after Christmas when, of course, in February he attacked me. She jumped on the plane in two days and was here. With her dicky heart, walking stick and everything but the Zimmer frame, oh dear. The last thing I wanted was her worried or involved or anything.

She's a real Trojan. My father wouldn't get involved. He's not the sort that would get involved. Even if you speak to him on the telephone, he never says 'love'. He never signs a letter 'love'. Mother's a star. She's courageous, she is Boadicea with a Yankee accent.

It was crucially important to Tessa, Candace and Anne that their mothers gave them an unequivocal message that the domestic violence they were experiencing was unacceptable. Barbara's description of her mother shows the extent to which women who are so quick to act on behalf of others seem, at the same time, unable to help themselves. And I suspect that a lot of women, like Barbara and, in the end, Elizabeth, may be getting mixed messages from their mothers, not just about domestic violence, but also about their roles as women.

It is clear from the experiences of the participants in this book, as well as many other women I have met over the years, that the ability to leave abusive men does not so much depend on whether or not our fathers abused our mothers – or even whether or not our mothers were immediately supportive – but the extent to which our expectations of being adult women were bound up with and limited to the images of womanhood we saw as we grew up.

Samantha found her husband's calculated emotional withdrawal from her the most distressing form of abuse. She now believes that the way she responded to him was a result of the confusion about adult relationships rooted in her childhood.

Mum was very religious, Presbyterian Scots. She didn't agree or accept the fact that I was an atheist from an early age.

She was very submissive. My father would actually just wave his hand in the direction of a cup of tea and she'd sugar it and stir it. In fact, she would panic if she hadn't ensured that everything was built around him and up to his standards – including me and my brother.

I never saw him violent with her, but he was very much the master and very much in the traditional role of the patriarch of the family – the husband you did everything for. He would let his underpants and shirt drop wherever they fell. And they were in the wash, ironed and back in his cupboard before you could say 'Thanks very much'.

I had a very mixed view of being a woman. I thought you could have a career, you could have ambition, you could do very well and you could better yourself. There was also a thread of looking at what my mother was doing and part of me being quite contemptuous of her: 'Why subjugate yourself to that extent?' But part of me saying, 'If I diluted that and made it more acceptable, then it must be quite nice to be a wife and mother and a partner and have a nice home and do things together.' I had very much a view of an equal relationship within the home.

My husband wanted me to leave the Job [quit the police force] and have children quite quickly after we got married. I didn't. I wanted a career first, because I didn't want to do all the blaming of children: 'If I hadn't had you, I could have been, I might have been.' It was a subject of some heavy discussion when we went on holiday overseas with my parents.

There were three of them quite similar in their attitude that, 'She needs to have children now. It's about time. You've been married long enough.' And I was trying to defend my corner, with no support whatsoever. 'Can't you see, I want my career first.' It felt very much like a conspiracy. I felt very much like my parents supported him. That I should have children, that's what a proper wife did.

But it wasn't until I'd been married five years that I got pregnant, but didn't know it. What actually happened was the beatings were getting worse and we had had a huge row.

I followed him up the stairs, because he was going to bed or getting changed or something.

There were two small landings. I got to the first-floor landing and he turned around and literally pushed me, and I went backwards down the stairs. And then he went upstairs, washed his face, cleaned his teeth and walked out. Later I found out he'd gone to the pub. I lay on the floor bleeding and lost the baby. I wasn't sure what had actually happened and had to ask a friend some days later. She said, 'You're pregnant.' I was on the contraceptive pill, so I actually thought I was safe. Obviously I was quite forgetful with working different shifts. I mean I would leave it four days and then swallow four pills and hope to God. So I had no idea I was pregnant and that affected me quite badly.

Christine blamed her husband's abuse on his unhappy childhood. She thought it would stop if they got married. But it didn't. Christine believes that by acknowledging how she denied and minimised her own experience of domestic violence, she is able to understand why mothers seem to want their daughters to stay with violent men.

As a refuge worker, mothers can be one of women's biggest problems. Because a mother says, 'Look. He brings his wages home, you've got a nice home, what more do you want? Get back home to him.' That happens time and time and time again. Mothers do not want to know about violence and about the abuse. Because they've probably gone through the same situation and stuck it out. They don't see why their daughters should get out of it: 'It's part of life.'

Many people believe that there is an inevitability about abuse. That nearly all male abusers were abused or witnessed abuse as children, that boys who are abused or who witness abuse are likely to grow up to become abusers, and that the majority of women who were abused or who witnessed abuse as children are particularly likely to seek out abusive men. Other people do not address gender as an issue: they think that all who were abused or who witnessed abuse when young grow up to be abusers and that all abusers were abused or witnessed abuse as children. The notion that being abused in childhood leads to such patterns in adult life is commonly known as the 'cycle of abuse' – a very powerful piece of ingrained 'common sense' in our society, as well as a psychological theory that has generated much academic and clinical debate.

Inside the relevant professions, a highly complex and even dynamic framework of literature and practice has been built up around the 'cycle of abuse'. Unfortunately, this work is based entirely on 'cases' that have come to the notice of one or other of the services – social workers, psychiatrists, police, etc. Some professionals are concerned that their work doesn't bring them into contact with women and men who have survived abuse successfully, essentially 'breaking' such a cycle. There is a growing belief that all relevant professionals need to have access to those survivors, in order to develop a wider understanding of abuse and more effective working practices.

In any case, it seems to me that the aspect of the 'cycle of abuse' theory that is most important for the rest of us – and for those professionals sympathetic to providing a better service to women – is not its theoretical dynamics, but how we are directly affected by its existence.

Throughout the world, the most scientific and largest-scale studies of the 'cycle of abuse' have failed to prove that those who suffer violence in childhood automatically encounter it as adults. Girls who first survived abuse as children, and then as women, have sisters with no experience of domestic violence and brothers who did not grow up to be abusers. It's just not that simple.

These studies show that not all children who have witnessed or experienced abuse go on to become abusers – no more than those who had abuse-free childhoods find they grow up to enjoy lives without violence. Neither do those who have had violent childhoods, in any significant numbers, seek out abusers as partners. Abusers do not necessarily come from violent homes.

Even when they do, other factors are seen as just as significant – sometimes more so – in determining whether or not they become domestic violators. In fact, there is some evidence to suggest that as they get older, those who endured child abuse or who witnessed domestic violence actively avoid potential abusers and seek out jobs that allow them to make up for the pain of their childhoods: social work, nursing, teaching, home help. Maybe people who like finding behaviour patterns should consider examining the possibility that there is actually a 'cycle of healing'. Look at the jobs of the participants in this book.

Though a lot of believers in the 'cycle of abuse' make some distinction between the reactions of women and men to violence in childhood, they ignore the key gender differences. Whether abused or not, women most frequently take whatever is bothering us out on ourselves. We cut ourselves, use drugs, become anorexic/bulimic/compulsive eaters. Irrespective of childhood abuse, men tend to externalise their problems. Though only some become domestic violators and child abusers, all men have a broader range of aggressions at their disposal. They bully people at work, get into fights at football matches, in the pub, at the golf club. They expose themselves, sexually harass or rape colleagues, acquaintances and strangers. And they *threaten* all kinds of sexual and non-sexual violence.

I believe that the powerful hold of the 'cycle of abuse' is to do with each of our own very deep-seated fears about the violation of our personal safety, about the consequences of that violation and about our need to have scapegoats. To protect ourselves, we must distance ourselves: if we can't see (or can stop ourselves from seeing) any abuse in our childhoods, then we are experiencing (or for abusers, perpetrating) none now. For abusers and others trying to avoid the systemic and endemic roots of abuse, individualising, medicalising, pathologising and off-loading blame on to other causes is highly convenient.

The 'cycle of abuse' theory also reveals the extent to which victim-blaming penetrates and clouds our wider perceptions, not just those about abuse. We regularly read, see and hear news reports where people are described as 'innocent victims'. Though this odious phrase is used mostly in war reporting, to differentiate soldiers from civilians, it is frequently applied to everything from divorce cases to criminal activities. The idea of innocence, of social and sexual virginity, of purity in all fleshly and earthly matters, underpins our most basic notions of good and evil. If to be innocent is good, then to be tainted in any way by abuse makes us evil.

Yet many supporters of the 'cycle of abuse' claim that it is, in fact, about *not* blaming children and women for what has happened to them and for what they supposedly go on to do or experience. But the reality is that the 'cycle of abuse' is often invoked by those defending male abusers – suggesting that somehow the men can't help it. This regularly allows judges to let abusers off on the grounds that a girl as young as five could have seduced them (somehow it must be the child's fault) or that women have endangered themselves or failed to protect their children. Indeed, the main result of the 'cycle of abuse' really seems to be to *not* blame (or, more accurately, hold responsible) the abusers themselves.

So the 'cycle of abuse' theory fits neatly into the whole woman-/mother-blaming syndrome. The good mother is one who safeguards her chastity and the innocence of her children. The bad mother is the one who endangers both. For nearly all the participants in this book, as well as for so many other women (and men), being able to understand and come to terms with our most intimate experiences means we can see that we have (had), and have been, good enough mothers.

5
Families don't need fathers

When I was forty, I gave up on my abusive father. I finally realised he was never going to stop and all I was doing by continuing to have contact with him was to subject myself to more abuse. Looking back, I realise I wasted a lot of emotional energy over the years, hoping he would change without any evidence that he even recognised what he was doing.

Because I'd been in psychoanalysis for four years when I made that decision, I thought I had examined it thoroughly. There seemed to be few problems in actually ending the relationship.

In fact, the physical and psychological relief I felt was so profound that I only wish I had been able to do it many years before. I became more self-confident, happier and much more at peace with myself. There is something about continuing contact with an abuser that is uniquely undermining. It means not only that all the abuse becomes effectively one's own fault, but that the actual imprisonment within the relationship itself does too. That by failing to get out, I had no one but myself to blame.

Achieving emotional independence from my father did, however, leave a psychic residue – a multi-layered anger that has taken me a while to understand. The top two strata were directed at my father and at my mother, and were the easiest to identify, to come to terms with and to peel off. Below those was the anger at myself for putting up with the abuse. This has taken longer to understand and to own up to. Buried deep in the core is the hurt, insecure little girl who both wants to make it all better and can't believe that she's so bad she deserves it.

Abuse is difficult to come to terms with for anyone who's experienced it. Nearly all women are brought up to believe that they have an overwhelming responsibility to be emotional healers. Though we know that children of both sexes blame themselves for family break-ups and go to great lengths to try to mend them, as they grow up the burden of holding the family together nearly always falls on women.

It is women who are seen as the preservers of social values, without which there would be moral anarchy. All over the world and throughout most of history, men are portrayed as having un-self-controllable behaviour that must be reined in by women: their mothers, sisters and eventually their wives. Men are wild, uncivilised beasts, programmed to behave as individuals. It is women who must tame them and ensure that their passions are channelled towards a collective good (that of the family and therefore the state) – and so often it is our fault if they fail to conform.

The verb 'to mother' is defined as female parenting, the verb 'to father' means to impregnate or sire. Parenting, though implying partnership and sharing, apart from perhaps supplying money and ultimate discipline, almost always ends up meaning being mother. Motherhood is simultaneously venerated and denigrated: it's supposed to be a woman's greatest achievement, yet anyone who doesn't absolutely conform to statutory rules about motherhood is vilified and increasingly denied financial support. In fact, few mothers are allowed to believe they would be judged more than just passable.

From early childhood, girls of most cultures are encouraged to play at being mothers because it is our destiny, while at the same time we are inculcated with the notion that we will need constant supervision to ensure it is being done properly – that it is a difficult and probably impossible perfection to attain. Curiously, even if others hail a woman as a great mother, she acquires no power or status through such recognition; the 'achievement' of greatness is meant to be its own reward. And in her heart she probably thinks she's a lousy mother anyway.

Fatherhood is a potent talisman (the most powerful political leaders, for example, are always fathers of their nations – mothers of nations are rarely more than purely ceremonial). In contrast to motherhood which is, confusingly, something for which women are both biologically determined and yet must also constantly strive to be good enough, it's as if men have a divine right to be fathers and fatherhood is something that just magically happens to them: each man's manifest destiny.

All men have to do to become fathers is to perform a single sexual act. Automatically, their rights to fatherhood are created. Though women can and often do successfully challenge men's unequivocal prerogatives of fatherhood, it is striking that, unless a woman does protest, it is usually assumed that such wide-ranging power is a man's automatic due.

Most cultures encourage everyone to prize the 'natural' wildness in boys. And when they grow up, it is marriage and fatherhood that will civilise them. Indeed, prison authorities are more likely to release a man on parole if he has a family to go to, because they believe that families (read 'women in the presence of children') will have a positive effect on curbing his savage behaviour. I can't understand how men can ever be socialised in this way; it would require the exertion of control over them, while, as fathers, they are the ones with absolute power.

It would seem that motherhood is obligation without power and that fatherhood, with the sole exception of a financial contribution, is power without obligation. This concept is challenged most vociferously by so-called fathers' rights' organisations. These are pressure groups of various sizes in places like Britain and America, largely made up of divorced men. They complain that men are being castrated by women who deny them their children. So it's not surprising that men involved in a leading men's rights' group were caught by *World In Action* television cameras offering to kidnap such children. In America, a hero of an equivalent group is serving a fifteen-year prison sentence for raping his wife.

To those who believe that the absolute rule of the father is sacred, children are irreparably damaged without one. All the evidence shows that, though one-parent families headed by women are invariably poorer and experience the concomitant effects of such deprivation, when the economic and social effects of single-mother parenthood are taken into account, children show little apparent differences in such areas as criminality and success in education.

In fact, the only striking differences that can be found between children depend not on the number or gender of parents, but on the stability and security children are able to get from caring, loving people. Growing children do prosper by being able to choose from a variety of adult role models. Not just different women and men, but people of a wide range of ages, races, sexualities, classes and abilities. In a British study published in 1993,[7] when poverty was included as a factor, poor single mothers were shown to produce children who presented no more problems for society in general than those from wealthier, two-parent families.

Despite the lack of hard evidence, all British governments and political parties have promoted the rhetoric that nuclear, heterosexual families are 'best'. This article of faith continues to underpin legislation and practice that directly and indirectly disadvantage all those who do not fit into that family structure – particularly women and children trying to break free from domestic violence.

Allowing people the choice of living in non-nuclear families means potentially weakening the power of abusive men. Politicians' commitment to the rule of the father is reflected in successive British governments' refusal to spend more than a pittance on any work to reduce domestic violence. This eloquently expresses their indifference to the women and children at the receiving end of the millions of reported incidents every year. Yet if only politicians would implement the findings of the research that they themselves have sponsored, follow the recommendations from their own parliamentary committee reports over the past twenty years, let themselves be guided by some of their very able civil servants, a dramatic and immediate improvement would be seen in alleviating the suffering of those subjected to domestic violence.

As a result of feminist pressure, the Canadian federal and provincial governments have spent hundreds of millions of dollars in recent years on a wide range of high-profile services, legislation and enforcement to reduce domestic violence. By contrast, though hard-pressed local authorities in the UK give women's refuges and other initiatives as much as they can, central government's total direct contribution to independent, long-term, secure domestic violence projects amounts to a few tens of thousands of pounds annually.

And just in case the rest of the British cabinet didn't get the message to block all attempts to eke out more cash for battered women, it is said that, in 1993, two of the most notoriously 'pro-family' ministers persuaded their colleagues that any money spent on domestic violence would result only in the utter destruction of the family. Ministers in a variety of government departments consistently refuse to listen to the evidence presented to them by their own research: that the risks faced by women and children exposed to domestic violence could be greatly reduced by putting money into housing, legal, educational, health and employment services for them.

So the state, as Our Father, works hard to ensure that families cannot escape the rule of man the father – ignoring the plentiful evidence that abusive fathers present a constant threat of danger to the psychological, emotional, physical and sexual safety of women and children.

Children are a hundred times more likely to be killed by the fathers and stepfathers they live with than by anyone else. Women are at greatest risk of violence from the men they live with, have lived with or with whom they have visiting relationships. And though there has been no large-scale research in the general population on the correlations between different kinds of abuse, evidence from Canada, Australia and the United States, as well as Britain, suggests that there are strong links.

Some studies show that those who perpetrate domestic violence are likely to abuse children. Other studies suggest that those who physically and sexually abuse children frequently commit domestic violence. Women who are made to watch their children being violated feel like it's happening to them. So do children who are forced to witness the abuse of their mothers

– getting hit themselves if they intervene. And abusers often use domestic violence as a prelude to the sexual abuse of children.

But the samples for such studies are small and taken from people already known to one statutory service or another. So though it is probable that sometimes there's a connection between different forms of abuse, it isn't always true that a man who perpetrates one kind will necessarily commit another.

All research does show, however, that all kinds of abusers are predatory planners and schemers, sometimes spending months and even years lining up victims. Nearly every day there are stories in the media about headmasters, teachers, care workers, scout leaders and choir masters – men who often assume a fatherly role – who are exposed as child abusers. Equally sinister are abusers who prey on single mothers in order to become stepfathers to potential victims. This cold calculation is also true of the overwhelming majority of domestic violators. By institutionalising the absolute power of fatherhood, the state solicits male abuse and imprisons women in nuclear families behind whose closed doors men act with impunity.

Most of the women who participated in this book revealed their abusers' predatory and insidious behaviour. Those who have children described how the children were abused too. The women also reported a range of other ways in which men deliberately made family life hell. These included exerting obsessional control over every aspect of the women's lives, accusing women of infidelity when the men themselves were persistently unfaithful, and constantly denigrating the woman, her family and friends. Yet the economic and psychological pressures on women to preserve the heterosexual, nuclear family unit are so great that they keep on managing and coping with the abuse. And for many women, the belief that families need fathers at all costs often means staying with an abuser.

Staying

Tessa went home to her parents when she was pregnant, having left her first husband in the 1950s. In the late 1960s, she didn't have that option.

My youngest child's father, I think, was the worst relationship I've ever been in. I don't know how I got into it, but I wanted to conform.

I wanted to conform because I was this black woman that had had all these kids, six kids by that time, and I thought here's a man willing to keep you. He's not good-looking, but he's got a good steady job and he gives you a good wage every week. Because regardless of what kind of trouble we had, that money on a Friday was put on the table and to me that was security. I didn't have to drag the kids out at six o'clock in the morning to baby minders. I didn't have to look where the next meal was coming from and – in one certain way – prostitute myself. Not in the way of being actually an out and out prostitute, but prostitute yourself with boyfriends to get a bit of extra money off them.

So I wanted to conform, to be a housewife, a mother and get a nice home together. Now he would give with his hand, but take back with his mouth – mental cruelty. Plus he got very violent in the end.

He was very, very – I wouldn't say jealous, I'd say possessive. If we went for an evening out, I had to keep my eyes down. I daren't say hello to people, because if I said hello to somebody, I'd been to bed with them. After we got home, he'd lay in bed and he'd wake me at three in the morning just to nag me. And I knew when the abuse was coming, 'cause he used to start rubbing his feet together. And I'd think, 'Oh God, I'm gonna get it – gonna get nagged.' The nagging didn't go on for one hour, it went on for hours and hours. Even when he was working as a docker.

This went on for over five years. In the sixth year I'd had enough. My eldest sister who lived five doors away, she hated him. She used to say, 'You're looking like an old woman. You're not caring for yourself. Your hair's a mess, you're getting lines across your forehead, look at you.'

Twelve years after I left him, I discovered that he had sexually abused one of my daughters. I went berserk. I got a knife and went to kill him. Actually I went to cut his balls off. I cut his privates, I cut the top of his leg. He never reported it.

I took myself off to the hospital for therapy. It took me a long time, a long time. Because I used to say, 'Why didn't I know?' I want to know why as a mother I didn't see the signs. I used to drum it into my kids. 'Any man, I don't care who it is. Come and tell your mother. Don't think your mother is frightened of anybody.' I'll never trust another man as long as I live.

For Elsa, the physical violence got worse after she started work in the 1970s. She had come to England from Barbados twenty years earlier, on the same boat as the man she would eventually marry. Though she had no interest in him when they first met, he pursued her until she finally gave in. Elsa describes the situation she found herself in in London and the Midlands during the late 1950s and early 1960s.

I was nineteen and it's strange, but I never liked him from the beginning. I couldn't stand him – the sight of him – and he knew that. He was determined and I tried to do everything to get away from him. He used to pester me so much. He pursued me for more than six months. Why did I give in? I do not know. I always wanted to get married and have children.

In many black families, there wasn't divorce. So I tried, I think for the children. I always thought I wouldn't like the children to grow up without a father and they were quite young at the time. When I did divorce, the youngest – she wasn't even quite three yet.

I was dependent on him for money and at that time I had no confidence. I'll be honest with you, things had got so bad that I was sure that I couldn't go out and face the outside world.

Eleanor, like many women, believed she was a failure because she was unable to change her abusive husband. She tried to manage his abuse instead.

You get to this state where you manage to control the big things that you know are going to upset him. If you know he doesn't like corned beef hash for his tea on a Wednesday, or whatever, you don't give him corned beef hash. You give him the steak and the mushrooms and everything. And you live on bread and butter, because that saves an argument.

You learn how to manage all those big things, but it's always the little things that you've got no control over. What I've learned since is that battered women become good managers, they manage situations. You do learn to manage the situation. You can control it, for weeks or maybe months on end. But then the little things happen, you may have left too much fat on the steak, you've got no control over that whatsoever.

Probably I was trying to be a 'normal housewife'. I didn't really know any divorced people. I know my aunt was divorced, but it was all hush-hush. You didn't ask why, it was never discussed.

I was so wrapped up in survival, I didn't realise how bad it was for the kids – the way he treated them. They used to get shouted at, they used to get chastised, he used to belt them. Now I've spoken to my kids and my eldest daughter said, 'I've had one shitty life, partly through my dad knocking us around, I've had one shitty life.'

Janie was able to admit she was a battered woman when she realised she was trapped – that her husband followed her everywhere. She describes why she married and stayed with him, and how her daughter was affected.

I was never in love with him. I realised after I left him. I mean when I was with him, I thought I was in love with him. But I was never in love with him. I married him for all the wrong reasons. I married him for security. I thought I'd get security and I didn't. I married him because I thought nobody else would want me with a child – my daughter. I was never in love with him.

A friend noticed something herself. She called round one day, and we were going to pick up the kids from school. He opened the door to her and he just said 'Right', and shut the door in her face. Me and him had had an argument. Then I came out and she asked what was wrong.

I started telling her everything that had been happening. She said, 'Why don't you leave him?' So I said, 'Where am I going to go? I've got three kids.' And she said, 'There's women who've done it before.' And I went, 'I know, but I'm not strong enough.' I really felt I wasn't strong enough to manage on my own with three kids.

By this time, he was out of work. And she and I used to take the kids to school at ten to nine. If I wasn't back for five past nine, he'd want to know where I'd been and what I was doing. I had no life of my own. Everything I did he was involved with. My friend stopped calling round. Nobody called round to see me because of the way he was. I couldn't go out anywhere, not at any time. Unless he was with me, I couldn't go out.

I knew where I could go for help, I just didn't have the courage.

After his first child, my oldest son, was born, my husband went very, very serious and he started picking on my daughter for the slightest thing and she obviously resented him for it. The time I left him in 1990 and then went back to him, my daughter said, 'I'm not coming back.' In the end she did come back. She came back because of me.

He used to chastise her. There was one incident where I stopped him. He started off smacking her. I don't know what she'd done – something wrong in school. He started smacking her and then he started punching her. And I had to go and I had to stand in between them. I said, 'No, you're not doing that.' And he went, 'Get out my way.' I went, 'No, I'm not moving.' I went, 'I'd rather you beat me than beat her.' So I got a beating. It wasn't long after that that she ran away.

We didn't know where she was for three days. The police found her staying at this girl's flat. She was twelve at the time. She said, 'I'm not going home.' Point blank. 'While my mother's with him.' So she went into care and there was no way she was going to come home because of him. She said, 'I can't take any more. I can't sit there any longer and watch what he's doing to you.'

Possession and control

Eleanor remembers an incident of possessiveness when she was eighteen, just before she married in 1963, that would resonate later in the marriage.

I think I must have loved him, probably for what he was – his social standing, really. Probably because he was tall, he was dark, he was handsome – he was the one all the girls in school wanted. I suppose I was flattered and I worshipped the ground he walked on really, originally.

We had an argument and I went away. And he wrote me a letter saying, 'When we get married, you'll never be able to leave me.' I was like a lot of women, I thought, 'Oh, God, he must really love me, he doesn't want me to go away.' Hindsight, you realise it's possession, not love.

You're like a stone that gets worn away or a pebble on the beach, by the time I left him. I mean, I had six brothers, I went to a mixed school. But when I walked along the street, I walked with my eyes down. I never looked at anybody in the face. If I did and it was male – after all, I had six younger brothers and if I let on to any of their friends or he had two brothers who had friends – I was having affairs with them.

So I looked down. And I always ran everywhere. People were always saying to me, 'You're always in a hurry.' And, everywhere, I never stopped to chat, whatever, outside schools or wherever. I was straight to the shops and straight back. Because I was timed. 'It takes you five minutes to get to the shops and five minutes to get back and five minutes to get served – that's fifteen minutes. You've been half an hour, where have you been for the other fifteen?' 'I was talking to so and so.' 'What did you say?' 'Oh, we were just talking about the kids in school.' 'That's took you two minutes to say, what were you saying for the other eighteen minutes?' If you didn't give an answer that pleased him, that was it.

It's also never knowing the right thing. I used to sit and watch television, and I'd have the kids in bed, and he'd have gone to the pub. I'd be sitting there thinking, 'Have I got the right station on? Am I watching the right programme? Shall I go to bed?' If I went to bed, I'd have had somebody there. And the bed was examined, because I'd had a man there. But if I stayed up, one, I didn't have the right television programme on – because I never had what he wanted to watch on, ''cause you *know* I want to watch the other side' – two, I was staying up to spy on him and I'd had somebody there. So you never knew which was the right thing and which was the wrong thing to do.

Christine works in a refuge where she sees the influence that their mothers can have on women experiencing domestic violence. It was her husband's obsessive, controlling behaviour that had an especially profound effect on Christine.

When my husband was there, everybody had to be there and dance attention on him. The kids couldn't go and play in their rooms, they had to be there. When he wasn't there, I'd let them have friends in or go out and play. But they always had to be somewhere where I could get hold of them if he came in. 'Cause if I didn't, then he'd start.

He had a habit, when he was coming home, he would never knock on the door. We lived in a square – on the corner of the square. He would enter on the far side of the square, and then he'd whistle. By the time he got across the square, I used to have to have the door open. If it wasn't open, he'd boot it in.

I used to have to keep the television turned down so low, so I could hear his whistle. I could never go to bed, I used to have to sit up and wait for him. If he came in and he didn't want to go to bed, if he fell asleep on the couch, I couldn't go to bed. If I'd gone to bed and left him lying on the couch (or if I hadn't covered him up – towards the end, I used to go to bed) he'd come and drag me out of bed and ask me what the fucking hell did I think I was doing leaving him downstairs to freeze.

When a friend realised that her apparently smudged mascara was a bruise, Molly admitted that her partner had hit her, but she said she provoked him. Somehow Molly hoped she could manage his abuse by trying to be what she imagined her partner wanted.

He wanted me to be really submissive and he wanted me to do everything. I always looked after him. I cooked for him and I cleaned for him and ironed his shirts and did his washing. When I wasn't working, I had nothing else to do. But that used to get on his nerves after a while. Because I was just at home all the time. Sometimes he'd say, 'You're too available. You're there.' And I'd say, 'What do you expect me to do? I can't go back to work at the moment. With a small child, the situation I'm in at the moment is really difficult.' And he used to say, 'There's no challenge left because you're always available.'

But then if I made myself unavailable – if I purposely wouldn't be in when I thought he might ring or I'd go out and come back a lot later than I told him – it would cause merry hell. 'Where have you been? Who have you been with?'

Anne sees her mother as Boadicea with a Yankee accent. Like many women, rich and poor, her mother was her greatest support. Anne's experience also shows that the way abusers use economic control affects women of all social classes.

He turned my room upside down and he took my credit cards, my chequebooks, the lot. He tore my room apart and took everything of value. So I was effectively trapped. He was, in the mean time, being sweetness and light, despite this latest outrage. He also took the key to the petty cash, so I couldn't even get money for the kids' music lessons or anything. But you see, *I* was being unreasonable, because I was enraged, because my bedroom was a tip. It was perfectly obvious.

He thought he was perfectly entitled to take my credit cards, my chequebook and he was quite entitled to take the petty cash key. The only thing he said was, 'I haven't taken the car keys.' But he had me under his thumb. He said, 'How are you going to support your horses? Now, see, but I'm a reasonable man.' It was all sweetness and light. 'And how are you going to support your horses now?'

Her mother is unable to understand why Candace allows her abusive ex-partner to visit their sons in her home. Candace believes she sets clear boundaries for the men in her life. She sees the effects of men's controlling behaviour on the women in the refuge where she works. She also feels the effects of such behaviour when she's at home.

Women think, 'What have I done? It must be my fault because I must have done something.' A lot of the time a man is manipulative and he will say to you, 'You're no good.' It's been pushed in her brain. 'You can't cook, you can't wash. Look at the house, look at the state of the house.' I mean this woman is working her arse off every day trying to keep the place clean. And though he's out all day and she's got the children, he'll say, 'Look at the condition of the children, it's your fault.'

And women start to believe it's their fault, because there's no one else telling them anything positive. Because they look up to the man, the man's always telling them, 'It's your fault.' So they believe it eventually.

We've all been – it's not so much our parents, it's the rule of life, isn't it, it's very hard to go against. A woman's supposed to do this, that and the other. I mean even yesterday, I went out and I came back late and I didn't do any food shopping. If you had seen the look on my boys' faces. I said, 'Can't you cook for yourselves?'

Tessa, Eleanor, Christine, Molly, Anne and Janie's descriptions show how abusers try to control their victims' lives totally. These women reacted like many others in their position: striving to be the best wives, the best mothers – to manage the abuse in order to achieve some measure of safety for themselves and their children. Men, it seems, largely exert power over other people in order to gain or maintain their own dominance, while women's struggles for control are mostly on behalf of others as well as themselves.

Treatment

Clearly the only way to eliminate male abuse is to change men. Despite much publicity, the law stops few abusers. Offering them 'treatment' looks like becoming the most fashionable option. Yet, in Britain, men in general are less likely than women to ask for any kind of professional support for personal problems (like GPs, or psychotherapists, etc.) and are older by the time they do. The average woman seeks help when she's thirty or less, while men wait until they are in their mid forties. Only one of the participants in this book said that her abuser ever indicated any wish to change. Even if others had, voluntary or mandatory programmes for domestic violators in Britain, outside prisons, are a relatively recent and rare phenomenon – there are perhaps fewer than 100 places in the whole country.

But we can really only guess at overall numbers, in the same way we can only guess at the variety of programmes and the quality of the service they provide. There is no central regulatory and governing authority for such programmes. The few that can even begin to be assessed are those with some connection to the criminal justice system, statutory agencies and academic institutions. And most of these are not very inspiring.

Anyone can set up as a treater of male abusers. And a curious bunch they often reveal themselves to be. I have sat in the audience of criminal justice and statutory agency conferences and been appalled at the amount of discredited and discreditable nonsense that is spouted by some of the masters of men's programmes. They produce flow charts that purport to explain the causes and cures for abuse. These elaborate diagrams manage, nevertheless, to simplify and reduce all women (and all men), as well as the dynamism and complexities of human life, to bite-sized bits of behaviour. Each chunk rigidly follows on, one to the other, like a nightmare game of snakes and ladders.

Male abuse is then explained away as the sum of an individual's problems and personal inadequacies, that will be magically treatable by whoever is on stage. The theories on which these programmes are based are either unproven, unprovable or utterly rejected by experienced, responsible professionals. And if a woman or the abuser doesn't 'fit' into the pattern (as most real women and men inevitably won't), she will feel that, indeed, it must be all her fault. But that's only part of it. Despite their lack of experience and unregulated status, men's programme workers are frequently invited to address sexual violence conferences. There are a disturbing number of stories about how these men routinely use such invitations as an opportunity to play soundtapes of abusers recounting their crimes in salacious detail. Women who attend are said to be sickened and some walk out. This practice itself seems like a form of abuse to me.

These sound tapes usually come from a part of the programme process. The majority of places on men's programmes are for child abusers, child sexual abusers and rapists. Of those programmes in the UK open to domestic violators, all but two of the ones outside prisons are voluntary. Rarely do the courses last longer than a few months. Some programmes call themselves therapeutic and often connect with a particular psychological theory or practice. Others are more vaguely named counselling services with equally imprecise goals. Still others are only helplines. Current flavour of the month are so-called 'anger management' courses which are often run by probation services. Programmes can be organised around groups or on a one-to-one basis. The vast majority of therapeutic and anger management courses focus on getting men to express their feelings; there's often a lot of hugging involved. What these programmes don't do is get the men to take responsibility for their offending behaviour within a context of gender and power relations.

In the UK, the only two mandatory programmes connected to the criminal justice system – that is ones that men must attend as an alternative to prison – are in Scotland. They were also the first programmes to have allowed themselves to be independently evaluated. Neither has been going for more than a few years, so it's still too early to form any definite conclusions.

Untested and unmonitored, the majority of British men's programmes nevertheless seem to have an easier time finding funding than women's refuges. Many are privately run for profit – bilking statutory agencies and private individuals alike. Yet no one has the least idea what difference, if any, such programmes make. Not only do we have no overall information about who's doing what to whom where, there is no follow-up – independent or otherwise – that would allow us to know what really happens to the men when they leave.

In Canada, they appear to be more organised. Having invested so much cash in reducing domestic violence, they ought to be interested in knowing if they're getting value for money.

Like those in the rest of the world, the vast majority of Canadian programmes involve a course of therapy or treatment. Abuse is seen as a psychological or medical problem, a physical or psychic defect of individual men. And the courses are short: even programmes which are not based on a therapeutic model and emphasise the social context of abuse, trying to get each man to take responsibility for his actions, rarely last longer than a few months.

With more men's programmes available in Canada, there is more apparent evaluation. Unfortunately, little of it is independent of the programmes themselves and most is worthless. Canadian women involved in non-treatment programmes for men criticise evaluation as sloppy and unscientific. Much of the follow-up work merely records whether or not men come to the notice of the criminal justice system or other statutory agencies. Attempts to look at changes in behaviour usually only occur four to five months after the man finishes the course – not long enough by any standards. On the rare occasions when women are asked about the effect of men's participation in such programmes the evaluation is done over the phone or by post. There is no way to gauge what effect the possible presence of the men themselves may have on women's answers.

Evaluation, such as it is, of treatment and non-treatment programmes in Canada and in the US indicates that men who take part have apparently lower 'recidivism' rates than those who don't. This is indicated by men not coming to the notice of criminal justice systems and statutory agencies, and the women known to have been abused by them allegedly reporting less physical violence.

What all this really means is anyone's guess. It has been suggested that men's treatment and some non-treatment programmes – in and out of prison, voluntary and mandatory, whether for known rapists, child sexual abusers or domestic violators – only produce more skilful, cunning and clever abusers who swap techniques with each other, thus avoiding getting caught again. Male programme workers have been discovered routinely colluding, minimising and otherwise letting men off the hook. They are allowed to excuse their behaviour by blaming victims, mothers, drink, drugs and the whole range of social and personal pressures as well as themselves being neglected or abused as children. Physical violence is thought to sometimes decrease as a result of these programmes, being replaced by more 'sophisticated' psychological, emotional and verbal forms of abuse.

In Canada and the US, there are a tiny number of pro-feminist programmes for abusers. Some are court-mandatory, lasting years rather than months. All are distinguished by factors never built into any British versions, such as being directly accountable to refuges and other services for women. Abusers must go out into their communities and openly commit themselves to allowing other people to monitor their behaviour. The goals for such programmes are set by battered women, and women's safety is a primary element of their construction. Those who run them recognise that follow-up evaluation based on women's experiences is difficult to implement. While they cannot gauge whether or not their programmes work after men complete the course, they hope their connections to women's services will, at least, give them some feedback.

All research points to abusers being serial and often simultaneous perpetrators. But if programmes for abusers are not even evaluated on the basis of the experiences of women *known* to have been abused by the men on such courses, what about all the other women these men may be violating at the same time and those they go on to abuse?

We need to ask whether there are certain points in abusers' careers when they cannot change. Consensus in research and practice has shown that these probably exist. However, research is also beginning to indicate that, rather than mainly fund programmes for adult abusers, it would be more effective to put greater resources into spotting and acting on the first warning signals (young children torturing animals, for instance). Early intervention work with boys and adolescent males looks increasingly promising to those with long experience of dealing with abusers.

Those abusers experiencing extremes of mental illness (and these are very few indeed) deserve our support and secure care. But the vast majority of male abusers have made the choice to do it: they are cold, calculating and in control. There is no indication that either limited prison terms or treatment programmes ever stop abuse. We have a right to our safety and to demand that society protects us from these men – permanently. We need to ask if their actions and the threat they pose mean that they have forfeited any right to contemplate unfettered freedom. Is it simply not worth the risk to women and children to ever let them out?

Some politicians have a knee-jerk repugnance to locking people up and throwing away the key. Others have a religious-like belief in innate human perfectibility. Still others believe that if women stayed at home where they belong and if feminists stopped making trouble, male violence would disappear. Women's safety is never high on any political agenda. Male politicians are far too worried about depriving themselves and other men of their property (women, children, homes), and their freedom to abuse.

The truth is, men's programmes on their own are never likely to work – certainly not without other changes being made. No one ever gives up power voluntarily. Since men's place in society is based on their ability to dominate others, nothing will alter until there is a shift in the balance of power between men and women, and until we revise the characteristics by which each are valued.

Even if a few men do stop abusing for short periods of time as a result of these programmes, isn't the temptation to abuse again once they leave almost irresistible?

Because most cultures prize and encourage aggressive, dominating behaviour in boys, male abuse will continue. Instead of spending so much money treating abusers, shouldn't we be using some of it to study men who *don't* abuse? This might enable us to begin to understand how we can create a society where abuse and violence are neither allowed nor valued: to raise sons who'd have no need to abuse and daughters who wouldn't live in fear of them.

Successful men have always been defined as those who achieve material prosperity, ascendancy over other men, social status and who keep their women (and children) under control. If, instead, their success was gauged on what women and children wanted, I believe the world would be, at the very least, a safer place.

Despite the depressing statistics that tell us that the average female wage is still only two-thirds that of men, and that though the percentage of working women has risen men do as little housework as ever, I believe there is hope. All around me I see women continuing to make demands that increase the possibilities for men now and for boys growing up to become good fathers. Demands of politicians, statutory agencies, the law, employers, community leaders, educators and the media. And most importantly, demands of the men in our lives.

These demands don't simply include eliminating the most gross forms of abuse. They also include demands for men to be emotionally reliable, not to use sex and money as weapons, to have no need to control anyone else, and not to threaten to use state sanctions, like immigration regulations, against women.

But until we are successful in securing acceptance of our demands, whatever else they may need, I believe families just don't need fathers.

6

Till death us do part

Like millions of other rather ignorant white girls throughout the last sixty years, when I hit puberty I fell in love with the novel *Gone With The Wind*. I wasn't troubled by its obvious racism (though I fancied myself a liberal at the time) nor its class prejudice (America? Social class?). I was oblivious of its imperialist message. I just wanted to be (no, I *was*) Scarlett, at Tara, to be loved by every man on earth – especially Ashley and Rhett – and to live melodramatically ever after.

Of course being rich, beautiful and endlessly resourceful – never mind constantly triumphing over adversity – held their attractions. But lots of stories have feisty heroines. I think the special attraction of *Gone With The Wind*, for me and perhaps for other women, was the proximity of love (sex) and death: Ashley going to war – and Scarlett's desire for him; the forced march from Tara, the acres of dead and wounded at the railway station, the burning of Atlanta – and Rhett's desire for Scarlett; the ruin and renewal of Tara – and Ashley's desire for Scarlett. And of course there was all that highly charged childbirth, passionate attachment to the land and dying for The South which seemed to stir my emotions. I chose to ignore the more problematical conjunctions: Ashley's vigilante murder of the freed slaves who may have sexually threatened Scarlett's (white man's?) honour, and Rhett's rape of Scarlett after the death of their daughter (for which he held her responsible).

And then I saw the film. Suddenly all those fantasies had human form. They were 'real' people: speaking, laughing, crying, yearning, loving and dying. Tara and Atlanta were 'real' places I could imagine living in. The pictures that had only existed in my imagination were now shared with countless other like-minded girls. Though there is always a part of every collective dream that each of us keeps secret, communing in the dark with those who have the same passion makes it all the more vivid.

Every time I saw the film, I'd start to cry as soon as the first frame of picture came up. I have a friend who began weeping even earlier – in the dark, before the screen lit up, just after the opening bars of the theme music. Many other women have also said that they cried throughout, in the happy and sad moments, for the pleasure and the pain (and the pain of the pleasure as well as the pleasure of the pain). The connections between sexual love and death became validated by that collective experience. ('*Cal*', a British film of the early 1980s, was trailed on television with the female protagonist lying in bed with her voiceover endlessly asking 'Would you die for me?')

The impact that works of popular culture like *Gone With The Wind* have had on countless women around the world is unquantifiable. But the way they reinforce the romantic connections between sexual love and death holds clues, I believe, to understanding the difficulties women encounter leaving abusive men.

The extent of men's passion and their willingness to die for us are nearly always seen by women, initially anyhow, as positive examples of female desirability and male devotion. We start out believing that this must be evidence of the perfect relationship. They cannot live without us, they want to be with us as much as possible, they have eyes for no one else, cherish every particle of our being. But how often does that apparent devotion really just disguise jealous, possessive, domineering, controlling violence and abuse? (Remember the hit song that went 'Every breath you take, every move you make, I'll be watching you. Oh can't you see, you belong to me. My poor heart aches with every move you make.')

Romance is as much a weapon of reality as of our imaginations. Nearly every woman I know, whether or not she's ever been involved with an abuser, will seize on anything positive, however minor, that makes her feel more secure about a relationship. Because so many of us complain that men run away from emotional commitment, to find one so utterly devoted seems almost too good to be true.

To have a relationship with someone who appears to want no one but her nearly always signifies that a woman may just have attained that female romantic ideal of getting and keeping her man. Even if the attention becomes overpowering possession, the adoration turns jealous and threatening, she may still keep hoping that what she believed to be the original love can be rekindled. And the spark is almost always sex.

Sex, with or without love, and death have a complex inter-connection. The sex act is at once an affirmation of life, but the release, the letting go in an orgasm, has also been likened to dying. In a healthy relationship sex is also an expression of love, unity, boundlessness and, paradoxically, a denial of the death of something precious. For everyone, it renews and strengthens the feelings that lovers have for each other. The denial of death can be even more paradoxical if the relationship that sex is reaffirming is an abusive one.

Death as a concept, as a threat and as reality plays an important and intricate part in abuse. Many women (and children) describe feeling as if they've died inside as a result of it. Abusive men use any pretext to threaten to kill women and their children: an innocuous incident during the most mundane, daily activity; the belief that the women and children might (want or try to) leave them. Nearly every week, it seems, I read at least one news story of a man, often described as estranged from the woman and children, who kills them and then himself. Not, I believe, because he fears them or is in despair, but as the ultimate act of revenge. Men do not kill women and children in self-defence, as a last resort, feeling threatened by their superior strength or potential for violence. These men are out to punish those they worry and imagine are beyond their control.

Women, too, kill their children and then themselves – though with much less frequency, and rarely at the same time as killing the man. Overwhelmingly women kill when they fear that an abusive man will succeed in gaining custody or access to their children; when a woman is terrified he will kill her and the kids; or when women believe that they are helpless to prevent the state taking their children away from them permanently.

When a woman kills a man it is nearly always because he has been abusing her or her children. Often she does it when *his* threats to kill are not taken seriously by anyone but her. When there seems no other means of escape.

Revenge

Years before she was raped and then told her mother, Elizabeth used to escape by thinking about her abusive partner's death.

> I never actually sat down and thought, 'This is how I'm going to do it.' But I used to wish to God he was dead. I used to fantasise about car accidents, bricks falling off tall buildings and things like him falling under a double-decker bus. And how much I would grieve!

Gradually Barbara built up strategies towards achieving her independence – getting an 'O' level, dealing with all the family's business, negotiating with her children's schools and the like. But though her sexual feelings for her husband were ambivalent, they didn't preclude a desire for his death.

> He was very, very demanding, sexually. I went to see the doctor on one occasion and said, 'Look, you know, is it me, is it him, what is it?' And he said, 'What's the problem?' I said, 'He wants sex in the morning. He wants sex – I'm not exaggerating – at teatime and then he wants sex when we go to bed at night.' And the doctor said to me, 'What does he do for a living?' I said, 'When he's working, which is rarely, he's a building labourer.' And this doctor said, 'And is he like that when he's working?' And I said, 'Yes.' And this doctor said, 'I wish I knew how he did it.' Which wasn't helpful.

Sometimes I would allow sex to happen. It wasn't rape, I allowed it to happen. I mean I would say, 'OK.' If I had said 'Absolutely no way', he would not have forced himself on me. He would have complained, but he would not have forced himself on me.

He wouldn't generally cast up. There was neither the physical nor emotional blackmail present in that situation. At the time when he was pursuing me sexually, it would be difficult to sustain saying 'No'.

But it was a side of the relationship that, no, I didn't want sex as much as that, but when we did have sex it was good. He was very considerate. He might suggest something. If I wasn't in the mood for that kind of thing, that was OK.

He would never dare come before me. From the very start, I asserted that I would not tolerate a man – him – having his satisfaction with my body, because that's what it would become for me. I suppose because we were both very young and very inexperienced – I had no experience and he had had a little – I think he thought that this was quite normal.

Since then I have discovered – after I left him, because I've had several relationships – I've discovered that it's not normal. I've spoken with other women. I've heard what other women put up with. And I think, 'At least we got that part of it right.' Which seems like a terrible contradiction, but that's the way it was.

I felt like killing him and planned it three times. I was a keen gardener. I had started to keep a small herb garden. I had gotten herb books out of the library, found that there were various herbs which were poisonous and the first time, I had thought, 'Right, I'm going to do a job on him.'

I didn't do it, because I thought, 'I'll get found out. It's not worth it.'

Then on another occasion, the house was being insulated and between the outside wall and the inside wall there was a huge cavity and they were pumping stuff in. So I thought,

'What I'll do is I'll somehow murder him, get him dead, put him down the cavity. Because there's a hole in the wall, put him down the cavity. When they pump this stuff in, what will happen is it'll stop any smell. And that'll be the end of him.'

The third way was that the next time he hit me, I was going to pick up something and I was going to let him have it.

There was only one occasion where I tried to hit him back and he battered me. I knew from experience that if I was going to hit him back, I would have to hit him to make sure he went down and stayed down. I would have to put all my eggs in one basket.

Samantha believes her husband's violence – that caused her miscarriage – and his total indifference to her pain were significant in the build-up of her murder attempts.

I put bleach in his tea for three weeks once and all he came down with was diarrhoea. Prior to that I threatened him with a knife. And after, I actually stabbed him.

The bleach in the tea came before the stabbing. So I think the knife was the final accolade. I think I'd been cleaning the sink, the bleach was out and he'd asked me to make him a cup of tea. I'd gone and made the cup of tea and thought, 'Bollocks to you.' And put a teaspoonful of bleach in his tea.

He said, 'Oh this tastes funny. Is it that bloody Earl Grey shit?' And I thought, 'Aha. With a little help, how many spoonfuls does it take?'

It was almost like a child sticking out her tongue. It wasn't meant with intent. It was just, 'Notice what I'm doing. Ask me why and then I'll tell you and you'll suddenly realise that you've been a bad boy. And you'll change and you'll be what you should be and not what you are.'

At this stage we had got to the point where there was no conversation. There was no actual verbal between us. We were two bodies living in the same house and there was very little conversation, unless it was absolutely necessary.

When I stabbed him, I did it in the leg, not somewhere personally serious that he was going to die.

He would refer to it as a joking thing. 'I'd better not push you too far because you'll stab me or you'll take a knife to me.' He was very wary around me after that, because it was that one point, 'There but for the Goddess, go I.' I could have perpetrated domestic murder, because had I actually got the knife near his heart, I would have killed him. There is no two ways about it.

I was going for him in the chest and torso. He actually raised his leg to deflect the blow. It wasn't a serious wound. A stabbing sounds serious, but if I could have, I would have killed him.

I think it was the last straw. We'd had a friend coming to visit and I'd had to clean the house from top to bottom. I think I'd had about three hours sleep. I was incredibly tired. I was very, very run down and things were just horrific between the two of us.

It was a red mist job. The red mist descended. The final thing he did was he closed the bedroom door on me. I was changing the spare linen and I turned around and said something like, 'Why the fuck don't you help me?' And he walked over towards me, turned around and then walked out and shut the door on me.

Just being in this room with the door shut on me was this massive symbolic distancing – 'closing down of shutters' – everything. And this red mist came down on me and I walked into the kitchen and picked up my best boning knife, my meat knife, and walked into the lounge and looked at him and said, 'I'm going to kill you.'

I was absolutely deadpan. I was deadly serious. I just went towards him and lunged at him. He lifted his leg and I caught him, nicked him in the leg.

I was sitting there whilst he was in hospital thinking, 'Oh God. I'm going to get arrested in a minute and my career is going down the toilet. He'll have told the police at the hospital and there'll be a detective on my doorstep arresting me for attempted murder.' And I phoned a friend of mine who was a really nice old-fashioned guy and said, 'What am I going to do? I've cut his leg with a knife. He could do me for attempt murder.' And he said, 'Plead pre-menstrual tension and you'll get away with it.'

So I thought, 'Right, I'll compose my defence.' So I sat there with a piece of paper and wrote down all the reasons why I had pre-menstrual tensions two weeks before my period was due. Or a week after, whatever it was. At the time it wasn't right for pre-menstrual tension.

I thought, 'Maybe they'll do a test on me, a medical test, to see when I menstruate.' I was really so chewed up.

He was stitched up in casualty and told them he fell off his motor cycle.

Then he came back and it was as though nothing had happened. He just said, 'I'm sorry I shut the door on you.' That was the first time he'd ever said, 'Sorry.' He didn't modify his behaviour, he walked with a limp for a while.

But things were going from bad to worse. He found it very difficult that I was the next rank up. He was obviously the subject of quite a lot of ribbing and good-humoured jokes and banter, and perhaps the odd malicious jibe at work, because the wifey was actually a rank above him – a supervisor.

That was the death knell. No correspondence that was addressed to 'Sergeant' Me could ever come through the door. I never wore my epaulettes home from work. Nothing ever was in the house that showed him I was a sergeant. *I* did that. I chose to do that to myself, not him. So it was pretty strange.

Molly tried to be the perfect housewife. That didn't work and her partner complained that she was too available, so she tried playing hard to get, which didn't work either. She couldn't face up to what he was doing and though Molly didn't try to kill her abusive partner, she did want some kind of revenge.

> I used to tip his aftershave away sometimes and I put it on his toothbrush once and I scrubbed the toilet with it. And I was scrubbing away at the toilet and I was really cursing him. I felt so resentful towards him. I felt really bitter and really angry. These are little things I can do when he's not around and I feel better for it.

Even though her husband was a rich farmer Anne was as financially dependent as much poorer women, especially when he took away her credit cards and closed her bank accounts. And like women of every social class, she lived with his abuse. During all the time she was with her abusive husband, Anne's determination to be vigilant was important to her.

> I meant to have him. Many a time I would have a knife to hand. Because he's the sort that comes up and literally almost puts his nose on your nose and screams full blast and spits in your face and would push you. I would not have that any more. So I always made sure I had a knife to hand or a pitchfork if I was mucking out.

> For the last three years, I slept with a butcher knife under my bed, which he knew about, as I said, 'You'll never hit me again.'

> And we went to his shooting dinner – pillar of society and sporting gent. He isn't a drinker. My doctor now assumes he's a psychopath which really cheered me. But he had one of his rages on the way back from his shooting dinner.

> I took the babysitter home, went to bed and he came in and attacked me. He was stupid because he knew I'd been sleeping with a knife for some time and he started to knock me about. For the first time ever, I knocked him off balance, off the edge of the bed. 'Cause he's quite heavy. As he was picking himself up off the floor, I went for him with a knife.

He raced for his life because he's a coward. A lot of bullies are cowards. I had the grim satisfaction of him running for his life wearing only his T-shirt, streaking through the top floor of this rather large house, trying to slam doors in his wake. 'Cause I was going to have him.

And he locked himself in the master bath. In the master bath, my dear, there's a rather large skylight set above the big doors. So I got one of the chairs from the bedroom and I climbed on it and proceeded to go through the skylight, cutting myself in the process, which is neither here nor there. But I was going to have him, there was no doubt.

Whereupon he turned the volume right up and started to scream to my son to call the police. 'Your mother's mad, she's trying to kill me.' Which in a sense was true. Poor child phoned 999.

In the mean time, my husband was trying to open the door and overpower me. And we had this Laurel and Hardy farce of the door opening and shutting. Every time he tried to overpower me, I'd take a slice at his gut. And I missed him, damn!

By this time he was waving a bath towel. It is quite amusing if you think back, but it wasn't particularly at the time. But I had him cornered in the master bath. I had this lovely long knife and he was sat on the loo in nothing but his T-shirt and not quite a smile.

And the next thing I knew two total strangers, two ruddy-cheeked baby policemen – this is two in the morning – are knocking at the bathroom door. My son had let them in the front door and they are there. And they're taking the knife off me. And there was my blood all over the bathroom from going through the skylight.

There was a baby-faced girl and a not-much-older-looking boy policeman, bless 'em, and they were trying to check my eyes for concussion. And they said, 'Your husband says you're mad, is that right?'

And I'll be quite frank. I said, 'Mad? I'm fucking furious! What else do you want to know?' They said, 'Right, OK, at least you're not insane. That's what he has told the child.' I said, 'He's never going to hit me again.'

After they'd interviewed him and interviewed me, I said, 'Oh come on, get out of the way. Let me pick up the glass and clean up the blood. I don't want the children walking on this.' They wanted to cart me off to hospital. I said, 'Don't be silly. I've had more knocks than you've had hot dinners.' They said, 'If we leave now and if he attacks you again tonight, what will you do?'

I said, 'Do you want the truth?' And they said, 'Yes, please.' I said, 'I'll kill him. I've had it. I'm not meek and mild. I'm not cowering. I'll kill him. He's never been able to cower me down, but he will never hit me again.'

So they told him to get dressed, took him away and they locked him up overnight. I don't know why. He's never said. I haven't asked and I never saw them again.

He was delivered back the next day. 'Cause I said, 'I'm not picking him up.' Two days later was when he turned my room upside down.

Suicide can feel as powerful a weapon as murder. Anita's abusive partner admitted that he wanted to control her. She saw her own death as a form of revenge.

I actually wanted to commit suicide in front of him. I wanted him to witness it, what he'd done to me. That's a nasty thing to do. But that's how angry he made me.

Eleanor didn't realise how her husband's abuse was affecting their growing children. Her eldest daughter has now told her that she has had 'one shitty life'. Yet Eleanor felt she tried everything.

After I tried the doctors, the solicitors, the court, suicide, the lot, I thought the answer was, 'Get rid of him.' And me and my friend sat there one night, we weren't drunk or anything, and actually planned it.

I was trying to find a way where they wouldn't trace it. I thought, 'If he comes in and he starts tonight, that is it. We'll do it tomorrow.' As simple as that. I honestly didn't think for one minute they would arrest me and put me in prison. Or that my children would be left without anyone to look after them.

We couldn't decide whether to use rat poison or weedkiller. I wasn't brave enough to stab him or anything like that. I tried once (after I found out he was having an affair) and it didn't work. I had walked downstairs and picked the bread knife up. He was in bed and I went back upstairs and I put it under his chin and I said, 'Right, you bastard, wake up now.' He woke up and he said, 'What's the matter? What's going on?'

And I turned my head and that was it. I got banged from pillar to post after that.

Kiranjit did kill her husband. She was sent to prison, but was released when a feminist campaign, led by Southall Black Sisters, kept up the pressure for her case to be re-heard. She describes her experience with the criminal justice system in Chapter 7. Here she remembers the days leading up to the murder.

Things were getting worse day by day. During the previous six months every day he started by beating me, abusing me sexually, verbally and physically. It was every day for six months. That last six months, I couldn't sleep or eat or play with my children. I was right to the end of my tether, depressed, losing weight, shaking all the time.

I lost touch with my husband's family and my sister, friends. Nobody wanted to know, nobody was helping me. I wanted to sleep, wanted to forget.

I was drinking whisky with water. I didn't know how to mix it. I was drinking it as a medicine because I wanted to sleep so badly. In fact, I hid all the drinking and sexual abuse from the police. I hid it from my original solicitor. I thought they would blame me and say, 'Aren't you drinking?'

Isolation and support

Since Kiranjit was released from prison, she has dedicated herself to helping other battered women, especially those who are still inside for killing their abusive partners. She is determined that the isolation she experienced, that allowed her husband to abuse her unchallenged, should be eradicated.

Isolation itself can feel like a form of death, as well as the death of love. So many aspects of a woman's ordinary, daily life are eliminated when all her supporters have been shut out and support systems cut off. Her existence is entirely controlled by the abuser's unbending will. Elizabeth describes how, before she was able to tell anyone, isolation denied her support.

> I didn't have any close friends. He didn't want me to have close friends. I wasn't very good at making close friends at that time. I didn't have many social skills. I was very nervous, very shut down.

> We had friends, but we only ever saw them in his company. I'd never sit and talk to them. I wouldn't have known what to say to them, anyway.

> I couldn't admit what was going on. They thought he was this wonderful new man, sort of helped in the house, et cetera, et cetera. I never dissuaded them of that. I never said, 'Actually he's lying. He never does anything in the house.'

Eleanor was also cut off from any support. But even though the abuse made her more and more physically debilitated, she felt that fighting the isolation would have put her at greater risk.

> It got to where I didn't go to my family when I had bruises. He stopped me from going to my sister's wedding and things like that. In the end you give in, 'cause it would cause a fight if you go. So you don't go.

> All my children were gradually born more and more premature, from one week right down to about eight weeks. He never once saw any of the children in hospital, or me there after I had them.

It was only when I had my sixth child, his mum was on to me about going on the pill. He said, 'Only women who are no good, who want to start going out with other men, go on the pill.'

The more Carmina tried to do what her partner seemed to want, the more he rejected and abused her. She hoped that by moving house the abuse would end.

I said, 'If we take this house none of this must go on any more.' When we went there, that's what he vowed, it would never happen again. But it did. It was worse, because he took control of everything.

He opened all my letters. But I'd nothing to hide, so it didn't really bother me. I'd nothing to hide at all. I wasn't allowed to mix with anyone. If I went to mix or anything, he'd say, 'You haven't got any topic of conversation. What the hell are you talking to them about? You haven't got any conversation. All you do is clean the house, make my tea and that's it. What have you got to talk about?' I went, 'Nothing. I just clear the garden, clean the house and stuff like that.'

The first thing he made a point of was that it was too expensive to have a phone. So he was not going to have a phone. So he ripped the wire out and left it outside.

The house was so rundown that if anybody was ill, it was that, 'We do not take a doctor in here. It is unfit for a doctor to come in.' My children and I weren't allowed to take friends in. He didn't want anybody seeing the place as it was.

But he wasn't going to provide anything for the place. He told me to scrub the house from top to bottom – it was covered in old wallpaper. I did. He said to the kids, 'Here's the scraper, scrape it all off now that your mother's washed it.' I scrubbed the floorboards, 'cause he wasn't putting in carpet. I had them polished up with Pledge and everything. I just had to stay home all day doing that.

It takes great courage for a woman to break the silence and ask for support. The risk of rejection is very real. But most women who experience domestic violence show enormous resilience, even when their efforts to get help are met with indifference or hostility. They also learn how to choose supporters. Having seen what has happened to other women, especially in the Women's Aid refuge where she works, Alabee believes she was lucky with the support she got. After she was sexually attacked, as well as beaten with a cricket bat, the openness and the closeness of that support was vital to her. And it has important implications for everyone who wants to become a successful supporter.

> My brothers were really good and my sister was brilliant. My friends were great. I have to admit I was very fortunate, more fortunate than a lot of girls I know that have been in similar situations. But my family were really supportive. Really great.

> My sister slept with me for about three months, in the same bed, cuddling me, because I suffered from nightmares afterwards. She literally slept in the same bed with me and moved into my house, lock, stock and barrel. I used to wake up and she'd be cuddling me.

> If I wanted to go into the area where the abuser lived, my brothers were always, 'I'll take you.' They were quite happy to talk to me about it as well. The only one who had a problem about talking about it was my younger brother, because every time you talked to him, he wanted to get up and go and find a gun and shoot the man.

> I think it was good for me to have a family so supportive. It made me realise that from then on, I can go to my family about anything that's happening in my life. And they're always there for me.

As a black woman, Elsa felt it was important that her children should have (and be seen to have) a father. At that time, she was also financially dependent on her husband and she lacked self-confidence. Elsa's family had given up on her, but she was able to find support from others.

My family weren't supportive. Because years back they'd criticised him and I stood up for him. They didn't like it and we weren't on speaking terms. Strangers were supportive, but not my family.

I had a friend and she used to say, 'Bring over your children and stay the night or something.' She was very, very good to me. So I went over and stayed the night and so on.

She never talked to me about divorce or anything. But if I went out, he'd be the type to chase after me and phone all my friends to find out if I'm there.

If I went out to her house, the next minute he would turn up with some excuse. And that would get her really cross. So one night, she was really cross. She said, 'Your husband fools around so much, but as soon as you come out, he's doing all this.' Though she never really took sides, this was something that really upset her.

Marian wanted to believe that her 'real' partner was thoughtful and generous. She had great expectations of her friends whom she saw as her only source of support: she was hopeful that they would stop the abuse from the 'other' (not really) him that was deranged, evil.

People who were close friends, I told. In fact, it got to the stage where, when it was actually happening, I'd end up phoning mutual friends in the hope that somehow they would convince him he shouldn't be doing this.

We had a friendship with another couple. He was extremely close friends with the man of the couple. Very, very close friends. And I would phone up this man and say, 'Look, he's doing it again, can you . . .' I just assumed this man would do something. And this man came round a couple of times and took him off. They had a drink. I suppose they must have talked about it. But men don't, I think, talk about things in the way women do.

I wanted my friends to do what I was failing to do. I wanted to stop his behaviour. I wanted them to somehow show him that he should be stopping this. Because I wasn't managing to do that, I wanted our friends to do it.

I wanted somebody to stop him behaving this way. But somehow, I wasn't expecting him to work on it.

I feel a bit shameful about this, but a couple of times Women's Aid was mentioned to me. And actually going to a Women's Aid hostel would have been worse for me. Because I'd done a little bit of voluntary work and the more I visited them, I knew what they were like.

I knew they were just dreadful: battered furniture and loads of kids and smoke-filled rooms. I knew it would be hell for me. It would have been admitting defeat, I think.

The other thing I found hard was when I was living in this shared house, there was a Women's Aid hostel just round the corner. And I had a bit of free time and I thought to myself, 'I've gone through this. Perhaps I could go round there and I could do something.' I went to a couple of meetings and I found it absolutely impossible to be there. It kept telling me, 'This could have been me. I could have been living in this awful place.' I found it absolutely impossible.

Marian's confusion about seeking help and her aversion to refuges are not uncommon, especially for middle-class women. There is no doubt that a chronic shortage of money affects the conditions of many refuges. But the stereotype that Marian describes, as she herself readily acknowledged, consists as much of her image of herself as it does of what was inside the actual refuges.

Because this sort of predicament is not uncommon, it's important to examine *why* we choose particular people and support systems. By simply rejecting any of the scarce resources available, we risk reducing everyone's options and weaken efforts to lobby for more and better services. Though middle-class women often have more money and richer supporters, this doesn't necessarily buy them protection.

Candace believes social class plays an important part in women who choose to use the refuge where she works. And she describes how the support offered there could be of benefit to women of any class who don't leave abusive men.

> We've never had a woman in there who is middle-class, who drives a nice car, has a big house. I've been there for three years. They don't come to refuges.
>
> We do sit down in the refuge, all the workers and say, 'Oh my God, she's still with him.' We talk about it, but we won't say to the woman, 'You've got to leave him or you don't come back.' We've never said that.
>
> We've been to clinics with the women and they've had venereal diseases and we know where they got the disease from – it's from the guy. I've had one woman talking to me, she's been to the clinic and she says, 'I'm going to have a baby for him.' It's the same guy she's running from.
>
> She's realised that if she lives with him, it's going to be a fight and an argument. But if she stays away from him, he's going to say, 'Where does she go?' She's sort of becoming like him. Because a man can just get up, go out, spend two days out of the house, but a woman can't do that so easily. Especially when she's got children.
>
> But when she can go to a refuge, now that is a way of doing it. Now he's going to say, 'Where is she?' He doesn't know where she is. He can phone her, but she's not dependent on him. And that's the main problem. Because you're always around the man. 'When I come in you're sitting there, you're so lazy.' That's how some men are. 'You've got nowhere to go, so I can abuse you.'
>
> But a lot of women have found that when they're there at the refuge, they can still go and do what they want with him and come home to the refuge at night time. And they're happy. And I say, 'That's great, if that's what they want.'

Sometimes the hardest thing for supporters to resist is giving conditional support: only offering help if the woman agrees to do things their way. By their unquestioning acceptance of what women want, the workers in Candace's refuge are not only giving more women a safe haven, but they are helping women to (re)gain self-confidence in order to make decisions for themselves. For Elizabeth it was a person, rather than a place, who provided that crucial beginning.

> I was very lucky that the first person I told completely understood and supported and knew the right things to say. She was a very strong, very grounded, down-to-earth woman.
>
> I knew I could say anything to her and she wasn't going to be shocked and she wasn't going to judge me. She was just going to say, 'I understand.'
>
> Then she started talking about what had happened to her. She'd let out little bits every now and then. She did say afterwards, 'I had a feeling there was something going on and I didn't know how much you wanted to say or how ready you were.'
>
> But still, even then, it never occurred to me that I could go to a women's refuge or anything like that. I still felt if I walked in a women's refuge, they'd take one look at me and they'd know that it's all my fault.

Anne has described how living in the countryside can be particularly isolating. But once the police were called and she was determined to leave, the intimacy of a rural community paid off.

> The police did tell me to contact my solicitor which I went to do, but she was on holiday for a week and I didn't feel like spilling the beans to a total stranger in a rather gossipy office.
>
> So I left it a week and changed horses – I went to a very smart law firm in the Gray's Inn, Lincoln's Inn, wherever they are. Of course I'd missed the boat as far as getting a restraining order, which he was crafty enough to work out.

But interestingly enough, at the same time, unbeknownst to me, somebody must have talked in the police station. Because two days after my son called the police out, there happened to be one of those big horse sales in the next county and I had a phone call later that afternoon from someone who'd heard about it there. I had told no one. It was all over three counties that he'd been taken away and locked up.

Now that can only have come from the police station, which wasn't a bad thing, because I'd always been so painfully private. I was there without cash, without anything. I was just coping. I was still winding down from the stress of this latest bit – and the shame.

And this old friend, the one who'd given me a good shake, she said, 'Anne, don't bother to even try to hide it any more – it's out. The cat is out of the bag. You don't have to pretend everything's all right. Next week we'll be gossiping about someone else, but today, kid, you're number one. It's not rumour, it's fact that he was locked up. Everybody's known over the years that he's knocked people about.'

Because they heard through the grapevine, I had people just arrive in the yard, open the stable door if I was mucking out, or push past one of the brood mares, and give me a hug. I was absolutely gob-smacked. I'd been walking around like an automaton.

Of course this enraged him, but he would say nothing and do nothing. He would see people arrive, just look or nod at him and come straight to me. He's used to having people come to him. He's used to saying to people, 'Anne's up the yard.' Or, 'Don't know where Anne is, don't think she's about.' And they would come and find me.

These were the people who moved my horses, moved my trunks, even kept him talking the day I bolted. I made a single phone call. A friend sent her husband down and he took my husband off, talking, down the farm. I had half an hour to throw stuff in the car and go. But I wouldn't have been able to and I was extremely touched.

Now he's socialising furiously, throwing barbecues and parties. There are still an awful lot of people that have to do business with him. I get cross with myself when I think, 'Spineless sods. It's as if, as in the past, you're turning a blind eye and condoning his behaviour, because you need his service. "Oh best not anger him."' It makes me angry, but then I think, 'I don't have to do business with him, they do.' It makes me cross from both sides.

I shouldn't feel resentment. Yes, I want him banned, I want him shunned. Particularly now it's common knowledge. But for all I know he could be coming out with all the sob stories that I heard before: 'People don't understand me. I've had a hard time.'

Support has many aspects. It can be quite specific, like the man who kept Anne's husband occupied while she packed up her car. But it is also about understanding that different kinds of help might be useful at different times. Sally finally decided she could not bear her daughter to be brought up around her husband's violence. She is now able to assess what her needs for support were then, and how these changed over time.

It's a very shaming thing. I think that's one of the reasons why you don't tell anyone, 'cause you feel ashamed that you're in that situation – that you're allowing someone to treat you like that. When I thought about it afterwards, I was thinking really the most helpful thing would have been if I'd been able to find a group of women who were in the same situation. An on-going kind of support group.

The idea would really in a way not even be to focus on how to get out or to focus on what was happening, but to focus on why we were in there. It would be about giving women support in developing their self-esteem and feeling powerful.

It would have to be a group of women who'd either extricated themselves from that situation or were still in there – at different stages. If you're listening to another woman's story, you can really feel for that woman and you can very clearly see that she deserves better than that. But you can't see it for yourself alone. There's something about seeing another woman's situation and seeing what she deserves, and seeing what she's allowing to happen to her – it's easier to make connections with yourself in that situation. I think you can recognise that in a group.

You can say, 'Oh my God, that's awful, why does that woman put up with this? Why doesn't she get out?' Even when you're in the situation yourself, if someone else describes themselves in that situation, although you may not be able to see it clearly for yourself, you can see it clearly for them. But in seeing it clearly for them, you also see it for yourself. You do make connections and you think, 'Oh my God, I'm in the same situation.' So you can say, 'Why am I in the same situation? I think I should get out of it.'

The first person I really talked to about it had a violent relationship herself and had got out. I met her when my daughter was one year old, so it was a year before the marriage ended.

She listened and she shared her experience. And I suppose really in a way it was the first time I realised that this happened to other people.

Maybe because of her I made an appointment to talk to somebody at a refuge for battered women. I met her, but I felt like, 'This isn't me. I'm not really one of these women.' So I wasn't really identifying myself as being in the same situation.

Some supporters are exactly the same as the women who get into abusive relationships. I had a friend who was in this role. It was really because I felt like I identified with her. She was like me. I felt she was like me and she'd been in the same situation.

So in a way I think that was probably the most supportive thing there was – somebody else who was talking about her experience. It was like my experience and it made me feel like I'm not the only person that this kind of thing happens to. And it's not OK. That's not how things should be.

She was very, very supportive at the time. Now I feel like I'm in a different place and maybe that was the most useful kind of support I could have had at the time. Now because I feel like I'm a rather different person, I'm not sure that would be the most useful support. But at the time, it probably was.

Sally's experience illustrates the fact that not only do different women have different needs, but each of us has different needs at different times. That is partly why theories of 'learned help-lessness' and 'battered women's syndrome', allegedly constructed to help, are so dangerous.

Both theories – often used by lawyers defending women who kill abusive men – allege that battered women become helpless as well as emotionally and morally lobotomised by abuse. The focus is entirely on the *woman's* behaviour, which is seen as withdrawn, distant and unreachable. Such notions suggest, paradoxically, that though abuse is entirely the problem of each woman individually, large numbers of women somehow feel and respond to it in exactly the same way. These theories detach a woman's very immediate environment from everything else. What has happened to her and what she is trying to do become isolated, not only from the man's behaviour and her personal circumstances, but also from the wider social and economic context. Each battered woman becomes an over-simplified list of medical or pathological symptoms, almost always imposed on her by those who hardly know or, in some cases, have never even met her.

These theories are also suspect because research has been unable to find meaningful and significant differences between women who have experienced violence and women who have not. In denying the complexity, dynamism and diversity of over half the population, they reinforce women's isolation and distort what are often successful coping mechanisms into examples of pitiable passivity. For instance, as participants in this book have described, blanking out the pain is often crucial for survival – a necessary stage in order to get to a place of less pain and greater safety.

It is a measure of misogyny, and the fear of women's potential to run our own lives, that such unproven notions as 'learned helplessness' and 'battered women's syndrome' have been so readily adopted by criminal justice systems and other statutory agencies throughout the world. The result of legitimising such theoretical models is that they become the only officially acceptable responses to abuse, perpetuating it as solely the woman's problem and potentially punishing all women who do not or cannot fit the stereotypes. This can range from being denied statutory services such as housing, as can be seen from participants' experiences in Chapter 8, to women like Sara Thornton being kept in prison for murder. She refused to present herself as a pathetic and downtrodden victim of the abusive husband she killed, and has consequently been vilified by much of the media and the criminal justice system. Unlike other women in similar circumstances, who were either never sent to prison or who have been released, she languishes there on a life sentence. There is a more detailed rebuttal of 'learned helplessness' and 'battered women's syndrome' in *Women, Violence and Social Change* by Dobash and Dobash.[8]

Leaving, going back and staying

Leaving, going back and staying are usually taken as evidence that women can't make up their minds and are therefore failures. Though every woman is the principal expert in her own safety and is the best judge of how to protect herself, there are certain things many women know from experience that are also backed by research from all over the world. One of these is that when a woman threatens to end the relationship and, even more so, when she does finish it, she is at greatest risk of being killed by the abusive man. More women are murdered in the months immediately after breaking up with such men than during any other time. Though I am clearly not arguing that any woman *should* stay with an abusive man, what is obvious is that only the woman who has experienced his abuse can know the full extent of his danger. Supporters involved in decisions about whether a woman stays or leaves should begin by acknowledging her expertise.

Leaving is also about emotional separation. It is very difficult for most women – who are brought up to believe, or at least to aspire to believe, that love conquers all – to confront the possibility that it might not. Marian thought about separating for some time before she acted.

> Later on in the relationship, one time I did actually tell him to leave. This was about four years into the relationship and he left. Then he told me that he went to the doctor for help because he thought he had psychological problems and what was discovered was a brain tumour.

> So I'm then in the position of, 'I have thrown this man out.' I felt, 'Oh my God, this excused everything. This is why he behaved the way he behaved. He's got a brain tumour.' And he was such a pitiful figure then. I'd thrown him out of this wonderful flat. He was living in this slum, this squat. And as far as I believed him, he was having to have radiation therapy.

> I pleaded with him for me to actually be involved in his treatment. I wanted to speak to the doctors. I wanted to know about it. So obviously I must have been very, very much in love with him. Or at least emotionally attached. And he excluded me completely.

> There was always that bit that makes me think that it was all a fabrication in order to make me feel like I had to have him back. Eventually we did get back together.

Christine lived in fear of her husband's psychological as well as physical abuse. Forcing her to keep the children near and quiet, and the television so low she could hear his whistle across the square, were a daily feature of his abusive behaviour. Christine also believes she stayed because she confused jealousy and violence with care.

I never wanted another man. I was never interested in anyone else. I'd have gone to the ends of the earth for him.

Now I know I was besotted with him. I had rose-coloured glasses on. He was violent. But I looked at it like this: my first husband was never violent – he was good and he'd always been demonstrative, but he'd never shown any signs of possessiveness. Somewhere along the line, I started thinking that my second husband wasn't jealous, that his attitude was because he cared for me. He was showing that care by laying the law down, telling me what I could and couldn't do.

After I left him, I found it hard to cope, because I had a free hand in what I chose to do or not to do. I'd been so used to doing things, like housework, the way he wanted – if I didn't there'd be rows and I'd get a beating. After I was free, I realised I'd forgotten how I had taken pride in how I did my chores – or not do them, if I chose. There was no one to say anything if I didn't do them – just my mother if she was visiting.

Barbara left and went back many times. Though there was always emotional pressure from her husband, that wasn't necessarily what drove her back.

I decided I was going to leave him and I went back to my parents. He talked to me and said things could be OK between us. 'I'll try harder. I'll try not to leave you on your own so much. I'll try not to spend so much money.' Because by this time he was getting into gambling.

I said, 'OK' and went back. I think it was only a matter of a week that it lasted. In the long term it didn't get any better, in fact it got worse.

He was gambling more, stealing household money. He was staying out. This is while we still lived in the cottage. The feelings of loneliness and isolation didn't get better. I was still saying that I wanted to go to night classes and I was saying to him that I would be prepared to go out to work if he wasn't, to get money, because by this time we were in debt.

I left him on many occasions after that, for a day, two days, maybe one night, maybe two nights. By this time, I had taken a job cleaning a chip shop. So I would get the child up about five o'clock in the morning, get in the chip shop with the child in the pram, clean the chip shop for two hours and then go back home again.

And things just got worse and worse. When I got pregnant again, I almost became devoid of emotion. It was very easy for me to leave. It was very easy for me to go to a Salvation Army hostel. It was very easy for me to sustain that.

I thought, 'Right, I'm going to get a flat of my own. I'm going to have the children put into a day nursery,' as you could then as a single parent, 'and I'm going to get myself out of this rut.'

I was in the Salvation Army hostel and I didn't know how he found out I was there, but he did. And he came to the door and threatened suicide. I said to him, 'If you commit suicide, it's your responsibility for what you do with your life, it's not mine. Don't put that on me.' And shut the door. I was shaking, but not feeling sorry for him or any of those emotions. I was shaking, but wasn't emotionally strained by it.

My son got croup and was admitted to hospital. Eventually it came out that I was homeless. The social worker and medical social worker said to me, 'There is no way that we will discharge your child from hospital into a homeless situation. And when he is better, if you are not out of the homeless situation, he will have to be put into care.' So I went back.

In the late 1960s, twenty years before she discovered that the man she'd lived with had been sexually abusing her daughter, Tessa was conscious of wider pressures on her as a black, working-class woman with seven children.

Especially in the fifties and sixties, when everybody was coming up with these theses about West Indian women having half a dozen kids – leaving three back home and then bringing three over. Remember I was born and brought up in Blackpool which was a small town, it wasn't a city. The norm was Mum and Dad and 2.4 children.

Big families were looked down on. They'd say, 'It's the Irish that have big families.' When we moved to Manchester 'blacks had the big families'. So when I met him, I thought, 'I've got this big family, at least if there's a husband, it'll be a so-called man and wife and children.' I was trying to aspire to something that wasn't even there.

I didn't want the kids to have this mother that had all these kids. I always felt guilty about my life because England has this thing about you're not supposed to go around and have kids to different men. That's not the norm.

I was thirty-three when I met him. I was thirty-five when I had my youngest daughter. I had got to this age where I thought, 'No, you haven't led such a moral life. You're leading an immoral life.'

I don't think that now. 'Cause now I couldn't care less. But at that time, somehow, I was going to give my children a stable, happy family life. Even though he wasn't a real dad, he was a hard worker. He was the type that he would take the kids out and buy them the best clothes – always had to have the best.

I had to be the best dressed girl. When he took me out, I never had to put my hand in my pocket. I had my house-keeping money and I could have any money left over from that, no questions asked, that was in my purse.

I wasn't even allowed to buy a round of drinks. That was the man's place. That's how he was and I thought at first it was all right. I used to think, 'It'll get better. He might change. He might stop his nagging, if he sees I've changed and I'm not the "going-out-girl".'

I learnt to knit. I knitted for four years and never went out of the house. When he used to say to me at weekends, 'Are you coming out?' I'd say, 'No.' 'Cause I knew if I went out – and he wouldn't go out if I didn't go out – if we went out, we'd have an argument. So to keep the peace, I'd stay in.

After she had come back to Britain from India for her father-in-law's funeral, Kiranjit felt worn down by the competing demands of her husband and mother-in-law.

My mother-in-law expected me to be a typical daughter-in-law. I'd do everything for her and her children. On the other side, my husband said, 'She's my wife, she's not going to do those things for you.' They were arguing over me as if I was their property. I knew if I took my mother-in-law's side that my husband would beat me. If I took his side, she would make my life a misery.

My husband kept his promises not to hit me for a few weeks after the funeral. My family in India had told me to get divorced, but I knew I would be a burden again. And then after my husband promised to stop, even my relatives in India changed their mind about the divorce. Like my family in Britain, most of my relatives said I should try again.

Mary's means of escape was almost always inward – even when her partner brought other women into the house to get a reaction from her. She now sees that she had an overall plan in leaving, going back and staying.

I think I moved out more than five or six times. Either stayed with friends or in the refuge. It was quite a few times in the eleven years. I was using the Women's Aid refuge like a support network at the time. I needed to go back, I couldn't live in the refuge.

I needed my space and my son's stability for his schools. And plus, this person was so flaming persistent. I couldn't get away. My ultimate dream became leaving the country. But I didn't have the courage to make that kind of break.

I had mood swings. I was in a mess emotionally and in a frantic state most of the time. I was living with a person who was really violent while I was going to college and getting all my qualifications. Doing that made this other part bearable. The actual physical attacks on me were extremely violent. The police were involved nearly every time. The attacks were quite sadistic, quite horrible.

I was building strategies which I didn't realise I was doing. I would say knowing about all my strategies came later in my life. Each time I left, I would gain some ground.

Eleanor also finds that it is only now that she can make sense of why she went back and stayed.

I'd got brave enough to leave him a couple of odd nights, but he would never let me through the door with the children. It's only now I can look back and see what happened. At the time, he used to always make sure he had one of the children with him when he went out.

He used to take the second child. I used to think it was because she was the apple of Daddy's eye. Then I had a son and he always managed to have one of them with him. I think it's only in hindsight I realise he knew I wouldn't leave without them.

I remember arguing with him and saying, 'I do love you. I do want the marriage to work, but every time you hit me, you're knocking a bit of love out of me. One day I'll end up going.' Then I went to my mum's – and I still didn't tell her. I just said, 'We've had a bit of an argument.'

I felt very washed out. I got support from the fact that she let me stay. But then one night, I was encouraged to go back. It was that the children might be worried.

I wanted to go back for the children, not for the marriage, but for the children. I didn't even think about it being a failure or not a failure.

Like Mary and Eleanor, Anne remembers surviving despite debilitating psychological pressures to stay.

> Frankly I thought about myself, 'Right, you bastard. You're stuck here, you're on your own, you put your back firmly against the wall day by day. You fight or you die.' And I felt like that – that my back was firmly against the wall, that I didn't dare move away from it and I would fight.

> But of course, that drags you down constantly when you rise to every abuse, until you get so exhausted that you let it slide for a bit, physically and emotionally. I think that's when I lost the block of time.

> I remember being obsessed with suicide. 'How would I do it? How would I make it tidy?' By this time, my daughter had been born and I'd had an abortion as well that upset me terribly.

The attachment each woman has to an abusive man often feels very personal to her. Most women are all too aware of being bound by economic, social and cultural constraints, as well as concerns for her own and her children's safety. Yet isolation often prevents the realisation that other women are in the same position.

Even women who feel no affection for the abuser still experience the shame and humiliation of having failed to have a successful relationship. For women who loved men who became abusive, and for all those women who retain some happy memories, coming to terms with the full implications of abuse is a painful process.

Support as we have seen, comes in many forms, and the right kind always believes the woman, listens to her needs and never abandons her. No matter how rejected you may feel as a supporter, persevere. Maybe not this week, this month, or even this year, but someday, the fact that the woman knows you're there, that you haven't given up on her, will make a positive difference.

When trying to support a woman who's being abused, don't be shy of telling her that you are concerned for her safety or of offering things for which she hasn't asked. But don't push her if she rejects your suggestions – unless she has specifically told you she wants pushing. If you can find a safe way that she approves of telling the man publicly that his violence is unacceptable, do so. This shows that you support and value her and has alerted him to the fact that his abuse will not be ignored or tolerated.

But most of all, be there without judgement or criticism. Do not be bossy. Otherwise you risk her feeling controlled and extending the abuse. Remember that research in Canada showed that, on average, women experienced thirty-five episodes of abuse before going to the police and asking for help. Leaving, going back and staying do not necessarily signify failure. Women often build up strategies and self-confidence over long periods of following such apparently fruitless patterns, whilst maintaining protection against the abuser's lethal danger.

But that protection doesn't always work. And because the odds are so often stacked against her, a woman may decide that it is only through the man's death that she will be parted from his abuse.

7
The law against women

There was one particularly aggressive male police detective I met while setting up *Partners In Crime* – my film about the policing of domestic violence. He was hostile because he was forced to treat domestic violence as a crime and because the BBC thought domestic violence was important enough to warrant a prime-time documentary. In all the months I spent researching the film, he was my most persistent (but by no means only) sceptic. Usually I managed to avoid his unwanted attentions by trying to keep up with the two very over-worked female domestic violence officers. But one day, after months of being told by policemen that domestic violence was not 'real' police work, I finally cracked.

In the hallway outside a charge room, I challenged him to explain himself. He said that investigating domestic violence was as much of a waste of police resources as looking for stolen milk bottles. So, I replied, if I was walking down the street and a stranger broke my jaw, you'd happily arrest him and see him charged with GBH (grievous bodily harm). But, I continued, if my husband did it, you wouldn't be bothered. He readily agreed.

Journalists and film-makers are used to police officers winding them up. But having observed a lot of police officers, men especially, all over Britain for more than twenty years, I am confident that not only did this man speak from his heart, but that his thoughts echo those of many who work throughout the legal system.

Since the mid 1980s, the message of the high-profile public relations campaigns conducted by the police is that domestic violence is a crime. But like the rest of the legal system, they aren't actually taking domestic violence any more seriously than they did before. Home Office research, conducted in 1993, revealed that on the beat they're making no more arrests in domestic violence cases. Rates of charging haven't increased either. Those at the top of the system continue to compare domestic violence with 'serious crimes like burglaries'.[9] Though the Crown Prosecution Service finally produced guidelines in 1994, implying a commitment to dealing with domestic violence, Home Office research indicates that many cases of serious (imprisonable) assault are still being dropped or charges reduced to common assault (where the penalty is just a fine), especially if the women are deemed not to be innocent victims.

The law's requirements of 'proof', 'evidence' and 'corroboration' define these terms in such a way as to make it virtually impossible for actions to succeed where there are no witnesses and no signs of struggle. Women (especially those who know the abuser) who accuse men of sexual violence routinely find their own characters put on trial by the defence, whereas the prosecution is either unable or unwilling to question the accused's probity. Judges have been known to advise juries that abuse from someone the woman knows is not as bad as an attack by a stranger.

Police officers often see women who've experienced domestic violence as difficult customers – dropping charges and/or withdrawing at court. Yet they never question why it's the woman who must bring charges. (Imagine an armed robber going free because the bank won't prosecute.) Women are rarely informed if charges against the man are changed or if court dates are altered. And they are almost never told when or if the man is let out on bail or released from prison. Yet police officers expect women to come forward, putting themselves and their children at even greater risk.

The majority of male police officers and many female ones believe women who back out are 'still in love with the man' or are 'addicted to violence'. The fact is, abusive men pursue and kill women, and the police and courts offer little or no protection.

The creation of domestic violence units inside police stations was supposed to be the panacea for previous police neglect. Ideally located in their own offices and staffed by sympathetic officers, the units were intended to alleviate domestic violence by providing support to those who had been abused. Crime prevention and positive arrest policies were meant to be implemented where appropriate. The best units also offer help with housing, solicitors, doctors and social services as well as ensuring that legal sanctions are enforced and perpetrators arrested.

My film, *Partners In Crime*, was about the first such unit set up in Tottenham, London, in 1987. It was staffed by two immensely dedicated, competent and effective policewomen. Throughout Britain there are now over 100 'domestic violence units'. Unfortunately, the quality of service that they give varies dramatically.

Some units are staffed by officers with the skill and experience to support women through the legal system and to enable them to find safety. But these usually older, more long-serving uniformed policewomen are on the decrease. They are being replaced by younger, inexperienced female officers – (or even, in some cases, male officers) those who senior policemen find easier to control. That this is intentional is not just my view, but also that of many sympathetic police officers and Home Office officials, as well as criminologists.

There are no national guidelines for domestic violence units. Some are just answerphones where all that happens is that women may get a return phone call or letter some weeks or even months later. Too many others just dole out tea and sympathy without offering advice or positive action. The effect of such units is to minimise and trivialise the seriousness of women's experience. Even the Metropolitan Police in London, who do have guidelines, only call them 'best practice' and rarely refer to, never mind try to enforce them.

You don't have to look very far beneath the surface of their flimsy public relations exercises to discover the overwhelming hostility of the police in dealing with domestic violence. Most officers still see it as a private matter, the result of weak men failing to control their women properly. Police mainly 'don't want to take sides' and still see their role as 'offering advice even-handedly to both sides'. Picture that bank robbery again. See the police offering impartial advice to the man with the stocking on his head?

Dedicated domestic violence officers are increasingly dealing with cases where policewomen as well as civilian women have been subjected to abuse by policemen. In a disturbing number of instances, domestic violence officers who refuse to roll over and 'get rid' of charges against policemen are targeted as trouble-makers and often subjected to systematic harassment, threats and accusations of mental illness. As crazy, perhaps, as the Home Office-funded research, completed in 1992, which showed, nationally, that policemen themselves perpetrate serious sexual violence at a rate three times higher than the national male average.

The most common legal action in cases of domestic violence in England and Wales is for a woman, via a solicitor, to take out an injunction (in Scotland it's called an interdict). Most prohibit the man from physically attacking the woman, children and other named people. Few injunctions are issued that actually bar him from where she is living (judges frequently make a point of saying they don't want to deprive a man of *his* home). And when such 'exclusion' or 'ouster' orders are issued, even the most violent and dangerous men are often given as much as two weeks to move out. Very few injunctions have a power of arrest attached to them. And when they do, it only applies for a specific and strictly limited period of time. The woman almost invariably has had to prove that the man has caused injury amounting to at least actual bodily harm and is likely to do it again. In breaking an injunction without a power of arrest, a man is simply in contempt of court. Generally, the worst he risks is being summoned back to the court to get his knuckles rapped. By being remorseful, he can usually purge his contempt.

Even if a woman succeeds in getting an injunction with a power of arrest attached, many frontline workers, sympathetic police officers and solicitors believe police enforcement is poor.

Injunctions are a low priority and police stations routinely lose them, so officers can often be sent on call-outs without realising an injunction exists. Even if they know there is a power of arrest, individual officers, many of whom don't think domestic violence is a crime, can use their discretion not to arrest. In any case, whether an injunction exists or not, the police cannot be there twenty-four hours a day to protect every woman at risk from domestic violence.

In January 1994, a civil (district) court judge wrote a vitriolic article ('It's My Ex Parte And I'll Cry If I Want To') in the professional journal *Family Law*. He condemned women who go back, after being granted injunctions, for wasting the courts' time. Such women, he said, should be denied any further legal protection from violence. He also said that he was only one of a group of like-minded judges who would be prepared to put this into practice.

And the longer a woman leaves it, the harder it is to get any injunction. And, of course if anything does happen to a woman who hasn't managed to get an injunction, the police, Crown Prosecution Service and the courts – not to mention social services, housing departments and education authorities – routinely hold it against her.

There are plenty of civil and criminal laws specifically concerned with domestic violence, as well as other legislation that could be used to help victims of abuse. In reality, there is little protection. Despite the fact that most of us are taught to believe that the rule of law is paramount, it can't and won't protect us from domestic violence. Since the 1970s, though considerably more legislation has been passed, we've hardly had much better protection. It may be that we have too many laws and that we keep inventing new ones as a way of avoiding the real issue, which is enforcement. Law is a resource, not a solution. The vast majority of women experiencing domestic violence don't resort to the law anyhow. The ones who do, like the women who participated in this book, mainly find it wanting. And in any case, how desirable would it really be to have our homes patrolled by policemen twenty-four hours a day?

Nevertheless, we have been brought up to believe that somehow the law is meant to cover all of life's eventualities. So that when something does happen to us that isn't recognised either as a crime or capable of remedy by civil action, we probably don't report it and, too often, we think it must be our fault.

If the courts, the police and many domestic violence units are that hopeless, why bother with them at all? Because the legal system is the only service available at all hours of the day and night that has the potential to give women some protection from abusive men. Because there are some very good police officers and domestic violence units that are providing an invaluable service. Because to deny any woman the possibility of seeking help or redress would be wrong. It is therefore crucial that all of us take an informed and active interest in all aspects of the law, particularly in areas of sexual violence. We should continue to make demands on the system and to insist that we have the right to the protection we need. We should automatically ring 999 when we hear a woman's screams and go out to meet the police when they arrive, to try to ensure that she gets a decent service. It's the least we can do.

The participants' experiences of the legal system – both when it worked and when it didn't – testify to the need to make the law more responsive to women.

On patrol

In 1988, Saroj came to Britain from Fiji to get married. She was deeply in love with her husband. Despite his abuse and the hostility of his family, she tried everything to make the marriage work. Immigration laws say that a woman like Saroj must stay with her husband for at least a year before being allowed to even apply for the rights most of us take for granted. Unlike nearly everyone else resident in Britain, such women cannot use social services or receive housing and social security benefits. Government legislation officially imprisons these women with abusive men. If a woman like Saroj does leave her husband within the first year, she is automatically considered not to have a valid marriage, to have violated the rules and is likely to be deported.

But Saroj did not leave her abusive husband. In 1990, he

deserted her and she was then evicted by his family. At the time, Saroj was working as a cashier in a catering company at Heathrow airport.

> When I came here in 1988, my passport was stamped for one year. What I didn't find out till 1990 was that in 1989, my husband had written a letter to immigration saying he didn't want me any more: 'Send her back home.' By the time I found out he'd done it, I had already got a solicitor to act on my case, because I had had a letter from the Home Office threatening to deport me. I used to carry my passport with me everywhere, because my husband once took it away from me.

> My husband told immigration where I was working. The immigration people came to my work to deport me. It was so embarrassing, I was in tears, because at that point, no one there knew I had a problem.

> Four people came. They had handcuffs as well. One of them said, 'How come you're working here?' I said, 'Because I've got an insurance number, I am allowed to work.' He said, 'Have you got a passport? Could I see it?' So I said, 'Yeah.' He said, 'I would like to take you to the police station.' I said, 'No, I'm not going. I've got a solicitor, you can talk to him.' He said, 'Once you get to the police station, then you call.' I said, 'No, I'm not going. I want to talk to my solicitor first.'

> Then they called my solicitor. There was some confusion because I had kept my family's surname and immigration had my husband's surname on the file. So they said, 'We have made a mistake and they went.' And that mistake lost me my job.

Since 1992, with the support of Southall Black Sisters, Saroj has continued to fight Home Office attempts to deport her.

Mary suffered from mood swings and stayed in the relationship with her abusive partner for eleven years, from the late 1970s till the late 1980s. Yet she still managed to go to college and gain qualifications. She recalls her experience with the police during that time.

> I must admit, I give the police round there all credit. They were there every time. And they never got pissed off with me. Even though I think they would have quite liked to, but they were there every time. I think that's because he was a black guy and I was a white girl. I could see that's what was happening.

In many of their campaigns, African–Caribbean and Asian women have related police racism, racial attacks and immigration activities directly to domestic violence. Some Asian and African–Caribbean women are reluctant to go to the police because of the very real possibility that all they'll get is racist abuse and/or that the police will simply beat up the abusive (black) men. Others are discouraged by their experience of official failure to deal with racial attacks and police collusion in violent treatment by immigration authorities. Also, women who do not have full leave to remain in Britain, or who are resident by virtue of marriage to the abuser, know that any help they seek is likely to result in *their* being investigated and subjected to deportation proceedings.

Apart from pouring his aftershave on her boyfriend's toothbrush and cleaning the loo with it, Molly contacted the police in 1992.

> When I rang up, the police were brilliant. The domestic violence officer said, 'The first thing we've got to do is get you into a safe house. But can you come down to the station?' So I went. And this policeman who works in the domestic violence unit, and his sergeant, came back to my house to get my belongings.

> They came in the house and I got my stuff together. Then they dropped me off somewhere, 'cause even they didn't know where the refuge was. I met up with a woman from the refuge and she took me back there.

> I'd been there no more than half an hour when the phone rang, and I didn't click, it was my boyfriend pretending

to be my brother in Spain. And the refuge worker said, 'Do you have a brother in Spain?' I was really panicking, 'cause I thought, 'Yes, I do. What's happened to him?'

But at this point, my parents didn't even know where I was, so I took the phone and said 'Hello', and it was my boyfriend. I threw the phone and said, 'It's him.' After that he left two messages on the refuge's answerphone.

I couldn't work out how he'd got the number. But after I'd been home with the police to get my belongings, he'd broken in and pressed the re-dial button on the phone. 'Cause the police had phoned the refuge from my house to say, 'Molly's got her stuff, we're on our way.'

So when he phoned up, the refuge worker had obviously said 'Women's Aid'. Because of that the number is available to anyone. I had been sitting there thinking I was totally safe and it was really chilling to hear him leave a message on the answerphone. The refuge workers said, 'If this continues you'll have to be moved to another county.'

I was still at the refuge when I gave my statement to the police. And I said to them, 'I can't stress to you how dangerous he can be. When I go back, if I'm in the house, 999's not quick enough.' So they said, 'We'll give you a panic button.' But I said, 'I'm not going back there.' And they said, 'It's OK, you can have one anyhow.'

I was then expecting to hear that he'd been arrested, when I got a phone call from the police to say they couldn't find him. Then this policeman who'd been dealing with the case rang me and said that he'd phoned my boyfriend in his car and identified himself as a police officer. He told me my boyfriend was 'flying at fifty thousand feet, he was totally off his head. If I had tried to arrest him and bring him into the station, there's no way I could have interviewed him because of his state of mind.'

I was really angry, 'cause I wanted him arrested. I wanted him remanded. I wanted him sectioned. But I said, 'Oh, I see.' And the policeman said, 'If I'd attempted to put him in a cell, he might have done something to himself.'

I found out about three weeks later that my boyfriend had then gone out to a night club and he'd been boasting to his friends that he'd found the panic button and he'd dismantled it by ripping out a fuse. He knew exactly where it was. Before the policeman had spoken to him in the car – when I wanted him arrested – he'd broken into my house again, 'cause the bolts were all buckled on the back door. He'd obviously seen this thing in my bedroom.

I was really terrified of him still, he's so unpredictable. He was finally arrested and charged. He was taken to court and he was let out on bail. I wasn't very pleased with the result at all. The police said, 'We had to get him into court to set his bail conditions. It was something we had to have him for.' I don't understand the legal system at all.

Molly's experience shows up a number of limitations of the legal system. She clearly felt well served by the domestic violence officers (despite their obvious slip-up in making that phone call from her house). Later on, whether or not the policeman could have got a statement out of the abuser, Molly believed that her safety did not figure in that officer's calculations. He said his concern was that the abuser would harm himself in custody. Molly's sense of powerlessness, of not being listened to, of being marginal to police considerations, shines through. I also feel there was male collusion involved – that the policeman was more in tune with the abuser's feelings than he was with Molly's. And perhaps the policeman was himself scared of the abuser's violence. It is not unusual to find policemen and others, quick to condemn a woman who doesn't leave an abusive man (but giving no thought to the woman's safety), who do nothing because they themselves are frightened of being assaulted by the man.

Elsa's family was unsupportive, but she had a good friend who always welcomed Elsa and her children into her home. Elsa also had contact with the police in the 1960s and 1970s.

My husband came one night to make an argument. It was midnight. I was in bed and he came and grabbed me out of bed to come and warm his dinner – at that time of night! I couldn't believe it.

When he grabbed me, I knew he wanted to hit me, so I ran to the police station. He followed me and said that he didn't do anything to me. He tried to make out to the police that I was mad. But I told them what he'd done. They said to him, 'If you are doing this, it's enough to get her off her head.' But they did nothing.

But the police used to come to the house more often than anything else. One night, this would be in the seventies, after I started work, I was in the sitting room. Just sitting down and he started an argument. The argument was about money.

He came to me for money and I said, 'I'm not giving you any money. I don't have any money.' He came to grab me and I screamed and I think it's the neighbours next door called the police. So when the police came and saw him, he told the police I was trying to jump through the window – the ground-floor window! He told the police that he had to grab me to stop me.

The police came in and talked to him. They said to him that if we don't get on well, why don't we see solicitors. They didn't arrest him.

One night another policeman came and asked if there was somewhere else I could go for the night.

It was some time after Janie's young daughter went into care, because she could not bear what was being done to her mother, that Janie was able to be honest with herself. She faced her lack of bravery, her fear of being on her own, and finding a place for herself and her three children. Janie describes her experience with the police, which took place well after their supposed conversion to an enlightened attitude to domestic violence.

After I got my own place and he found out where I was living, there was an incident where he came round. This was 1990, during the divorce proceedings.

He came round and started arguing. So I said, 'Get out. This is my house, get out.' And he threw a metal bin at me. It caught and bruised all my elbow. So I went to the police station after he'd left and told them about it.

'Oh we can't do nothing, it's a domestic.' I went, 'Wait a minute. I'm not even living with him.' So they said, 'It's still a domestic. He's still your husband. There's nothing we can do about it.'

For Tessa, staying in and knitting for four years may have mitigated the violence temporarily from time to time, but it didn't end it. She got the same response from the police in the early 1970s that Janie did nearly twenty years later.

And even one time, I ran in the police station and they said there was nothing they could do because it was domestic violence – that was '72 '73. He beat me where he busted my lip. It was usually kickings in the legs and stomach, he'd never got me in the face before.

Trial and error

Kiranjit had experience with the police in the late 1970s and 1980s, before she murdered her husband.

I tried to run to the police, but my husband caught me. Then I got turned off the police because of what happened to my husband's sister.

She tried to go to the police a couple of times. The third time she was bruised, bleeding badly and had a big lump on her head. One of the policemen took her husband to one side and told him, 'If you want to hit your wife, hit her on the head where nobody can see it.' Even after that, she went to the police. But they told her, 'It's domestic violence, we can't do anything.'

So I decided to forget the police and to go straight to court. I went to see my solicitor, showed my fractured finger and said I wanted a divorce. But when my husband got the court summons, he got really angry. Then his mother and sister made an endless fuss and put pressure on my sister and her husband.

So I got my husband to sign an undertaking. He promised my solicitor, and then in front of his solicitor, that he wouldn't touch me. 'Please let me stay in this house,' he begged me. 'Don't chuck me out.' Because he knew his mother wouldn't keep him. So I let him stay, but then I got an injunction in court with a power of arrest.

For a couple of months he was all right. He knew that if I went to court, then I could get rid of him. From the day I married him and the violence started, I was losing my confidence. I was scared of him and his mother. I became so weak, I couldn't do anything for myself. I couldn't even go to see the doctor, I couldn't explain what was wrong with me. I thought I had become illiterate, handicapped without my husband. I couldn't do anything – he would beat me.

After she poured petrol on her husband and set it alight, Kiranjit immediately gave herself up.

I think I was very badly treated by the police. Whatever I did, I never disguised it. I never tried to run or hide. I went to the hospital in an ambulance and I went to the police. I never hid anything.

One of them shouted over and over, 'Tell us how you planned it.' I was so frightened. I was terrified. Being an Asian girl, I'd never talked to a white man before. They kept telling me, 'You planned to murder him. Make a proper statement.' Imagine an English statement. At that time I could barely speak English. I could feel their hatred.

I was admitting I'd done it and they were so rude. After every single question, I told them, 'He was beating me for ten years. I was taking pain the way you are giving me pain.' I told the person who was frightening me that what he was doing was just like what my husband used to do.

I kept saying to him, 'I'm telling you the truth. I'm not denying it.'

But they wanted more. They wanted to find out that I was a bad person. In fact, they couldn't find anything against me except what I'd done to my husband. I was admitting what I'd done, but apart from that, I wasn't a bad mother. I'd never done any crime before. I didn't have any boyfriend or a man involved who I'd got the idea from.

I don't know where I got the strength from. I wanted to give him pain, so he would remember that I'd done it. They wanted to punish me. They should punish me, I deserved some punishment. I admit that. But who suffered? My poor sister, her husband and my children. They suffered.

I spent three years four months in prison. I was free in prison. I got more freedom in prison. My confidence came back to me in prison. I got more friends than when I was out. There were some sympathetic prison officers. One of them used to ask me, 'What are you doing in here? I don't believe that you're serving a life sentence. There must be a strong reason behind you.' I told them my story and they ended up in tears. They used to be in shock, those prison officers.

Eleanor's husband controlled her by never letting her take all the children out of the house without him. She describes one occasion in the 1970s where she sought help from the legal system.

I remember going into the police station loads of times. The night before I went for my judicial separation, there was a big argument, 'cause my solicitor had told me not to cook for him, not to clean for him, all that sort of thing. That was probably seven years into the marriage.

I was quite confident that I was going to do it, that the law was going to be on my side. And a big argument developed and I ended up with a large shiner.

Then the next morning he said, 'I'm not going.' I said, 'I am.' And I went to court on my own. The judge was lovely. He said, 'Who did that to you?' I said, 'My husband.' 'Where is he now?' I said, 'Looking after the children.' 'Does he know the hearing's on?' I said, 'Yes, but he said to tell you he's not coming, that he's at home looking after the children where I should be.' And the judge said, 'Right, judicial separation granted.'

To me, I thought, 'Great.' In practice, it meant I went home full of smiles, told him I'd got this judicial separation. Then the children got thrown in the pram. I got dragged by the hair for a mile, mile and a half, back to the courts. We went into the court and he shouted all over the courts that where was this effing bastard who was going to split his family up, no one was going to split his family up. And we were right next door to the police station and he shouted all over the court.

Nobody came out. Not even a court usher. Nobody came out. Then I was just dragged back home again. Something along the lines like, 'You're mine, you're married to me and that's it.' From then on it went downhill.

Daksha did what her father wanted and married a high-caste Patel. She moved with him to Britain. He became abusive and she forced him to move out. In the late 1980s, Daksha found that until she got an injunction with a power of arrest that banned her husband from her home, she had no redress when he harassed her and smashed through her front door. Though the injunction didn't stop her husband from harassing her, at least it brought a response from the police and it meant she got a measure of compensation.

Three or four times over the three years he broke the glass in the front door. Finally, I put cardboard in it and said, 'Break it now!' He kept harassing me, 'Take me back. Take me back.'

Because I had an injunction with a power of arrest, when I phoned the police they came immediately. They took a statement from me and took him to the police station. And he always had to pay for the repair of the door.

But after a while, the power of arrest was gone. And he started harassing me again. I kept phoning the police. They came, but only talked to him.

With a group of women from Southall Black Sisters, we made a written demand to senior police officers to get better protection for women subjected to domestic violence.

Beyond the law

The support Alabee got from her family made all the difference when dealing with the legal system in the late 1970s. Nevertheless, she retained lingering doubts about herself.

Once my brothers had found out everything, the police were brought in. Because it was such a vicious attack, the hospital had wanted to phone the police. They were finding bits of wood in my head my face, my legs. What he did to me underneath, I could hardly walk. That's why I said I don't know how I got out of the house to the cab in the first place. Because the cab man actually near enough picked me up to put me in a wheelchair when I got the other end.

The next time I saw him was the first appearance in court – the magistrate's court. I went dead at first, totally numb. My eyes were focused straight ahead, I couldn't see anything else, it was just him. Then my brother turned me around, he must have sensed something in me, because I stiffened right up. He turned me around, and put my head on his shoulder till the abuser walked past me. The police said I didn't have to go into the actual court room.

I saw him again when we went back to court to get it remanded to the High Court. Then I went through the court stuff, where I was in the dock for the whole day. It was a strange feeling seeing him. I wasn't really frightened, because I knew he couldn't get to me, there were too many people around me. My brothers were sitting in line, like sentry duty. Then there was the police and all the other people in the court room and I knew he couldn't get to me or hurt me.

He got eighteen months. First offence. Which, at that time, I was just grateful he got something.

He was charged with actual bodily harm. They said, 'Near enough sexual assault.' Because I had only told them he stripped me off, nothing more. I never told them the rest.

I sometimes wonder if I was trying to protect him for some weird reason. Or protect myself. I felt I should have known it was going to happen. When I was re-living it, I kept thinking, 'I should have known. Something he said to me over the phone, "Don't bring your daughter".' That was very unusual.

I used to take my daughter everywhere. I sort of back-packed her. I went, 'Why?' So he said, 'Let's have a few hours on our own, because we need to talk.' I always felt afterwards that I should have known. That should have triggered off something in my head. And it didn't.

It sometimes seems that our capacity for self-blame is limitless: having once become involved with him, no matter what he does many women continue to feel responsible for the man's behaviour. Not only do we expect ourselves to be eternally vigilant, but if we slip up even once, we condemn ourselves for ever.

Barbara had overcome rural poverty and official lack of support by the time she decided she wanted no further connection with her husband in the early 1980s.

After nine years, he was playing up the reformed this, that and the other thing. He also got into a relationship with a woman who had three children. She moved into the house. She was out working full time. He was going to be at home with his two children and her three children. And happy families.

Fortunately, he stupidly didn't turn up at the High Court in Edinburgh. Everybody toodled through to Edinburgh and they were all waiting. The judge allowed that to happen on two occasions. Now you're talking about a date for the High Court, months and months ahead. This had gone on for four or five years.

Finally on the last date, he didn't turn up, so the judge said, 'On this occasion I'm hearing the evidence. I don't care if he's not here. He's had ample opportunities to get here.' The judge took evidence from my mother. He took evidence from me. The children were supposed to give evidence, but the judge decided not to take evidence from them. His brother was supporting me and was now prepared to stand up in court and say, 'I saw him assault her.' But he didn't have to give evidence.

The judge simply said, 'I grant you your divorce and I give you full custody of the two children. And I believe that you don't want any maintenance.' I said, 'That's right.' He said, 'You already have interim custody of the children. I realise that the sheriff had decided that you were not the state's responsibility, you were your husband's responsibility. Even though you didn't want maintenance, they awarded you maintenance.' I said, 'That's right.' He said, 'What's your view now?' My advocate stood up, but the judge said, 'I'll hear it from the petitioner.' And I said to him, 'I don't want maintenance for me. If he wants to voluntarily give money for the children, then fine. But I don't want anything. I'm cutting all ties here.'

In 1974, Christine still felt controlled by her husband's rules about doing everything, including the housework. She also discovered the particular problems in dealing with the legal system when there are complexities of domestic violence, child sexual abuse and rape.

He'd been sexually abusing *my* fourteen-year-old daughter. Apparently, he'd been blackmailing her: 'Do this for me and I'll buy you a new sweater,' or, 'You can go out with your friends.' Of course, I'd brought them up to be subservient to him, and she'd done it. It turned out that when I thought about it, over the years from when I'd met him, it was 'Come and be Daddy's teddy bear. Come and give him a cuddle.'

I thought, 'Right, come on, we're going to the police.' He said 'OK.' So the three of us – the police station was only just down the road – we set out for the police station. On the way he said, 'Of course, I might go down for seven years, but you know you'll be dead when I come out.' So we turned around and came home. And I thought, 'Well, he'll never touch *his* daughter, she'll be all right.' And I thought I'll make sure he never has an opportunity again to do anything to *my* daughters.

After I had my hysterectomy, my mother asked me to go and stay with her in Liverpool so she could look after me. So I took the children, the two youngest ones and my eldest son, and left where we were and we went to my mum's. *My* daughter missed it 'cause she was working and she didn't live with us anyhow. While we were there, on the Friday night, my husband had gone out and he'd seen her in a club. He'd said, 'You pack your bags and get back home.' She'd packed her bags and went home. And he raped her. She was seventeen.

Monday morning she turned up. My sister asked her what was the matter, my sister was a social worker. My daughter told her. My sister took it right out of my hands and she brought the police in.

Suddenly my husband starts blowing up about he wants his kids and all this. The police said, 'Tell him to come up and get his children.' We were at my sister's which is out in the country and the police were hidden behind hedges and everywhere, you know. He drove up in a taxi and all these police swooped and arrested him.

We had to make these horrendous statements. They'd asked me all about our sex life, what we did. I'd made full statements, really thinking, 'He's going to be locked up.'

And my daughter had gone through the inquisition and examinations. I told them about the abuse when she was small.

They said, 'Sorry, we can't keep him. There's no evidence.' They'd come to the house with us, got the sheets off the beds and everything. But they said it was because it happened on the Friday night and she'd left it till Monday morning.

So I went to a refuge and I was terrified. I stayed there for four months with the two youngest children. And I was frightened to even cross the street, in case he was waiting for me.

Imagine having gone through the same humiliation and emotional turmoil as Christine and her family did in 1974 – with no result other than feeling totally defeated. You'd hope that maybe eighteen years later, with a greater public awareness about all aspects of personal and sexual violence, that things might have changed. Then consider how you'd react to the news that one man was sent to prison for twenty-five years for burning down an empty barn, but a child sex abuser was put on probation because his eight-year-old victim was, according to the trial judge, 'no angel'; and another man was also put on probation, forgiven, again by the trial judge, for battering and strangling his wife because she had failed to be a proper wife and mother. Where is the justice? What is the point?

All crimes of personal violence (except murder) have lower arrest, charge and conviction rates than those against property. This can partly be explained by the fact that the British legal system is constructed around protecting property and not people, and that crime is defined as that which offends against the State's (not an individual's) interest.

Personal violence that takes place between strangers in public places (football matches, pubs, picket lines) has a far greater chance of being recognised by everyone as crime. The vast majority of personal violence, though, takes place in non-public places, between people who know each other, and is rarely disclosed to the police. Government crime surveys routinely pick up huge amounts of this unreported violence. Most is perpetrated by men against women, children and the elderly.

I would like nothing better than for those people to inundate the legal system with their complaints of personal violence. Not only would this help weaken the grip of hidden abuse, but it would expose the inherent, structural inability of the law to act in the interest of those victims. But it is easy to understand why such victims are reluctant to come forward, when at the very least they risk being treated with disrespect and at most becoming even more endangered. What would certainly happen if they reported abuse from a known assailant is that his chances of arrest, charge and conviction would be less than if he was unknown, and that if, by luck, he was sentenced to prison, it would be for a much shorter term than if he were a stranger.

And women in particular often get a poor service when they go to the police and solicitors, because they mostly do so in the middle, rather than at the beginning or the end, of the abuse. The law just doesn't seem to be able to accommodate the nuances and subtleties of people's real lives.

Apart from the structural failures of the legal system, there is the functional misogyny of its practitioners. A few random, but significant examples:

In an inner London crown court, a judge excused a child sex abuser on the grounds that his wife was pregnant and allegedly denying him sex.

Rape victims regularly find the police, judges and especially defence barristers accuse them of advertising their complicity by the shortness of their skirts, the amount or style of their make-up, their friendly behaviour, their previous sexual activity.

A judge in a murder trial told a man that as a hard worker and good provider he was entitled to expect his home kept as he liked. It was understandable, then, that he had killed his wife because of her unreasonable behaviour in putting the mustard pot on the 'wrong' part of the dining table.

Far from easily withdrawing at court or casually asking for 'no further action' to be taken, women are regularly discouraged from proceeding by the way the police (don't) act in: not arresting, delaying investigations, giving wrong advice, having negative, over-bearing or bossy attitudes, intentionally keeping women ignorant of procedures so weakening their resolve, providing no support and marginalising women by giving no information about court hearings, displaying an inability to understand, care or deal with the risks to women of reprisals and further (and possibly escalating) violence.

Resistance to dealing properly with domestic violence is not just a feature of the British legal system. In America and Canada, where they have experimented with mandatory arrest policies, follow-up research revealed that in order to increase their figures, but to subvert the system, police officers were arresting *women victims* rather than abusive men.

The indifference and hostility of the legal system and its practitioners to domestic violence is further exacerbated by internal wrangling. When I made *Partners In Crime* in 1988, the police complained that, while they did everything they could to protect women and prosecute men, they were constantly let down by the Crown Prosecution Service who were given what had been the police's job of taking cases through the courts. In 1992, when I began researching this book, the Crown Prosecution Service was still treated with derision by the police, but the courts and particularly the judges were their new bad guys.

The real cynicism and hypocrisy of the legal system though is revealed in the collusion that took place in the summer of 1994, between the police, the Home Office, the Crown Prosecution Service and the Lord Chancellor's Office. Their enthusiastic participation in government cost-cutting measures presents one of the most serious threats to women's safety. To save money on the criminal justice system (especially prisons and courts), they agreed to reduce the seriousness of certain assaults – including those most often experienced by women in cases of domestic violence. Settable broken noses, black eyes, bruises and grazes, for example, will no longer normally be grounds for charges of offences that usually attract a prison sentence. They will be largely punishable by fines and classed as common assault rather than actual or grievous bodily harm. Those charged with common assault are rarely held in police cells or on remand. And they almost never go to prison. If they do, the maximum sentence is only six months.

The indirect effect of these changes may be even more devastating. By officially downgrading women's injuries in criminal charging, civil judges will be even more reluctant to attach powers of arrest onto injunctions and to issue exclusion orders. Tens of thousands of women will be denied even the rudimentary protection that used to exist.

With all these barriers to safety, protection and justice, it is a miracle that any women have the courage and stamina to go to law. And even though the rates of arrest, charge and conviction haven't changed, the one figure that has shot up as a result of the police claiming to take domestic violence more seriously is reporting. If not in droves, women are coming forward in a steady stream to register male abuse. A triumph of hope over experience? Desperation?

No. What it really shows is that women have guts. In the face of the most terrible abuse, women keep fighting. Now what we need to do is to focus that energy, and that of sympathetic men, to transform the law against women.

8
Guilty and innocent victims

When I was just eighteen I was raped. My boyfriend and I were each living with our parents, so once, in order to have sex, we went round to his older, married, best friend's house.

That night the friend's wife wasn't home. The three of us socialised for a while, so it was pretty late when my boyfriend and I went into the bedroom. After we had sex, I stayed in the bed while my boyfriend slipped out to a late night shop, some distance away, for cigarettes.

Moments after he left, his friend entered the darkened bedroom. I remember being drowsy, hearing the door open and recognising the man by his voice before his familiar features were lit by the street light filtering through the curtains. He put one hand around my throat, squeezed hard and said, 'Don't move or make a sound or I'll kill you.' With his other hand, I heard him unzip his trousers. Then he raped me.

Fortunately it was over in minutes and all he did was straight sex. When he'd finished, he got off me without a word and walked out of the room. I waited till I was sure he was gone, got dressed as quickly as I could, and ran out of the house.

By this time it was after midnight, when girls like me had had it drummed into us, that we should not be walking the streets alone. But I was so sickened by what had happened that for the only time in my life I was completely oblivious to any thoughts of other danger. I ran towards the store where my boyfriend had gone for cigarettes.

Meeting me on his way back, he demanded to know what the hell I was doing out on my own. When I told him what had happened, he started for his friend's house shouting, 'I'll kill him, I'll kill him.' I grabbed my boyfriend's arm and stopped him. 'Can I just break his legs, then?' he asked. Somehow I persuaded him to take me home, that I wanted nothing done to his friend. And it was left at that.

To those who know me now, that story may be surprising. I am usually both confrontational and assertive. So how could someone like me behave in such an apparently uncharacteristic way?

It took me many years to be able to ask myself that question, but when I did the answer was quick and succinct: because I thought it was my fault. I had, after all, had sex in that man's house, in his very bed, with his best friend. I had stayed, alone and naked, in the bed after my boyfriend had left. Surely I was complicit, even asking for it? The shame and the guilt flood over me even as I write this, every time I think about it, nearly thirty years later.

I would like to think that if I was raped now I would fight back immediately, and instead of rushing off to find my boyfriend would contact the nearest police station. But shame and self-blame are immensely powerful forces. I couldn't really swear what I would do until it actually happened.

The pain of sexual violence and the unbearable weight of self-blame are internalised in different ways by different people. But all over the world, judgement by the external arbiters of morality is largely unremitting; like the poor, victims of inter-personal violence are either deserving or undeserving. Help is only given to the worthy. It's not just denied to those who are seen as soldiers of their own misfortune, they're often punished instead.

Determining worthiness varies from culture to culture, country to country. Purity and innocence are most often used as indicators, but they are defined and weighted differently in different places. Nevertheless, though definitions may vary, each society seems to have a clear notion of what it means to behave like a 'real' victim. For a woman, this usually means being a passive, pathetic, pleading wretch. Assertiveness and self-possession are generally looked on with suspicion. A convincing female victim puts herself in the position of needing to be helped. To reject that begging role suggests wanting to take control, to make one's own decisions, to be free to live one's own life.

All statutory and many voluntary bodies are based on 'experts' dictating what is available to women who have experienced domestic violence. It is inconceivable that these decisions should be made by the women themselves, who inevitably feel like objects of charity. And charity itself, I believe, only exists so that those who give it can feel good when those who get it act grateful.

The criteria used for judging the 'deservability' of women who experience domestic violence differs very little between statutory agencies (such as social services, housing, health and education), members of the criminal justice system, civil law practitioners and traditional, professionalised voluntary charities (like the Samaritans, Victim Support, Relate and the Citizens' Advice Bureaux).

In 1974, 1979 and 1993, the Parliamentary Home Affairs Committee issued Reports about Domestic Violence. Though they reached liberal conclusions about increasing refuge space and extending legal provisions – even taking evidence from feminist organisations – the reports are all redolent with the underlying assumption that statutory agencies and traditional, professionalised charities always know best. Embedded in each such organisation is a rigid definition of 'victim', in which only those deemed innocent are deserving of help – demonstrated by their displays of weakness, subservience and supplicatory behaviour.

Victims must fit into specific slots in these agencies and traditional, professionalised charities. Unbending rules are necessary to sustain agendas clearly set with the main purpose of ensuring such institutions' survival. To get any of the services on offer, victims have to present the correct bunch of pre-determined needs. The very existence of these hierarchical organisations, in and of themselves, are barriers to women's voices even being heard, never mind demands for defining and controlling our own lives being met.

But professional supporters who are ambivalent about their roles do exist. There are many caring, dedicated people inside all these organisations, caught within institutional rules and limited by their own prejudices and good intentions. Some have tried to democratise their work by applying the concept of 'empowering' their 'clients'. Unfortunately, this often only consists of persuading 'clients' that they themselves have made decisions already actually taken on their behalf. Perhaps it's hard to come to terms with the fact that genuine power cannot be given up so easily within institutions, especially in performing that most basic function of gate-keeping: culling the 'guilty' from the 'innocent' victims. Real empowerment is about having statutory rights that no one can remove, not about simply doling out bits of power that can just as easily be withdrawn.

To overcome its negative connotations, some women have stopped using the word 'victim', preferring 'survivor' instead. Others have expressed the view that this risks denying women's feelings of being victimised – that it is not possible to leap from being abused to recovery without acknowledging the pain and anger of the experience. What I believe we need to eliminate is 'victimology' – the process by which an individual's right to self-definition is usurped by others purely for their own benefit. Ignoring a person's own wishes, desires or interests results in them losing control over yet another part of their life. Being a victim means different things to different women, and different things to each of us at different times. It is up to each woman to define herself, whether she chooses to call herself a victim or not.

Victim or survivor?

Christine remembers what happened when she went into the refuge in 1974, after her husband wasn't prosecuted for raping her daughter.

> I don't think I did feel like a victim. I'd been *put* in the refuge, which I think is one of the reasons I went back to him, a decision was made for me by Liverpool Social

Services. They found me a place in the refuge. The refuge was very good to me, though. I made a lot of friends and they gave me a lot of support. It was one of the best summers we ever had. We had outings to the seaside – but they were different outings. When we'd gone with my husband, we were always waiting for him to blow up. But these outings were relaxed and fun.

And I've thought about that over the years since, especially while I've been working at a refuge. 'Why didn't I go back to that refuge?' I never thought about it at the time. Perhaps I'd thought because I left I wasn't entitled to. 'Cause nobody ever said I could.

In our refuge we always make a point of saying to women, 'You can come back here. We understand why you're going back to him. You can come back here when you're ready.' And, unfortunately, some women sneak out to go back – 'cause they think you won't like it. So now we say to everyone when they first come in, 'We understand that you might choose to go back to him.'

Accepting that women have such rights rarely extends beyond places like refuges. There is a widespread view, not just among judges, that the effects of victimisation can be ranked on a distinct, hierarchical scale: that assault by a stranger is worse than an attack by someone we know. Policewoman Samantha disagrees.

To me, it's always been very convenient to say that you're either a victim or survivor of domestic violence. Now if you're in it and you're amongst the thick of it, then, to a certain extent, you *are* surviving – just by being on this planet. But you're still being victimised, because you're still within that power relationship, that abuse of power.

There's an intimacy, a trust. It's far more violating than a burglary by a stranger. I've been burgled by a stranger and, yes, felt violated and, yes, I felt a victim, and, yes, it adversely impacted on me. But it's OK to feel like that. It's OK to drink large quantities of brandy and feel rotten.

But with a relationship, there's intimacy and you also look at some of the good times. You sit there and you think, 'Hey, we could have that back. There is a possibility, no matter how remote.'

I think I would prefer another word for 'victim', but I don't think there is one. So therefore, we have to work with the word we have which is 'victim'.

I think women should self-define. I self-defined in my mind when I became a survivor. It wasn't when my husband and I separated, even though I went on to glow in my personal life and to glow everywhere else. I was still a victim a good two years after we separated. I would have classified myself as a victim from the time the violence started till 1989. My whole life was still being impacted on. My whole life was being victimised, because of what had gone on between him and I. Because it spills into other things. It spills into your relationships with other people, in that you worry if a friend doesn't phone when she says she's going to phone, because you think she hates you. Your low self-esteem, lack of confidence stops you going out socially.

Then I became a survivor. It was at my own point in my own time, when I looked at myself in the mirror and said, 'You're not a victim any more. You're a survivor.'

Before she murdered her husband, Kiranjit survived without having any friends or family to turn to.

I didn't go to social services. It was too frightening to go out. Even when I went to the solicitor for the injunction, my husband thought I was going to work. Apart from that, I was too scared to take a step.

We can't do anything. We are fully trapped. We are so weak, why I don't know.

Feeling trapped is intensified when support systems let women down. The practice of many statutory agencies, like social services, is to put the entire (over)burden on women to deal with domestic violence. The abusive men are never confronted. Some workers admit they do this purely because they are scared of the men.

The professionals?

The refusal of the police to act when Janie reported her husband's abuse in 1990 may also have been self-interested. Just before then, though, Janie had a very different experience when she sought help from a social worker she'd known since her daughter ran away.

> My husband got up and went to sign on. As soon as he was out of sight, I ran to the phone box and I phoned the social worker. I hadn't spoken to any of my family for months, she was the first person I thought of. I said, 'Come and get me. I'm leaving.' She said, 'What do you mean?' I said, 'I'm leaving now. I've got all my things packed. Will you come and get me?'

> She was there within five minutes. I just threw everything and the kids in the car and we drove off. She looked at me when I got in the car. She went, 'Are you sure?' So I said, 'Yes, I'm not going back.'

> She just seemed to understand what I was going through. It was only later I found out that she'd been through what I'd been through.

> She took me to her office first. Then social services gave me some money and I went to the homeless families and they found me somewhere straight away. I told them that I'd left a violent husband, so they put me in a place where they had a lodge at the gate with guards.

> Social services phoned ahead and said that I was coming and not to let my husband in if he came. When he found out where I was staying, every single day for three weeks, he came and left a flowery letter claiming undying love. After the first four days, I said to the men in the lodge, 'Next

time, put it in the bin. Throw them away, I don't want them.'

I felt quite safe. I felt quite secure, because I knew he couldn't get to me.

I did agree to go and see him, but I made sure there was someone sat outside in a car. He wanted to talk about arrangements for seeing the kids and he had some money to give me. I thought, 'Bleeding hell, all these years and I've never got anything out of you. Now you're starting to give me money.'

When I went in, he was stood there crying. I just looked at him and said, 'I can't be doing with this any more. I'm going.' I walked out and left him stood there crying. I thought, 'You're pathetic. All these years, I've been frightened of you and you're stood there in front of me crying. You're pathetic.'

Janie was very lucky she got such a helpful response from that social worker. The ability to use her own experience in such a direct and positive way is an example of the best kind of support.

Barbara encountered the social workers who threatened to take her son into care just after she'd received better service from another social worker. He was the very first person she ever told about her husband's abuse.

In order to get into the Salvation Army hostel, I had to be referred by a social worker. So I went into the centre of town and eventually found the social work department. I just walked in off the street, five months pregnant, with my son, a toddler, some clothing of his and a few bits and pieces of my own.

Now I realise it was the Duty Social Worker that I spoke to. I said, 'Look, this is what's happening. I need somewhere to go. I need to get away. I can't go to my parents' home.'

Oddly enough, my mother was away at the time, at some conference or other – probably the Scottish Trades Union

Conference or something. I think the Duty Social Worker phoned the major at the Salvation Army and said, 'Take this woman, she's kosher.'

British social service departments do not have statutory responsibilities for women experiencing domestic violence. Like many other government bodies they do, however, have a legal obligation to look after children. Janie and Barbara had positive experiences with social workers not just because they were believed and their rights to make decisions about their own lives were respected. The fact that they both had children meant that social workers were able to help them. It was also crucial that the social service and housing emergency departments had the resources to provide immediate and appropriate help. From the late 1970s through to the mid 1990s, when all public services have been reduced and squeezed for cash, their margins for providing such apparently non-statutory services have disappeared.

The guidelines from central government to local authorities say that those experiencing domestic violence should be a housing priority. But actual practice is often at variance from stated policy. Some local authorities offer alternative accommodation only if women provide proof that they've sustained a certain level of injury and that they have taken specified action on their own behalf. To receive support in the Women's Aid refuge where Candace works, women don't have to prove anything. And it is the woman alone who chooses whether or not she leaves an abusive man. But like most refuge workers, Candace's job involves trying to find women safe, permanent housing. In 1993, almost all the housing departments she dealt with had the same criteria in cases involving domestic violence.

For a woman to be housed, she has to have a doctor's report of all the bruises and everything she's had. If she hasn't had a doctor's report and even if the doctor's seen the bruises but hasn't stated that down in a letter, how many bruises she's had, there's no help for her.

You've got to have a broken arm, broken leg, some sort of bruise before the housing will even talk to you. A doctor's letter will say, 'Yes, this is official, she came here with a bruise.' That's why the first thing, as soon as a woman comes into the refuge, you say, 'Go to the doctor to show them that you've got a bruise.'

Then the housing will say to you, 'Did you get an injunction out on him, to get him out of the place?' Most men, if you say you're going to call the police and get an injunction on him, he's going to kick you, left, right and forward. And it's almost impossible to get an injunction out on a man. If a policeman tells him he can't come to his house, because there's an injunction out on him, if he sees you anywhere, he's going to beat you black and blue, because you got the police on him.

Then he does come anyhow. He decides, 'Oh, bugger the injunction, I'm coming into the house anyway. The police are not going to be here in two seconds.' He's in your face. The police are going to take their time. You'll be beaten up by the time they reach you and he'll be gone.

So it's really a hard thing to do, to go for an injunction.

You might be forgiven for thinking that there's an official conspiracy to prevent women leaving abusive men, since, in order to even try to get help from the criminal justice system, the civil law and the statutory agencies, a woman has to appear willing to risk intentionally exposing herself (and her children) to even more abuse. Unless she does so, she's got no proof that she's trying to help herself or that she's not making it all up. In any case, in view of most judges' reluctance to issue injunctions depriving men of 'their' homes and to attach a power of arrest when they do, the odds will continue to be stacked against women in the snakes and ladders of officialdom.

Barbara thought she'd escaped bad housing for ever, after leaving the isolated cottage in the Scottish countryside she lived in when she was first married. But a decade on, after her divorce, Barbara couldn't find any local authority housing.

Eventually I got a private factor [landlord] to rent me an attic in the top of an old tenement house that had been fire damaged. There was nobody living next door, there was nobody living downstairs. It was practically a derelict building. It had an outside toilet.

I was back to the cottage situation. Ten years on, with two children who were six and eight, but I stuck it out there. He was fighting for the custody of them. He was in the family home, he had the three bedroomed, semi-detached house. They would go back to their old schools. They would have their old toys. They would have their old friends. I was in this poky, wee, overcrowded, no running water, no bath, no toilet situation. And I was working full time.

Fortunately for Barbara, her husband's failure to turn up in the High Court three times meant she got custody. If he had turned up, remembering her experience with the social workers who threatened to take her son into care when he had croup because she was homeless, the result might have been very different.

When Saroj was in court facing eviction by her in-laws, she was lucky to meet a sensitive, pro-active housing officer.

The allocation officer in housing, he was in court. He heard the case and gave me the phone number of my local housing office. He said, 'Contact these people.' I didn't really know who he was. Though I didn't contact them, I kept the number.

But he got in touch with them and told them to write to me and to go and interview me. They wrote me a letter which I didn't receive, because my in-laws wouldn't give me any mail that came for me.

I had to be out of my in-laws' by the end of July, 1990. About two weeks before, I did ring the number. The man who answered knew who I was and all the details of my case. 'We'd like to make an appointment to interview you.' So they did and got me a flat.

Christine found that her doctor was able to provide a means of escape.

> I went to the doctor and told him how I felt. He asked was I on anything. So I told him I'd been on tranquillisers for twelve years. He nearly had a fit. I'd never taken tranquillisers regularly. I only took them when I got too tense, so wound up that I needed something – which I think was a good thing.
>
> Anyway, this doctor gave me an anti-depressant. Within two weeks of taking it, I felt much better. I got myself a job as a cleaner with social services. I was only earning seventeen pounds a week, but it was a lifeline.

Mary believes the police were responsive because she was white and her partner was black. She also used her doctor as part of her support network.

> My doctor was quite good. I had a good relationship with my doctor. And that was it apart from Women's Aid. It varied between what refuge I went to. I don't think I used any of the formal structure organisations apart from them.
>
> But it's also about being at that stage where you can take information and go 'Yes, no or I'll leave that on the shelf and come back to it in five years' time.' That freedom.

It was that freedom that policewoman Samantha felt unable to exercise.

> I never went to the doctor for the stairs [miscarriage] incident or for the beatings. I never went to the doctor. There were bruises, the odd abrasion or cut. A bit of Germolene and that was it.
>
> So nobody really in my doctor's or anybody knew. Even at the affidavit stage, which was about four months before we got divorced, I couldn't say anything.

The need that professionals have to control whether or not they give support often goes beyond the perceived innocence or guilt of the woman – or indeed anything within her power. Professionals may feel entitled to dictate a particular course of action for her or refuse assistance solely because of the *abuser's* behaviour.

In addition to consulting them about her husband's sexual demands, Barbara found the medical profession to be of varying helpfulness.

> I went to my GP and I specifically asked for the last appointment. I said to the receptionist, 'I'm probably going to be in with the doctor for a while.' She said 'OK, I'll give you the last appointment.'

> I went in and told my doctor everything. I said, 'I think I'm depressed.' He said, 'No way, your problems are not caused by depression. Your problems are caused by what's happening in your marriage. If I give you something to see you through your depression, which is a manifestation of what's happening in your marriage, then it will only postpone the inevitable. Really what you need to do, Barbara, is to go away and sort something out – with yourself and your marriage.'

> He refused to give me any kind of medication to get me through it. Women's Aid didn't exist at the time in my town. I didn't know about the rest of Scotland.

> In the early days of the final separation, my husband had attempted and threatened suicide many times. Once he slashed his wrists. After they strapped him up, the doctor in casualty sent him to a mental hospital. The psychiatrist interviewed him and then came out and spoke to me. 'Take your husband home. Put him to bed with a hot water bottle and hot drink.'

> I said, 'Hold on a wee minute, we don't live together.' She said, 'According to your husband, you do. This man's mental state shouldn't be played around with. You need to

take him home and put him to bed.' I took him to his brother's house and I sneaked out.

Two days later, somehow he managed to get me in a situation where I was with him again in his other brother's house. My husband stuffed tablets into his mouth in front of me, like about fifty of them, two mouthfuls. They were tiny white tablets that he had been getting from that psychiatrist on prescription.

We got into hospital. The psychiatrist was called from home. A policeman went to speak to my husband because he was refusing treatment. The policeman came out and said to me, 'He's needing a good kick up the arse.'

The psychiatrist went in and saw him, then came out and said to me, 'You know what this is about, Barbara, this is about control. He is saying he's not going to accept treatment unless you promise to go back to him. It's up to you. You can promise to go back to him and not go back, so as he'll accept treatment. Then is he going to do it again? Or you can go in there and say to him, "I'm not going back to you." And it's up to him what he does with his life. Or you can go in there and say, "OK, I'll come back." And you'll go back. You know you've got three choices here.'

The house doctor who was on duty said to me, 'A) I can't treat him [pump his stomach] because he's got a mouthful of teeth and he's not in a coma yet. B) I can't treat him while he's still conscious, because he can charge me with assault. I've got to wait till he goes into a coma. Once they're in a coma it's touch and go. I've got other patients and they're badly needing my assistance. I'm not wasting my time on this guy any more. I'm sorry that this is the situation that you're in and I can't do anything about it.' And he walked off.

The ward sister came into the cubicle and there were two student nurses standing at the other side of the bed from my husband. He was beginning to slur his speech. He was definitely going under. He was still saying to me, 'I'm not going to accept treatment unless you promise to come back to me.' These two student nurses were looking at me like I was some kind of a fucking bastard of a woman.

But the ward sister said, 'Right, you' – that was me – 'I want you off these premises in three minutes.' Then she said to the two students, 'And you two, get him off this trolley. Get him on his feet and get him out of this hospital. I'm not having this on my ward. That's it. If you want to commit suicide, you bloody well do it some place else, pal.' She said to me, 'But before that, I want you out of here now.'

It was as though she was saying, 'Everybody else that's spoken to you tonight has given you a choice. I am not giving you a choice. Go.' And I did. It was one of the hardest things I've ever had to do in my life. I didn't know whether he was going to make it or not. It was all that stuff about, 'He's the children's father and what are they going to think when they're older if he doesn't make it.'

Eventually he agreed to see another psychiatrist. The psychiatrist asked if he could see me as well. I said to him, 'Sometimes I doubt myself. Most of the time, I know that it's not me. Most of the time I know it's him, that there must be something wrong with him. But sometimes I doubt me. Sometimes I think that there must be something wrong with me that's making him like that.'

The psychiatrist said to me, 'I can assure you that there is absolutely nothing wrong with you, Barbara. And there's nothing wrong with your expectations of how your husband needs to change his behaviour.'

Choice is a very complex thing. The freedom to choose or giving someone a choice – and more so, taking it away – is not just about control over an immediate decision. It also means taking into account the future. In denying Barbara any choice, I believe the ward sister recognised that making her choose would actually risk Barbara becoming even more controlled by her husband and his abuse – and having less overall choice in her life. But as a supporter you need to be aware that any decision you even think of taking on someone else's behalf can only be done when you have first considered all the consequences – the immediate as well as the long-term effects.

The ward sister understood the delicacy and difficulty of Barbara's situation – an understanding entirely missing from health service rules and regulations, especially those regarding mental health issues. Though lots of practical guidelines and legislation cover this area, like the law they exist largely to protect property and the State from the individual. And as they are throughout the legal system, these rules are applied very differently to different people. There is a long history, for instance, of black people fighting against the racism of mental health practitioners and the racist way their regulations are applied. Women in general are often classed as mad when we rebel against female stereotypes. And when we try to use those rules to protect ourselves from abusive men, all too often it's the men who are protected, not us.

Anita's boyfriend actually told her that he wanted to control her. He demanded the comforts of a home, with her always waiting there for him, even though he wanted the freedom to go out clubbing and take drugs whenever he liked. Anita found that her interests didn't figure when she tried to protect herself from her boyfriend by getting him psychiatric help.

> I phoned MIND and found out I could actually be party to having him assessed for sectioning. So I initiated that.

> I came home from work one evening, saw the look on his face and thought to myself, 'You're not going back in there tonight.' So I didn't go in. The next morning, I phoned the local council neighbourhood office and spoke to the approved social worker [officially qualified to assess a person's mental health]. And things started from there.

> I stayed at a friend's house for about four or five days while this was going on. The approved social worker came round with a doctor. I had to meet them at my flat and let them in, in case he wouldn't let them in. Obviously I felt I couldn't discuss it with him, because he could have run off.

This was the one opportunity I had of actually getting something done.

So they came around. They thought he should be sectioned, but they had to get an independent psychiatrist to come round who could actually carry out the sectioning procedure.

I talked to her first, told her what had been going on, about his behaviour, et cetera. They were only in there about twenty minutes. I was waiting outside, terrified.

It was a boiling hot day. It was too hot to sit in the car, yet at the same time I was frightened that he would come running out and attack me for what was going on. The approved social worker and the doctors came out and left without saying a word to me. The police were outside with a van, ready to take him to hospital.

I just couldn't believe it. I couldn't go back into my flat. So I sat there. Then I drove the car a bit further down the road, so I was out of sight of my flat in case they came back.

I waited for about twenty minutes or so, puffing away on my cigarettes, thinking, 'Now what the hell do I do? I've gone through all of this and I'm just left here.' They knew I was outside.

Eventually I decided, 'The only thing I can think of to do is to go down to the local council neighbourhood office where they originated from.' That was quite late in the day, about six o'clock. When I got down there, the office was closed, so I just waited. Eventually they turned up. The approved social worker told me that the psychiatrist didn't think he was ill enough to be sectioned. However, she said that she had suggested to him that she thought he needed treatment and that he should go to hospital, that she'd got a bed available if he wanted to take it up.

I felt absolutely flattened. I couldn't go back to my flat. There were very few of my friends that I could talk to about things, that were understanding.

By this time I'd got more knowledge of mental illness. The next day I got on the phone to the approved social worker and said, 'Look, what's going to happen? I've got to get back into my flat. I can't let him, even though he's ill, keep me out of my home.' I had to stand really firm on these issues. She said, 'I think the best thing to do is, if you can, give him a couple of days to think about things, maybe he will go to hospital. Give him an ultimatum. I'll talk to him if you like.'

I was in a state where I was too upset to talk to him and I knew it would be difficult. She phoned him and made an arrangement for him to move out in five days. But he didn't. So I rang her again. She said, 'You have to get the police.'

I went down to the police station and told them what had been going on. They accompanied me to my flat, went in without me and talked to him. They came out and said he'd agreed to go in an hour and to leave the keys behind. They came back with me in an hour and a half and he was gone, but hadn't left the keys. But he had left me a note that showed he didn't understand what was going on. It said that he was going to return that evening for his suitcase.

I was too frightened to go back in. I had to get the locks changed as quickly as possible. I was terrified. I didn't know what to do. I didn't know where he had gone, how I could communicate that he couldn't come back that evening to collect his suitcase.

So I arranged for my cousin and her boyfriend to come to supper – they knew what was happening. He would very rarely cause trouble with anybody else around. He turned up, as sweet as anything. He tried to worm his way round me. But he went off with his suitcase.

Anita's struggles with the mental health system have continued. Through her persistence the abuser, whom she believes is mentally ill, was finally committed to a secure psychiatric unit.

But then she discovered the hospital didn't recognise that she had any right to be either informed or consulted if they were considering releasing him. Her security was of no interest to them. Anita is still struggling to be kept informed about his treatment. She has lodged complaints throughout the health service and is determined to get recognition that she has been mistreated and that her safety counts.

Before she threw her husband out and got an injunction against him, Daksha's GP was the first person she told about her husband's abuse. Though the doctor immediately believed her, his only advice was that she should leave her husband at once – the GP thought he was a hopeless drunk. Daksha explained to the doctor that she was too frightened to leave, but she still kept going to him for her injuries. The doctor reassured her that all she had to do was ask and he would provide her with whatever evidence she needed for court. Because she was diabetic, Daksha had an appointment every week with the nurse at the factory where she worked.

> I wouldn't tell anybody at the factory because I was frightened that my sister-in-law who worked there would find out and tell my husband. The factory nurse asked me all the time how I was. One day I decided to tell her, because she said, 'I'm not going to let you go home today until you tell me what's wrong. There is something on your mind that you won't tell me. I am a nurse and you have to tell me the truth. I won't tell anyone here. I know your sister-in-law is here. I will never tell her anything. You tell me everything and I will try to help you.'

> Then I decided to tell her. 'I'll tell you everything that has happened in my house.' She found Southall Black Sisters and rang them up. They told me to leave the job and get out of the house. I left the house the same day and went into a refuge with my kids.

Eleanor found that using the legal system only increased her husband's violence. Almost immediately after she succeeded in getting a judicial separation, he was even able to beat her up in the court building with impunity. For a long time, Eleanor felt trapped.

> I got a new doctor and I started telling him. I remember him saying to me, 'Eleanor, you've got to get away from this man. He's going to kill you, if you don't get away from him.' But I thought, 'Where the hell do you go?' I had six kids. My mum still had some of hers at home. There was just nowhere.

> Then I actually got quite positive, with the support of the doctor, and went to the local council. But they didn't want to know.

> The police were called up, I went to the police loads of times. They said they did not interfere with domestics. In the sixties and seventies, they didn't interfere with domestics. But if I wanted to press charges myself, I could do.

> Nobody ever explained that me taking him to court just meant I had to press charges. I thought I had to personally go and see a solicitor and take him to court. None of this was explained to me. I thought, 'No way could I do anything like that.'

> I remember going to see a solicitor a couple of times, then backed out and never went back again. Then I got positive, brave, and I went to see another solicitor. He explained all the things. That was the time I said I would have a judicial separation. I think I was trying to frighten my husband into thinking, 'She's going to leave, so I'll change.'

> Then I got this friend and I started telling her what was going on. She used to say, 'You're going to have to get away.' I said, 'Where am I going to go?' Then I went to the council again and I said, 'My husband's beating me. I need to get away. I've got six children.' 'Oh, I'm sorry, love, there's nothing we can do. If you go and ask him to sign his half of the tenancy over' – because both our names were on the

rent book – 'we'll let you have the tenancy.' I got bounced off every wall in the house for that, asking him that thing.

I went to the council, to the doctor's, to the police, to the Citizen's Advice Bureau, to the Marriage Guidance, to the social services who said they could take my children into care and that would leave me able to cope. I went to everybody I could think of, even went to the local church, and nobody, but nobody, could help. You get so demoralised.

I remember trying to pay him to go. 'Cause one thing I did succeed in doing was, we were on social security, I managed to get our money split. I told them that he was spending all the money, so I managed to get my money and the children's money. He used to claim his own.

I was starting to save a bit. If we had food in the cupboards and he had none ('cause he drank all his), he'd go to it and I'd say, 'Don't use any of our food.' I knew an argument would develop and I'd get a beating for it. But I was starting to harden up.

But the beatings continued. Then one day I was feeling so bad I slashed my wrists. I remember walking in to him, he was in bed. The blood was dripping, very dramatic. And he just started laughing.

I walked out of the house and into the police station. The blood was dripping, the walk was about a mile, mile and a half. The bobby said, 'Oh Jesus Christ,' and threw me in a police car and took me to the hospital. I was kept in overnight and bandaged up.

They let me out the next day and I went home. For the next three days I got beaten, he kept saying I'd spent the night with a man. It didn't matter that I had the bandages on my wrists. I told him to phone the hospital up, he still didn't believe me.

After three days, I wanted out. I took iron tablets, birth control pills, paracetamol, I took the whole lot. I told him what I'd done and he just went out.

I can vaguely remember him coming back. I was sort of groggy and I was on the back-kitchen floor. He started banging my head on the floor saying, 'Aren't you dead yet, you bastard? Aren't you dead?' Then I think he went out.

I don't really know, but I think I walked to the corner of the road and just happened to see an ambulanceman who said, 'Oh you're lucky we're here.' I got into it and was taken to hospital. But, I'm not really sure. It's like a dream.

I remember having my stomach pumped. They kept me in for about a week. They were waiting for my husband to come and visit me. They had a long wait, 'cause he didn't come. In the end, they wouldn't let me out till I saw a psychiatrist.

I went back home, I had nowhere else to go. I didn't dare tell my mum about it. I knew I couldn't tell my mum I'd attempted suicide. I don't know why, I just couldn't tell her. I went back home and he was very, very nice to me for a few months. Then the beatings started again.

For some reason, I got strong and argued back and really stood my ground with him. The beatings stopped, but the arguments and the mental abuse continued.

I went to visit my mum and somehow, I don't know from that day to this, I told her a bit about what had been happening. I didn't tell my mum all what was going on, I sort of outlined it. She said, 'Right, that's it. You get back tonight, you pack all the clothes and you get back up here with the six kids.' One of my brothers had a minibus and she said, 'He'll come down there, he'll pick you up and bring you back here.' I just said, 'Yeah, OK.' Because you want somebody to actually do it for you.

I went back and I packed all the kids' clothes, one change of clothes for each of them. I remember saying to him, 'I'm leaving you and I'm going to my mum's.' He said, 'Oh, go on.' I thought, 'This time I'm going to get out with the six kids. I am not coming back.' 'Cause I'd never got out with the six kids before.

I went to stay at my mum's and within ten days I had a house, 'cause I went to the council and really hounded them. I had got this inner strength. I went to my husband, quite cocky, and I said, 'I've only come down to let you know that I want half the furniture.' He started laughing. 'All right, you've had your holiday. Get the kids back here.' I said, 'No, the kids are in school and I've got my own house and everything.'

Eleanor stayed with her husband for so long, because neither she nor any of her family or friends had the money, influence or contacts to help her get out. Though what she describes took place in the 1960s and 1970s, her experience is increasingly typical of the lack of choice faced by many working-class women, white and black, in the 1990s. Despite fear of her powerful, land-owner husband and the isolation of being an American in rural England, being middle class did pay off for Anne.

About ten days before I bolted, two friends, well meaning I'm sure, said, 'Anne, he's going to kill you.' I was at such a low ebb, but I think that was the first time I recognised what would happen if he snapped, particularly his wallet being an endangered species. I think if I was still there, something dreadful would have happened. One of us could easily have been dead. Because if he didn't kill me first, there's no doubt about it. But you get past a point of caring, even though you're thinking 'Kids, kids, kids.'

So I moved out and found a London solicitor. They're stars, expensive stars. But they're stars. I found mine through another friend, a very strong personality, whose current husband had had the floor wiped with a very high-powered solicitor from a previous divorce in the mid 1980s.

I was sat there, I had gone down to seven stone, which is light even for my frame. I was sat there like a zombie with my mother and this friend, being propped up with a stiff drink. This friend called her husband who was absolutely crucified by this powerful woman lawyer and asked for her name. Good as gold, he went in, looked through his files and fished her name out of the file. But he also gave me a contact name – a man I'd never met before – this magic-door-opening name. He said, 'Use the man's name, this is the woman solicitor you want. Go for it.'

Doors were opened. 'I don't have a bean. I don't have a pot to piss in. Take me on.' They said, 'If you can scrape together a hundred quid, we'll take you on.' But for those friends, I wouldn't have had entree to this woman, who I hope will see me right.

Elsa's husband tried to persuade the police that she was mad and that all he was doing was stopping her from jumping out of a ground-floor window. She didn't let poor service from the police or from one solicitor put her off.

I think after a while, I had built up my confidence. Maybe not completely, but I had to do something to survive. Then I started going to the solicitors. The first one I went to, I never went back to him. I asked the solicitor to write to my husband to tell him if he didn't change his ways, I was going to divorce him.

The solicitor didn't write to him for three months, at which point things were calming down a tiny bit. It seemed to get out of hand again when he got that letter. It didn't make him any better, it only seemed to make him worse.

My husband got really cross. He went to the GP and told him that I was going off my head – that my husband would have left me except for the children. I didn't know about this the next time I went to the GP. He showed me what he'd written down that my husband had said and told me, 'You're not unstable and you're not mad. You could get a job if you want to.' So I said, 'All right.'

Then I came back home and I stood up to my husband a lot more. He couldn't walk over me as he would have. I went to a different solicitor and he was the type that although I'd be a bit wavering, he would push. When I said, 'Oh, I don't think I'd move to get a divorce.' I was a bit scared. The solicitor said, 'Do you think he'll change?' I said, 'I won't say he will change, but I don't think I want a divorce yet. Because it's so final.' I didn't want to think about a divorce, but things were so bad that you had to.

After that I went out to work. I had my independence. He was never home. If there was a fuse, I had to change it. Anything like that. I had to do everything myself. If the house needed repair, I had to do it myself, after I started working. So I think it was a good thing that I was going out to work. It gave me my independence back.

At that time, maybe if I hadn't been working, maybe I wouldn't have divorced him. I'd have been thinking, 'How am I going to manage?' But I could see that I could manage without him.

One day I had just come home from work. I was sitting down in the sitting room. It was a summer's day and I could hear him just outside telling a man that he was going to throw me through the window without opening it up. I thought, 'I can't take any more of this.'

I immediately went to the phone and rang the solicitor. I said, 'I know I keep putting off the divorce. I can't take any more. Go ahead.'

My husband didn't hit me after I phoned. He used to live in the house, but the arguments stopped. The solicitor put in for persistent cruelty. The solicitor was very fast, very efficient. He got things moving right away.

Self-help?

Saroj didn't get the kind of service that Elsa did from her solicitor.

I was depressed and thinking, 'What am I going to do when another deportation notice comes?' The solicitor never went through my full history. He just kept telling me that my case was weak and that I would have to go back to Fiji, otherwise they would deport me. I received another letter, giving me a date by which time I had to go back to Fiji. So I tried to cut my wrists.

In 1992, someone told me about Southall Black Sisters. So I phoned them and was given Hannana Siddiqui as my case worker. She took me through the case from A to Z – from what had happened in my childhood through all this time. Then she wrote a report.

I know I needed treatment for my depression, but in a way I didn't need treatment. Because I'd made up my mind and no one is going to change my mind for me. I needed more support than treatment. Which I got from Southall Black Sisters.

Though Sally got support from one friend who'd experienced domestic violence, she found others failed to acknowledge what she was telling them.

I think it was when I was pregnant. So now we're talking about ten years after I'd met him. I went to see a marriage guidance counsellor. I went to see my doctor. I wanted an abortion. I was referred to an educational psychologist at the hospital.

I saw her several times. I told her about the violence, but she didn't respond to it. She didn't talk about it at all. She just talked about my relationship with my mother and how I felt when my mother was breastfeeding me. I got really angry.

All those people were really unhelpful. It's like they didn't want to talk about it. I was getting messages from them that this was not an acceptable thing to talk about.

Jean was white and was born in Orkney in 1945. She lived in Aberdeen where she worked as a cleaner. As a child, she had been sexually abused by her grandfather, her uncle, her father and her brother. She had never told anyone outside her family, until she sought help for her drinking.

I saw a woman at this alcohol counselling place in 1991. For all the years, I never told anybody, except years ago, my mother and sister who didn't believe me. I never said a word to anyone else and this was the first person I'd said it to in all those years, about my childhood sexual abuse.

But I stopped going there, because after I had told this woman about my childhood, I was up at this friend's house who also worked at the alcohol counselling place and she said, 'Look, there's a new book I've got.' I said, 'What is it?' She said, 'Child abuse.'

That stopped me in my tracks. She'd never offered or said a book about child abuse before. I thought that first woman must have said something or that she had kept notes. So the next time I went to the alcohol counselling place, I asked her. After she said 'No', she said, 'Well, just enough notes to memorise.' I said, 'Does anyone see your notes?' She said, 'No, we all have different cabinets and they're locked.' I said, 'Has anyone ever been in your cabinet?' She said, 'No.' I said, 'See now, if you were off sick. I go up every Monday morning, say you were off sick that morning, I would see someone else.' She said, 'Yes.' 'They wouldn't know anything about me.' She said, 'But they would.' I said, 'How? Do they have a key for your cabinet as well? I never told anyone about my child abuse, you're the first one. Then this other woman I know who works here suddenly offers me a new book she had on child abuse. I've known her for years and she's never mentioned it before.' She had nothing to say.

Now I find I cannot trust anybody. I thought I'd got to know this first person and that I could trust her. I really put my trust in her and then I was let down, so I don't trust.

I suspect that this friend may even have rung my sister – she had the phone number. Because two months ago, my sister and I were having lunch and she suddenly said, 'Dad didn't actually rape you, did he, when you were young?' I mean after all these years. Maybe it was the recent stuff on abuse in Orkney that was on her mind at the time. I felt guilty because I never told my sister that I'd spoken to anyone else. I don't know, everything seems so twisted.

Five months after she gave me this interview, Jean died from the effects of alcohol and the medicine she was taking for epilepsy. It was the last interview that I did for this book and one of the most harrowing I've ever done. It had taken everything Jean had to open up to the woman at the alcohol counselling service. Despite that experience, she still wanted to find someone she could talk to that she could trust. But Jean had had a lifetime of feeling let down and abused by nearly everybody.

As Alabee left her boyfriend's flat, after being sexually assaulted and beaten with a cricket bat, she found that her instinct about trusting a stranger paid off.

> The minicab driver nearly died when he saw me. He went to storm right past me and said, 'Where is the bastard?' Because he knew it must have been a man that had done it. Then my boyfriend's brother came out and said, 'No, just take her, just take her.' Because he was screaming, this minicab man.

> But I was glad he'd done that, because it made me feel safe. I hadn't really felt safe about getting in the cab with this strange man. It was going on in my head that I shouldn't be getting in this cab, because I don't know this man and he might do the same.

> But he was really good. He took me to the hospital. He stayed there until my older brother got there. Then he said to my older brother, 'I know where he lives. Come on, I'll take you.' He was really great. And he came back after as well, to see if I was OK. I thought that was quite nice, actually.

> Initially when my older brother walked in, I didn't know what the minicab man had said. My older brother said, 'Who did it to you?' I went, 'I don't know who did it. It got done in the street.' I lied. I don't know to this day why I lied.

My youngest brother had turned up by this time and he went to me, 'Who did it?' I said, 'I don't know.' I told him, 'I don't know.'

He took my hands and he said, 'You can tell me anything. Who did it? Did he hurt you?' He didn't mean physically hurt me, he meant rape. I went, 'No, no, he didn't do anything, no.'

It took me months to even tell my brothers that he actually raped me. Even though my brothers probably suspected that I had slept with the man before, it still felt wrong that this man should have invaded me in that way.

It was a really strange feeling. I don't know why I lied. To this day I don't know why I lied.

All of the participants' experiences with both self-help and official and professional supporters lead to one simple conclusion: that the most successful were those who understood what each woman defined as her needs at the time and then did what was asked. Though lack of resources increasingly affects their ability to respond quickly and appropriately, the far greater problem is their refusal to accept that women are the experts in our own lives.

In the late 1970s and early 1980s, when there was more council housing available, the National Women's Aid Federation (now four separate Women's Aid Federations of England [WAFE], Wales, Scotland and Northern Ireland) did a survey of all of their then-150 refuges. They discovered that 60 per cent of women went back to the abuser because of housing problems. With the complete cessation of council-house building since then, the lack of alternatives in the private sector and the reduction in all forms of welfare benefit, the chances are that if the survey was undertaken again, fifteen years later, that figure would be much higher.

What WAFE did do in 1993 was to sponsor a report on how housing authorities in England responded to women and children who came to them as a result of domestic violence. Though over-worked and under-funded in many places, the main impression is of a service staffed by people who humiliate, intrude and send women back to unsafe homes. Even when they do offer accommodation, this is often in unsuitable and sometimes dangerous places.

Other organisations have undertaken smaller-scale studies – of doctors in Aberdeen and legal services in north-east England, for example. Like the WAFE Housing Report, these revealed that, while some doctors and solicitors had well-thought-out and constructive policies towards domestic violence, the majority did not. The services women got were mainly patchy and un-predictable. No doubt, comparable research into other statutory agencies and professional support systems would produce similar results, including a lack of coordination and inconsistencies between services .

Since the late 1980s, the fashionable official solution to the 'problem' of domestic violence has been the formation of 'multi-agency' forums. These are local groups of professionals – usually a mix of statutory agencies like police, social services, housing and probation with solicitors, doctors and even magistrates – and a sprinkling of voluntary groups like Victim Support and Women's Aid.

Multi-agency forums are often initiated by the police through their domestic violence units. Though local women's refuges are usually asked to send a representative, the majority of forum members are from statutory agencies. Of course there is some variation between them. But the ostensible idea of most is to pool ideas and information and to coordinate activities, in order to provide a more efficient service. Laudable, if limited, goals, you might think.

The effect of multi-agency forums has not been quite so benign. Having fairly successfully divided women into guilty and innocent victims, professionals are still being pressured by feminist groups like Southall Black Sisters and by the Women's Aid Federations to improve service provision for all women. By trying to coopt such groups on to multi-agency forums, and by promoting policies that fortify the self-serving nature of the majority of members, multi-agency forums can be a powerful force against real progress.

Multi-agency forums do not lobby for change or for the creation or expansion of services run by and for the benefit of those who experience domestic violence. They do not challenge the division of women into guilty and innocent victims, whose only position is as supplicants before professionals. Such notions have, if anything, become entrenched even more deeply with the creation of multi-agency forums: yet another layer of authority which further distances even the most well-meaning professional from women who are then even farther away from the power to control our own lives. Women remain the focus (and locus) for blame and responsibility. Men's violence, men's behaviour, men's culpability for their own actions are never addressed.

This is not to ignore the work of pioneering feminists in a number of local authorities and central government who have fought hard to force through guidelines that recognise the importance of women's voices in dealing with issues of sexual violence; who have worked tirelessly to create excellent services for women, children and men. But, on the whole, these are not seen as core activities by statutory agencies, local authorities and central government. When funding gets tough, these are the first to be cut.

And like efforts to 'empower' their 'clients', multi-agency forums merely tinker with the system. Real change can only come about through serious re-evaluation of the relationships between professionals and those they are meant to serve. It needs to be acknowledged that professional 'expertise' is mainly an artificial construct based on largely sterile, academic learning. Such field experience as they may have had in their training is usually only a tiny proportion of the curriculum – treating 'clients' like specimen rather than as having any valuable insights or knowledge to offer. Professionals' expertise has to be recognised as deriving from the power of the professional status itself – not from any intrinsic abilities or other superiority they may have. In order to provide as good a service as possible, it is important to address the issues of expertise and power directly.

Women who have experienced domestic violence and those who have worked in the frontline of independent and feminist groups dealing with sexual violence must be acknowledged as the true experts. Such recognition should be demonstrated by giving these experts real power within all statutory and traditional, professionalised voluntary organisations.

This would begin to redress the power balance, opening up the minds of professionals, perhaps reducing their tendency to blame women for domestic violence. It would not, as some believe, de-skill. Professionals might start to question their ideas and practices, replacing them as necessary with those from the authentic experts on tap – ideas and practices that would truly meet the needs of real women's real lives.

Nor would professionals be abnegating their responsibilities. In fact, this process should make them become more responsible: finding it easier to recognise the knowledge and experience of women who seek their support and better able to respond effectively. It would help stop 'victimology'. Coordinating activities between agencies could then be focused through refuges and other centres of expertise, rather than through artificial constructs like multi-agency forums. Dealing properly with domestic violence should then no longer be seen as a peripheral activity.

Of course this doesn't mean that problems are going to disappear overnight. The institutional biases, including racism and sexism, prejudice against lesbians, disabled women, working-class women and older women, will remain. But in beginning to question the criteria by which individuals and organisations make their judgements, we will be taking the first step: to stop dividing women into guilty and innocent victims.

9
Safe women and unsafe men

Afriend and colleague, an eminent feminist criminologist, has a party piece that she's performed on more conference platforms than she'd probably care to remember. She challenges one of the key orthodoxies on which criminal justice systems throughout the world are based: that all crime prevention, enforcement, judgement and punishment are predicated on 'crimes' of interpersonal violence being largely defined as taking place in public between strangers, whereas the overwhelming experience of women is that we are most at risk from men we know, in private. This 'revelation' greatly helps to explain why, for example, women's fear of crime rate is about three times higher than men's, while official statistics rank women as the least likely victims.

As a result of her speech, we were invited to apply for government funding for a video that would look at women's safety from our point of view. So we wrote a position paper which eventually formed part of our grant application to the Home Office. It was critical of all current crime prevention initiatives as largely irrelevant to women's needs and experiences. We said that existing advice ignores the fact that women already go to great lengths to protect themselves. We were also critical of all the experts in videos and the rest of the media being either men, celebrities or police officers, never real women.

Our video, *Safe Women*, we said, would begin to redress the balance. It would re-focus the debate about women's safety within the realities of our everyday lives. All our experts would be real women from a cross-section of society. They would reveal the real risks to women's safety. The Home Office approved the idea and gave us the money.

The finished video's challenge to the male orthodoxy of women's safety turned out to pose a serious threat to some Home Office officials. They hated *Safe Women* and reacted to it with shocked disbelief – which was strange, since the end product was exactly as described in the grant application they had authorised.

Every woman who appeared in the video saw and approved the final result. When the civil servants began to attack us, we were delighted at the depth of the spontaneous support from the participants, as well as from women throughout the activist, statutory, voluntary and academic communities. We were all united in our desire to get *Safe Women* into distribution for women who, at the very least, were entitled to see what their taxes had paid for.

When we met with six of the relevant civil servants we were amazed at the intensity of their anger towards us. One man actually spat with rage when he spoke, depositing globules of saliva on his chin.

The attacks came on three fronts. First they complained that the video didn't fit in with right-wing Conservative ideology (and this from the drooling government civil servant who is meant to be politically neutral). Then they accused us of being anti-male, when by every measurement (including their own figures) nearly all assaults on women are from men. Finally we were attacked for including such 'irrelevancies' to women's safety as concerns about protecting our children.

It seems we are never so scary as when we are trying to define our own lives. In this case virtue prevailed and *Safe Women* has provided increasing numbers of women with an alternative to all of the fear-of-crime-prevention-inducing materials previously on offer.

But though *Safe Women* represents a growing challenge to the idea that it's all women's fault, we are still lectured about curtailing our activities if we are at risk from men. No one would dream of suggesting that it is men who should be stopped from roaming the world, free to impose their will as they like. And women are often blamed if they are attacked: the nagging wife tried her battering husband's patience; the male rapist was driven to it by the woman's miniskirt.

Millions of pounds is spent every year by the British government and the private security industry trying to convince women that we are incapable of trusting our own judgement about personal safety. The subtle, underlying message is that our unsafety is not endemic – that there are 'safe' men and that we are often prey to hysteric delusions about our own danger.

If we feel unsafe in public spaces, we are exhorted to rely on men in uniform like police officers. Yet many domestic violence researchers have observed that men who work in the police and military seem to keep showing up as perpetrators of all kinds of sexual abuse in higher disproportion than those in any other occupations. All the frontline workers I have asked over the last twenty years say this is consistent with their experience.

The only official British study on the subject, completed in November 1992, was Home Office-funded research into the police in England and Wales. It revealed that, inside those forces, policemen were committing serious sexual violence at a rate three times higher than the national male average. More research needs to be done to find out if these generally hierarchical, regimented and inward-looking jobs attract and reinforce men who are more likely to think it's acceptable for them to express their power by violating women and children.

Whatever the reality of women's relative unsafety from men, the fact is that we are always being urged to seek protection from some variation of the very source of our danger. The media, the police and the security industry continue to bombard us with warnings about safety precautions we should be taking. As though we weren't already taking them or had no idea they even existed. The implication is that we cannot know what is best for us, despite the fact that we have the most experience in looking after ourselves and the greatest intimate knowledge of our biggest threat – known men.

At the same time, we are expected to leave men as soon as they become abusive – with virtually no help from anyone. And we are to assume, when we do, that predictable care is forthcoming. Yet as the participants in this book have shown, the barriers to leaving are formidable, and care is anything but reliable.

The most important aspect of ultimate protection from domestic violence – how women achieve safety and leave for good – is rarely addressed by these so-called experts. Maybe it's because the most successful strategies are the ones that women find when we are able to follow our own instincts.

Women's intuition

Candace has described the problems that arise when women are forced to get injunctions. Her belief that women are their own safety authorities derives both from her work in a Women's Aid refuge and from her own personal experience.

> I mean a woman can assess the situation. She knows the man, she knows if she gets an injunction out on him that isn't going to help, to get the power of arrest he has to be trying to kill her.

> What is an injunction? It usually says he mustn't come so far near your house. Now he might be round the corner and you've got your key in the door. Then he's got you and he pushes you in the house. That's it. You can't phone. He's beating you up and then he's gone.

> I've been there. Even though I was strong, I have been there. I thought, 'My God, I've left him, but I'm on my own now.' It takes a while for you to actually get up and say, 'I've just got to survive.' Because you're used to being with him, until you can't take any more.

> And it is until you cannot take any more. Some people can't take it at a certain stage. Some people, it takes more – that they can't take any more.

Before Eleanor enlisted the help of her mother and brother to move out for good, she remembers something that saved her sanity.

It was as if all my strength was used up going for that judicial separation. And when that didn't work, I thought, 'Well, that's it. I have tried.' Then I got a part-time job.

I suffered beatings and everything, but I thought, 'No, I'm keeping this part-time job.' It was in a cake shop just round the corner. My husband used to come and watch the deliveries, 'cause he swore black and white that I was having an affair with one of the delivery men.

He used to stand in the shop while the deliveries were going on. But I put up with the beatings. I was determined to hold on to that job.

Though Molly had a good experience with her local domestic violence officers, she felt let down by the rest of the criminal justice system, especially in matters of her personal safety. She was also torn between terror and love. Molly feared she would become more unsafe if she stood up to her boyfriend.

I went and stayed at a friend's. I went into hiding really. I went to the police station from half past nine in the morning till half past five in the evening. I wouldn't leave. I was trying to decide whether or not to press charges.

In the end, I decided not to, because I was frightened of the repercussions. I was advised to get an injunction out, via a solicitor, but he wouldn't take any notice of that, I know he wouldn't have done. Besides which, at the end of the day, I knew that despite what he'd done I still loved him. I still wanted to salvage our relationship.

He was writing me letters, he was getting messages to me. He was going out of his mind, he didn't know where I was and he hated that.

It all came out a few nights later when he went round to a friend's house and put a letter through her door, thinking I was there. She phoned me up, I was round at another friend's house. I thought, 'He's pestering everybody else now. I've got to stop this.' So I spoke to him. He was absolutely devastated. He said, 'Is it true what people have been telling me? Are your injuries that bad?'

I eventually came back home and then he started phoning up saying that he wanted to see me. I really wanted to see him, but I was still frightened of him. He was ringing me up every hour on the hour, saying, 'I really need to see you. I really want to see you.' It was like he was obsessed.

In the end, I decided, 'I'll see you.' So he came round to my house and he was very loving and affectionate and we went out to dinner. Then all he could talk about was moving in together. He didn't want to talk about what happened. He didn't want to talk about what he'd done to me.

I showed him the injuries I had. I had very bad bruising to the right breast. Even two months later it was still bruised. When he did it, it was black and it was swollen. It was awful and I had to go to the doctor about it and I had to go up to the hospital.

Even then he could not face up to what he'd done. He looked at what I'd got on me and he said, 'You must have done that yourself.' I said, 'How did I do it? Put it in a mangle and squash it?' 'Cause it was hideous what he'd done.

For many women, the first time really is the last, because they are able to end the relationship immediately. But love, as a number of women have said, is not something that can be instantly switched off. Molly just wanted the violence to stop. But she also felt tortured and controlled by it.

One of the worst times started when he walked over to me, very slowly, came right up to me and then just went mad. He got hold of my hair, he threw me on the sofa and he pulled me by the hair. Then he dragged me into the kitchen. He was throwing me from side to side. He was wild, he was totally and utterly uncontrollable. He was going berserk.

He belted me around the head with the flat of his hand. Then out of terror, I was absolutely terrified of him, I got a knife out of the cutlery drawer and I just pointed it at him. I wasn't going to do anything with it, but I thought maybe it would help if I showed it to him.

But it had the reverse effect. It made him worse. He came up behind me. I was still holding the knife, but he was holding my hand and he put the knife on my neck. He said, 'I'm going to show you how it's done.' He didn't do anything with the knife, but he was incensed and he pinned me against the fridge and the wall and he repeatedly hit me with the full force of his hand, round my head.

Everything went black and I saw stars. He's nearly six foot tall and twelve and a half stone, I'm eight and a half stone, there's nothing of me. He could have killed me. I was so scared, I actually wet myself out of total fear.

Then he put a cooker ring on. When I thought he wasn't looking, I turned it off. He'd seen what I'd done and he said, 'No, you mustn't do that, must you? You naughty girl.' That really patronised me.

Then he put both cooker rings on and he said, 'Let's see how well you burn.' He got my handbag and he emptied all the stuff from my handbag on to the cooker. So there was this little fire in the kitchen. I begged him to stop what he was doing in the kitchen, but he didn't. He just carried on.

I was just standing near the oven, 'cause I knew there was nothing I could do to stop him. I had to let him do it. People say, 'Why didn't you try and get out the door? Why didn't you hit him?' I said, 'You've got to be kidding. I would have ended up in hospital or dead if I tried to stop him.'

He started walking out of the kitchen and I followed him. He pushed me back in and then he shut the door. I tried to get out and I couldn't. He was standing behind the door. I thought, 'I'm going to have to smash a window.'

I was looking at the saucepans on the top of my microwave. I thought, 'I'm going to get a saucepan and smash it. I'll probably get cut to pieces, but I've got to get out of the kitchen.'

Then I screamed at him, 'I can't breathe.' 'Cause there was smoke everywhere. Then he opened the door and he came back in. He looked at me and put his fingers on his temples and he said, 'I'm mad.' I thought, 'You are.'

But not content with doing that, he then got my purse and he started taking things out of my purse. He didn't burn my driver's licence or my National Insurance card or anything, but any other bits of paper which he thought were insignificant, he burned them.

So everything was burning. I was really bruised round my head, I had a huge bruise on my leg and I had one on my back. I didn't cry. I went into the dining room when he was burning everything and I just sat at the table and I had to let him do it. I had to let him finish it, finish what he'd come to do.

When he finished, he came over to me and he said, 'You can tell all your friends what I've done, but if you dare tell my mother . . .' I can't remember exactly what he said, but he threatened me.

I said, 'Oh it's all right, you'll probably come back and kill me.' He said, 'You're not good enough for that, I'll maim you.' And with that he left.

Then he phoned up and he said, 'I'm coming back. I want you to cook me something to eat.' I said, 'My kitchen's on fire and I'm in shock.' He said, 'I don't care about that. You'll be in a worse state of shock if you don't do as you're told.'

Molly also felt ashamed. Ashamed that she still loved a man who abused her and ashamed that she put up with it. She found that this sense of shame silenced and isolated her. For some women, this is also coupled with a fear of having no one – that the familiar, even if painful, is less frightening than the unknown – and the possibility of being left with nothing.

Though Christine was in fear of her husband, especially after he got away with raping her daughter, on occasion she did stand up to him.

He said, 'Go on, hit me.' And I did, I hit him and I lifted him off the ground and he fell on the floor. He was so shocked that he did nothing.

That happened again later on in life, that I stood up to him, about two other times. He never retaliated, he just backed down.

I don't understand, I think I've got to ask myself about why I didn't learn a lesson from that and stand up to him completely.

Perhaps Christine didn't stand up to her husband more often because deep down she knew when it would work and when it wouldn't. Though Anita believes her boyfriend suffered from mental illness, she was glad she stood up to him.

I did put my foot down. I began to realise, having never been involved in that sort of situation before, you think violence is a one-off thing. Now I know it's not a one-off thing, once it's there it's there and it's not going to go away.

That's when it dawned on me and I did make it clear to him that I could not be in a relationship where there was fear and violence.

I wouldn't accept it and I was incredibly brave. I don't know how I was so brave. I don't think I could go through any of that ever again now. But gradually he was a lot better.

Standing up to an abuser on one's own is a very complex thing to do. The possibility of escalating or prolonging the violence is too great for many women to risk. And just because standing up worked once doesn't mean it will work again.

But the opposite can also happen. Some men become more abusive when women are passive. Indeed, nearly all the battered women and frontline workers I have ever asked said that this was often the case. Finding safety – wherever and however it is for each woman – is the only answer.

The last time

Southall Black Sisters found Daksha space in a refuge after she told the nurse at work about her husband's abuse.

> This place was really nice – fine and clean. There were three or four women with kids. They were nice people.
>
> I got the kids into school. We lived there three months like a holiday. I enjoyed that and didn't want to go back. Being there gave me strength. I got custody of the children. I got the solicitor to send my husband a letter telling him that I wanted him out of my home. I fought with my husband and got him out of my flat.
>
> After we were divorced, I saw him in the street and he started threatening me. 'I'm going to kill you because you divorced me.' Before I would have been frightened, but now I've got guts. People in the road asked me, 'Can I call the police?' I said, 'No. He's going, don't worry. I am not in fear of him now.'

For Eleanor it was a gradual process. It took a number of incidents, small victories and experiences to build up her strength.

> After the suicide and after the psychiatrist and everything, I went back. The beatings were still happening, but not as frequent as they were. I remember getting a beating one night and I went out, I didn't know who to turn to.
>
> For some reason, I rang the Samaritans. They said to me, 'Would you like to talk to somebody who'll be able to understand?' That was in 1973. I said, 'Yes.' They said, 'OK, can you make your way down to the Pier Head?'
>
> So I went to this particular meeting place and this minibus came and picked me up. We went round Liverpool, picking up all these other women. They took us to the refuge.
>
> It was full. They couldn't offer me a room, but they sat and they talked to me. They gave me cigarettes and they gave me cups of tea. They gave me bus fare to go to my mum's.

I told her, 'I've just come to visit you' and then I went back home again. But I think that's where I must have got my strength from – knowing there was somewhere to run. Just through going there that one night.

That's what I always said. 'If I ever win the pools, I'll open a women's refuge.' That's where the idea came from. I think it took about twelve, eighteen months after that before I finally left.

Though Eleanor didn't win the pools, she did open a refuge where she and Christine now work.

Anne was finally able to leave by confronting rural isolation and her husband's local influence – he even owned the church which was in the middle of his land.

That was a huge step. It was years of degradation, self-loathing, self-disgust at not being able to wave a magic wand. Mother said, 'Just walk out the door, leave the horses, leave grandmother's silver, leave everything.' I thought, 'No, sod it. I'm not going to just walk out the door with my two little kids, no clothes, no nothing. It has to be planned. I will plan. I will plot. I have got to stay healthy enough to stay upright, to be strong enough, to be sane enough.'

As an added humiliation, I was being doled out my shopping money, weekly, by the farm secretary. I had to go and ask her for it and be handed it out in tens and fives.

Because when you're told often enough that you're mad, you start to believe it. I thought, 'If I ever do get put in the mental hospital, that's it, he's got me then.' Not from the standpoint that they keep you there – it's the stigma. It was, 'I have got to hang on, I have got to look for building blocks.' There were no building blocks there, but I had to believe in fairies. I had to believe that there were building blocks there.

I dithered. I thought, 'Who do I ring? What do I do? Where do I go? How do I make a start?' Pride wouldn't let me go into a refuge – I would have had to be really desperate.

The first thing had to be a bolt-hole. For years I thought, 'How do I do it? He's dealt with so many land agents around here over the years. Who is not likely to ring up and say, "Oh, your missus is on the phone looking for a property".'

'How do I find a bolt-hole? You've got to have a land agent. How do you do it?' There were some people that lived locally, she is involved in the church and has always been a quite formidable woman. But I knew she was also secretary for a local land agent. I thought, 'At least I know her. I'm frightened to death of her, but I know her sort of. All I can do is be at her mercy.'

So I went to her office. I started to explain and I broke down. To my astonishment, just goes to show how weird – and that's why everyone must know that they've got to take the chance, somehow, and go directly to people – she said, 'Anne, stop. Put aside the fact that I'm a secretary to a land agent. Between you and me, I'm a Samaritan.'

Well, you could have knocked me over with a feather. She said, 'Now just take a deep breath. I've got plenty of time. I'll put my other calls on hold. The boss won't mind. Talk to me.'

And I just fell apart. She said, 'Anne, there's no such things as fairies, they don't have magic wands. But we are taking steps. They might be into the unknown, but thank God.'

She said, 'Anne, I'll start looking.' Now there was someone. I probably owe that woman my life. She took it out of my hands, bless her.

She rang around, wouldn't give my name. She combed the countryside. She rang me. She helped me spirit things out of the house. She and her husband propped me up with double gins and hugs. He plays the organ in church and she was always a very austere woman.

She said, 'I can't stand your husband. It was rubbing off on you. We've got to deal with him because the church is in the middle of the farm. But I can't stand him. It's not a very Christian attitude, but it obviously shows.'

I would just dissolve on her doorstep. She saved my life. She found me my bolt-hole. She did it all. She only rang people that she felt she could trust. She would not ring other large land-owners, on the off-chance they might have an axe to grind with him. She did the lot.

Policewoman Samantha feels that the support she got made it safe for her to take decisions on her own behalf.

So I said to him, 'Would you leave and go and stay with your parents or friends for a while.' He went and stayed with some friends which was really good for me. I began to have time on my own to look at what had happened and look at the way forward. And also to start picking up the pieces. Two women who were socially friends of mine, who weren't police officers, became very, very good and supportive. Both had been through a divorce themselves.

I got loads of very, very good advice. They were really wonderful. Stupid things like they would tell me stories about favourite sewing boxes they'd left behind and still bitterly regretted. 'Cause I was saying, 'Oh hell, he can have everything.' They were saying, 'No. If there's anything you really want, you must take that. You must take what you're entitled to. If there's something you particularly treasure, don't let him have it.'

They were very supportive. Even to the extent of just coming round, saying, 'Come on, put your coat on, you're going out for a walk.'

Anne and Samantha, like many others, emphasised the importance of not allowing the abuser to deprive a woman of her valuable possessions. He might not even want the things he tries to keep. It may be just another way of getting control: abusers often smash up the house – damaging objects as well as people – as a way of inducing fear. Life saving is, as it should be, nearly always at the forefront of everyone's mind when a woman leaves. But we also need to remember that women are entitled to furniture and other essentials from their homes, as well as those things precious and important beyond material value. It doesn't matter if it's grandmother's silver or a favourite sewing box.

Though Mary didn't use a formal structure to leave for good, safety did feature in her route out.

> I moved in and out of roles like the therapist, the mother, the lover. The lover went out about five years into the relationship. I was moving in and out of different roles to pacify or to make myself and my son safe within this relationship. Not good.

> But I couldn't get away. This person followed. All your energy gets drained away. Even though you have that little spark, you kind of get to the point, 'I can't deal with any more of this.'

> It came to an end very violently, but I was quite calm as well. I didn't want any more. It was like waking up one morning and it was, 'No more.' But it wasn't easy to end it.

> I went and had my tarot cards read. Not for the future – I don't believe in future-telling. But it was like I needed to build parts of myself.

> I met this very old Romany person. She read my cards. She was quite horrified. She thought I was going to die. She warned me that the path ahead was quite dangerous.

> The violence escalated. I got run off the road. I was followed. I'm walking down the road and then, suddenly, the van'd be there and it would be stopped right in front of me – from out of the blue. Then it would be, 'Get in, get in.' I would get in and he would aim the van for the next lamp post. It was very calculated.

> It wasn't like we'd had a row. I was still trying this softly, softly out of a relationship – trying this friends kind of garbage.

> He locked me in the flat one weekend with him. He'd said he'd come to see my son. If I'd kept the door shut, it meant

he would have been straight on through it. Then he was in here, not touching me, but sitting by the door with a Stanley knife pruning his fingernails – for a whole weekend. Then he covered himself in petrol and threatened to set himself alight. I had to grapple with him to try and stop him. It was quite a horrendous thing to me. Even though it wasn't thrown over me, trying to set me alight, it was as if it was done to kill both of us. To me that's so much more violent: 'This is what I've got. This is what I can do. This is what I'm going to do. No one knows you're here. No one's going to come and get you.'

I was in the flat for a whole weekend like a hostage. It was like I was working with a time bomb. I'm sitting here now, so I think maybe the way I worked round it meant luck went with me.

And I ended it. I wasn't in the relationship any more. I'd made that decision. I wasn't scared any more. Which I thought was quite strange, that fear had gone. It was like turning around and facing my own fear.

I'd got the person out of the house through cunning ways. I got him to go into work and then I'd stay behind. Then I got him to live down the road. There was still a lot of contact.

Then I said, 'If you don't go away and move out of London, I'll have you arrested.' A lot of people started getting involved, like friends. And I said, 'If you do not go, I'm going to press charges about this.'

The police called on two occasions. The fourteen-year-old girl upstairs heard all the commotion and she actually called them and they were there. It was a struggle to get this person away, but they had to go. And that's how it came to be ended, in the end.

Barbara had been reassured by a number of professionals that there was nothing wrong with her, it was her husband who needed to change. Finally, as she looked back over her past, she could see future unsafety stretched out before her and she left for good.

> Eventually he came home one night. He wanted to cuddle. I said, 'OK.' I waited until he went to sleep. Rolled on to my other side. I lay there and I thought, 'I could be knocked over by a bus tomorrow and my life is going to go in front of my eyes and I'm going to think . . .' And it suddenly occurred to me that the next ten years were not going to be any different from the past ten years that had just taken place. I got up out of bed and I quietly put my clothes on and I walked out. And never went back.
>
> From there the children and I went into the Women's Aid refuge. I'd been there once before. It had been in such a state that I went back home. But I knew what I was going to on this occasion. I knew this was the end of the line.
>
> I thought, 'If I have to go in there and I have to throw all that smelly furniture and that horrible stinking carpet out and buy disinfectant with my Giro cheque and bleach and scrub that place from top to bottom, I'm going to do it. I'm going there, because I'm entitled to that place and I'm going to be there until I get somewhere to live with the children and I will never go back.'
>
> I made a sincere promise to myself on that occasion. I knew it was the end of the line. Whereas on the other occasions when I left, although I didn't realise it, because I had nothing to compare it to, but now looking back, I knew then there was always the possibility that I would go back. But on that last occasion, I knew that was it. Definitely it.

Carmina's partner treated her like a slave, imprisoned in a rundown house that no one was allowed to visit. Afraid for her children's health and safety as well as her own, she got the abuser to leave permanently.

> I said, 'It's now time for us to split for good, because what you've done in the past can never be repaired. I don't think

you'll ever change. I'm the type of person, I'll always let you have your own way. So that's no good to me and it's no good to my health. You actually make me physically ill. I need you out of my life.'

So eventually he went to the bar one day. My daughter said, 'Now will you do it now, Mummy. I'll stick by you if that's what you need.' I said, 'Yeah, OK then.' So we changed the locks. But he managed to grab hold of us and was bashing our heads on the door.

Next-door came out, and he's a really big guy, and he actually physically pulled him off the two of us and he held him down. They took my daughter next door and I said, 'Get her to go down to the police, I'm going too.'

My partner goes to the guy next door, 'Will you get off me?' The guy next door goes, 'I'll let you up on one condition: you don't touch any of these women again. I mean it. This'll be the last time you ever do it. Not in front of anybody like this.' My partner says, 'I'm going to go in and pack. I'll be out by the time the police come.'

So my daughter and I went and got the police and they came back with us. He had packed two massive football bags. He sat down and said to the police, 'I've always said to her, "Just talk. Just talk." Now, I'm ready to talk. It could all be resumed and all be put back in its slot again. It'd be a happy family.' I thought, 'Oh, my God.'

The bobby went, 'Hey man. Up your bags and out.' Because the bobby was actually going to search the bags. I thought to myself, 'I'll just have to risk whatever I'm going to lose, 'cause it's not worth it. Whatever he's taken, I'll just lose it.'

He walked out with those two heavy bags. From then on, our life pulled up a lot. Even though we suffered a lot. We suffered starvation because he told social security he was going to feed us, so social security didn't give us any money.

We sat there a fortnight and we didn't know what to

do. There was never any money from social security, there was no money coming from him. What we did, we ate every day what was in the house.

Somebody came to visit us and she's got these little kids. They were screaming and screaming. She goes, 'Nina could you not feed my kids biscuits or something?' I thought, 'What am I going to do?' I said, 'Just go and look in the cupboard, look in the fridge.'

She went and looked and there was no food and she said, 'What's going on here?' I said, 'We've split up. I thought he was going to feed us.' She said, 'No, ring up Income Support and say two words, "We're starving", and they'll deal with it.'

I did and they said, 'He left here saying to us that he was going to pay money.' I said, 'He hasn't. I'll tell you something. I don't want to deal with it. Can you deal with him? And then when you come back, even if it's with two pounds, I can buy bread and milk to feed my daughter.'

Then they sorted out my money and whatnot. It's picked up from then. I've never dealt with him after that.

Janie remembers the lead-up to leaving, asking the social worker's help and the aftermath. Safety and self-confidence were closely connected in all three.

I'll tell you what triggered off my leaving him. We didn't have an argument on the day. The Saturday before we had an argument and he turned around to me and he went, 'You are insignificant. You are inferior to me.' I suddenly thought, 'Wait a minute. I'm not inferior to anybody and I'm not insignificant.'

I think that was behind me leaving him. All the beatings he'd given me, it was when he said that I was insignificant and I was inferior to him. I am not inferior to anybody and I think that's what clicked in my mind. I thought to myself, 'You're not inferior, you are yourself.'

I think I subconsciously decided on the Sunday. I went upstairs and I packed all mine and the kids' clothes into black bin liners and put them in the spare room.

I got up on the Tuesday morning. I decided, 'That's it. I'm going, I'm getting out.' It was the only day I could, because it was the day he went to sign on the dole. It was the only time he went out and I never went with him.

I wouldn't let anybody do what he did to me now. I would think about killing. Like the one I'm seeing now. I've told him, 'You ever hit me, don't go to sleep in my bed, because you will not wake up.'

I wouldn't let anybody do that to me now. I've got back some of my self-confidence and my self-worth. I know now I can do it on my own. I don't need anybody else. I'll turn to my mum for help when I need help. But I don't need a man to bring up my kids. I don't need a man to live. I can do it on my own.

Marian went back to her partner after his alleged brain tumour. Then she invested all her money in a rural business which they ran together. Though she felt isolated and trapped, she also felt permanently unsafe and knew she had to get out.

I think I had an absolute sense of helplessness. I had finally, after several years, got to the point where I knew I didn't want to be with him. I think that may have something to do with having a young child as well. Because she was witnessing all this. I knew I didn't want her to be witnessing it. There were times when he was holding her in his arms and kicking me.

I knew I had to remove her from the situation. I'd got myself completely financially tied up. It took me a long time to realise that if I was going to leave, I was going to lose everything. I think it took me about a year to eighteen months to finally come to the decision that I was going to leave.

I was quite calculated about it. I spent months sorting out my things. Every time he went off to wherever he had to go, I was sorting out our books. Which ones were mine and which ones were his. Putting mine in boxes and taking them over to this little place I rented.

When I had a roomful of stuff which was mine over at this rented place, by this time I decided I was actually leaving. I'd worked out the day I could have the car. He was out somewhere else. This friend went to the rented place and loaded up her car with all these boxes. I met her in a garage and we transferred all the stuff into my car. Still, I only left with a carful of stuff.

Self-protection

Elizabeth felt very lucky that the first person she told was so supportive sharing her own experiences and not passing judgement. For Elizabeth, the safety of leaving was intimately connected with self-discovery.

I started going to the women's centre and went to a couple of women-only concerts. I began to think, 'I feel quite comfortable here. This feels right. It's because there aren't any men around.' It wasn't immediate, but I said to myself, 'OK, this feels good.'

I started to feel good about myself. I started getting in touch with my own body. At that time I was working with my partner as a gardener. I found that the only way to get him to work was for me to work. If I was getting up in the morning, he'd have to.

My body was getting very muscular, very toned. I'd been very divorced from my physical self. I just lived in the top of my head. I didn't live with my body at all. I can remember quite distinctly one night my hand sort of brushing my leg and I jumped as if I'd touched somebody else.

Very slowly I got a sense of myself and what I wanted and where I was going to go with it. But I was still terrified, because I'd never lived on my own I didn't know how I was going to do it. I hadn't got any money. I hadn't got any job. I didn't know what I would do with the kids. They were in school, in college. I'd no idea. I just had this feeling, 'I'm going to be all right. I'm going to survive.'

I can remember quite distinctly being in the kitchen. I was going out and he was saying, 'You can't go, you can't go.' I literally felt my spirit sort of pull out the top of my head and I said, 'There's absolutely nothing you can do. Because if you hit me, I'll hit you. I'll hit you much harder than you can hit me. I'll fucking kill you.'

And he sort of stepped back, this was the first time he was scared of me, and that was it. I don't mean I stopped being scared of him, but it was like, 'I know that he is not this ogre, that he's not all-powerful, that I actually have got my own power and I can use it.'

I was thirty-four then and in the new year, I decided, 'I'm going to leave him.' I actually said that out loud to myself, 'I'm going to leave him and I won't be involved with men any more. I'm not going to be sexually involved with men ever again. I'm going to be celibate.'

I didn't think of women, I just thought I'd be celibate. I don't think it was possible to think sexually of women then, because I still felt so out of touch with myself. But certainly I'd opened something up. I was feeling a lot happier. I didn't know when I was going to do it, but I'd decided I was going to do it. Somehow or other, I was going to get away.

Every time I had time on my own, I'd sort of take the idea out, have a look at it and put it away. But each time I took it out it felt more and more right – and like me. At the end of two weeks, I just thought, 'Yes, that's what I am, that's who I am. I'm not mother, wife, sister, daughter, I'm a lesbian. And this is great, this is wonderful. I felt brilliant.'

He always knew exactly what to say to make me think, 'It'll be all right this time. I'll be able to confide in him and he's not going to throw it back at me.'

We sat down one evening. I felt safe to say, 'There isn't anybody I'm thinking about, but I'm absolutely certain that I'm a lesbian.' He said, 'Well, Elizabeth, you've got to go for it. You've got to find out if this is true. You mustn't waste your life.' He said all the things you're supposed to say, being caring and supportive. But that was the way he always was. Within twenty-four hours, he'd flipped. He was raging and screaming and shouting at me. He was as near as he got to physically hitting me again.

One night he actually raped me. Before it had been rape, but this was actual – me saying, 'No', and him saying 'I don't care', wallop, doing what he wanted.

Very few things that have happened to me are entirely negative. Even being raped by him wasn't entirely negative, because it gave me the power to say, 'Right, that's it. I'm never going to sleep with you again. I'm never going to be sexual with you again. Don't even consider it. I'm going to sleep with a knife under my pillow. I will kill you, I will maim you. This is the way it's going to be. I'm going to leave at some point in the future. I don't know when, but I'm going to get out as soon as possible.'

Elizabeth's experience is not uncommon. Women who come out as lesbians to (ex-)husbands, (ex-)boyfriends, (ex-)partners, male relatives – any men with whom they have had a close relationship – often find themselves subjected to sexual terrorism. Though Elizabeth's two teenage sons chose not to go with her when she left for London – they were at college and wanted to stay in the countryside – all three of them felt the pain of separation. Many lesbians with children face harrowing custody battles and lose because of their sexuality. If a male abuser manages to set up home with another woman, he stands a good chance of discrediting a lesbian mother. While a lot of men continue to harass women after they leave, many abusers take particular advantage of society's rampant homophobia by spreading poison about lesbians, threatening their personal safety, jobs, homes – potentially leading to their complete ostracism.

Tessa overcame her concerns about being stigmatised as a black single parent. She got her husband out of her house, but not out of her life.

> One night he'd been out somewhere and somebody must have said something and he hit me. He didn't say anything, just walked in and he hit me. But my daughters got involved and one of my daughters could have killed him that night.
>
> If it had been a glass bottle, he would have been dead, but it was a plastic bottle. They heard the argument, 'cause he hit me and I stood up for myself. I wasn't taking it lying down.
>
> It took me a while after that and I thought, 'No, I don't want my kids to see me being a punch bag for anybody.' A friend of the family lived in Rochdale and she came one day for tea. I told her I couldn't take any more. She said, 'Get the kids ready, all of them.' Imagine six kids and we all went to her house and slept on her floor.
>
> We stayed up there till the weekend and I said, 'I want him out.' Any man I've ever had, it's always been my house. I've always provided the roof. I said, 'I want him out.' My friend's husband and his mate came back with me. My husband must have been out the night before and got beat up and he was in a right state. I knew who would take the blame for that was me. So I said, 'I'm not staying there.'
>
> My friend's husband said, 'Yes you are.' He went into the house and he said to my husband, 'Out. She wants you out. You're getting out. We don't have to have the police involved. She wants you out of this house, you are getting out.'
>
> He left that weekend and he found somewhere to store his furniture. He came back and he ripped every bit of carpet up in the house that he'd bought. I paid half to some of these things, but he took all the furniture. The only thing I wouldn't let him take was the stair carpet. I said to him,

'It's your baby I've got. She's two and a half years of age. It's her feet, not the big one's feet that'll get cut on the stairs. If you take that you're the wickedest bastard on earth.'

He did leave the stair carpet and that's all he left me. Took everything. I said, 'In three months, I'll have it all back.' And I did. I got myself a job and built myself back up again.

But I had more beatings off him after I left him. I couldn't go down the street. He's beaten me up outside stores, outside shops. He's beaten me up in night clubs. That went on for a good eighteen months. Nobody stopped him.

I worked nights as a hospital nurse. I had to change from nights to go on to days, because he used to know what time I finished. He'd come and stand outside the hospital and follow me down the street. If I wouldn't talk to him, he'd start beating me up and people would just walk past.

My last husband hit me about six months before we divorced. We were in the kitchen and he slapped me. I took a knife out of the drawer and I said, 'Hit me again and I'm going to kill you.' He told me afterwards that day he was scared, 'cause he knew I meant it. I didn't just say, 'I'm going to kill you.' I said, 'I'm going to stick the knife in and I'm going to twist it and twist it. If you pick your hand up once more to me, I'm not taking it.'

Many women share Tessa's experience of the abuse carrying on after throwing the man out. Abusers often refuse to accept that they've been rejected. A woman experiencing domestic violence is most likely to be killed by the abuser from the time she tells him it's over for about eighteen months to two years after they're apart. Sally's husband also continued to threaten her after she left.

I'd bought this house after a year and he talked about coming to live here. He was being very violent. He was threatening to kill me and chop me up and bury me under the pond.

The threats got worse. I believed him. I believed that he could kill me and chop me up and put me under the pond. It felt to me, right from the beginning that there weren't any options. It didn't feel like there were any choices. It didn't feel like there was anything I could do.

I felt at the time very strongly that I'd destroyed his relationship with our daughter. I felt guilty for her and guilty for him. I wanted him to go, but I wanted him to stay in London so that he would still see her.

Marian also felt the threat of violence after she left.

There was no way I could have said to him, 'I do not want to see you, so I am going to leave our daughter outside the door, on the step, for you to collect.' He wouldn't have accepted that. He would have got angry, thrown stones at the window. He would have bashed down the door.

All the time what I was trying to do was keep the peace. Just keep everything ticking over. I knew that if I cut him off completely, he would explode.

I also knew that the woman I was staying with had gone through a violent marriage, too. She didn't want that at her front door.

Eleanor's husband didn't give up after she left.

After I left, it was loads of verbal. He found out where we were living and the phone number. He used to phone up and threaten that he was coming to take the kids.

He turned up one day with this nice, big double bed we'd only had a couple of months. I think it had only been used about six times, 'cause I'd started sleeping downstairs on the settee and he stayed upstairs in the bedroom.

I thought, 'No. If that bed comes into this house, he'll want to come with it.' I wouldn't let him in. We stood outside in the road arguing about this bed. He said, 'I'm not taking it back. I don't need it.'

I said, 'I don't. I've got my own single bed.' I was quite proud of these seven beds – like Snow White and the Seven Dwarfs.

My husband started to walk off, leaving the bed. The bin man was there, so I shouted to him 'Take this bed for us.' The bin man said, 'It's nearly new, love.' I said, 'I know, I don't care.'

My husband was just standing by his van going, 'You're fucking mental, you.' And I'm shouting back, 'Yeah, it's you that's got me this way.' I let the bin man take this new bed. It felt so good.

He came round often. He was very subtle and very persuasive on one occasion. I think I might have weakened, only the kids came in. Then he started with threats to the children. He was going to get the kids, he wanted the kids, I wasn't a fit mother. I was having affairs with Tom, Dick and Harry – the window cleaner and everyone.

He lived about twenty minutes, half an hour away. 'I'm going to be down there in half an hour and I want those kids.' I thought, 'I can't put up with this, threats and everything.'

So he came down and I said, 'Right there's the six kids, there's the bin bags, there's all their clothes. While you're at it, take the six beds as well. If you want them, you have them.' Then I had all the excuses in the world why he couldn't have them.

I had decided to call his bluff and from that day on he used to say to me, 'You're going to turn these kids against me.' I said, 'No, I won't. You'll do it yourself.'

When I left, I didn't take any photographs of the children when they were little. Now they're grown up and married and got children of their own, they want photographs to compare when they were little. I always tell women who are leaving now to take photographs, 'cause he wouldn't let me have them.

I rang him nearly twenty years later. Instead of saying, 'Can I have the photographs, please?' I got on the phone and I said, 'I want my photographs.' He said, 'I'll bring them round to your house.' I said, 'No, I don't want you near my house. There's a pub I often go to for lunch bring them there.'

I took Christine with me as well. Not because I was frightened of him, but because I didn't want to be intimidated by him. He brought some of the photos, but not all of them.

I told him, 'I've told you years ago and I'll tell you again: I'll dance on your grave, I mean that.'

In spite of government public relations exercises and media coverage of domestic violence, there is still a powerful force that keeps women imprisoned in danger, and that is society's fantasy that such women are hooked on abuse.

How many times have you heard the phrase 'She wouldn't believe he loved her unless he gave her a black eye'? A great excuse that says men's behaviour is really down to individual women's problems, personal inadequacies, even needs. The theories of 'learned helplessness', 'battered women's syndrome', female masochism and the 'cycle of abuse' are often used as justification for such remarks. But though research consistently fails to support these theories, they are used to sustain the myth that women are addicted to violence. For which, of course, we need to be given endless safety lectures and/or 'expert' psychological treatment.

If we are too stupid to look after ourselves, the police and the security industry need to keep selling us their ideologies and their products. If we persist in staying with men who hurt us, then we need to be studied, treated and monitored by the medical and psychological establishments. If we can't make our men happy, we need to be sold endless books, courses and gurus who lecture us on our failings and train us with easy-to-follow, step-by-step instructions to perfect womanhood.

Those who benefit most from this myth are abusive men who can use it to avoid responsibility for their actions. The myth also stops blame for the perpetuation of abuse being placed on societies that use it to control women. Men's dominance and women's economic subservience remain, and all those who make money from the myth get fatter on women's misery. And the end result, of course, is even more pressure on women to stay and greater obstacles to leaving.

Yet women keep resisting attempts to blame them for men's violence. Despite the money and power behind the propaganda, we know the reality of our lives and continue to survive efforts to turn us all into fearful, quivering wrecks.

To declare women safe and men unsafe is a highly subversive act and one which offers potential liberation from all forms of sexual violence.

10
A life of her own

By now I hope you're convinced that support is essential if women are to negotiate the external and internal minefields that stop them leaving abusive men. I don't know of any woman who has emancipated herself entirely on her own without help from anyone. No doubt she exists somewhere. And no doubt her struggle was lonely and painful and would have been made less so if someone had offered her support.

Deciding to take control of one's own life is both exhilarating and frightening – scary, because most women know only too well that they are up against powerful forces that would imprison them in abuse if they could. Even the prospect of freedom from fear and pain can seem threatening. Being totally controlled and isolated by a man's abuse can destroy the self-confidence necessary to make the smallest decision, to carry out the slightest independent action.

Women are often accused of collusion when they experience sexual or personal violence. Collusion is an immensely loaded, complex and often over-wrought term. Mostly it implies a kind of equality between the perpetrator and victim, in the same way that, say, the concept of 'family' (rather than 'domestic', 'sexual' or 'male') violence obscures the gendered nature of power relations. However, unlike 'family' violence which exists, it seems to me, only to build lucrative careers off women and children's pain and misery, collusion is a deeper, richer and more important concept to explore and understand – and it does, indeed, exist.

Collusion is about the role we play in our own oppression. On the surface, collusion suggests that at the very least we ask for it, and at the most that it is, indeed, all our fault. Somewhere in between is the idea that we are, on one level or another, willing participants. When someone is accused of colluding in their own oppression, the suggestion nearly always is 'You got yourself in it, so it's up to you to sort it out.' In other words, victim-blame. Women who have experienced sexual violence usually hear this accusation as a duet of their own inner voices in concert with those of the outside world.

But collusion doesn't appear out of nowhere. In women who don't leave abusive men, lack of self-esteem, of inner conviction, of self-confidence, of belief in one's own entitlements to life choices, as well as self-sacrifice, are some of the potent seeds planted in childhood that grow into 'collusion'. Collusion in these circumstances becomes a form of powerlessness – the belief that we cannot change things, that we have no choice other than to go along with abuse. In this way we apportion fault and blame to ourselves and/or let others do it to us.

Paradoxically, surviving abuse for a woman (and children) is often, against extraordinary odds, about accepting/taking/assuming responsibility for her own life and those in her care. This is especially true for a woman who spends years scheming and planning to leave, while being blamed by herself and others for staying.

Understanding that what others call collusion is often a combination of a woman's calculated strategy of self-protection and her feelings of helplessness improves our effectiveness as supporters. Also recognising that we may be confusing our own sense of helplessness and the frustration we feel at being unable to protect her with her apparent inability to help herself, or to accept what we have to offer, will enable each supporter to customise the suggestions in this book for themselves.

It is all too easy to give advice and offer help to someone without considering what that person actually needs or wants. In order to be truly supportive, we not only have to look at the needs of other people, but also at why it is that we don't automatically consider their wishes in the first place.

The desire to give support, like charity, is not essentially selfless. It makes us feel better to imagine that we are doing good for others. And we need to recognise that we get irritated, angry and feel like giving up when our support is rejected – that we are threatened when, after we decide what's best for someone else, she ignores us. And like charity, support can be both pernicious and insidious, imprisoning women in misery by imposing moral sanctions, by exploiting economic superiority and by dictating how they should conduct their lives.

In order to be effective supporters it's important to recognise the inequality in 'helping' others. This imbalance of power can only be shifted when supporters make a conscious effort to give it up, beginning with asking themselves *why* they are being supporters, *what* they are getting out of it and *who* will really benefit from their support. By questioning our own motives, we can learn to recognise what it is that women who have experienced domestic violence really want and need from us.

Redressing this imbalance also means we can begin moving on from ideas which suggest that women who experience domestic violence are somehow genetically programmed to be, or bred into, pathological creatures, individually treatable for a condition or a sickness that has 'driven' them to be unable to leave abusive men; that there will be a magic pill or form of treatment that will 'cure' the disease. We should be very suspicious of self-serving therapists peddling handy homily-like 'answers' to women experiencing domestic violence. I hope this book has already convinced you that staying with an abusive man is not determined by each individual woman's wishes or desires, nor that domestic violence turns women into unitary zombies.

All this is not to say that experiencing domestic violence is not enormously damaging. A friend once challenged me when I was unable to understand how those who had experienced oppression could turn around and oppress others. 'Whoever told you,' she said, 'that suffering ennobles people? Suffering,' she continued, 'damages.' As a supporter, although you should resist being controlling and condescending, you must also try not to turn women who have experienced domestic violence into martyrs. No woman will benefit from being atomised as a sufferer – whether in pity or on a pedestal. Tell her that you care, that she is worth worrying about, even that you fear for her safety.

An effective supporter enables a woman to make the choice(s) that she herself wants at a particular time. We all need different things at different times. Women negotiate men's violence for so many reasons and in so many ways. Not only do needs differ, the paths we take differ too.

We also need to understand that we relate to each other differently at different times – sometimes giving support and sometimes getting it. This is true even for professional supporters. Creating an absolute divide between 'us' and 'them' is false and damaging to everyone. As you have seen from the participants' lives, even women in the throes of abuse can be very effective in defending others. Every day isn't necessarily a disaster. It is both realistic and beneficial to recognise that support can be mutual.

The choices open to women are as wide and diverse as women ourselves. They range from the totally informal and sometimes necessarily random support networks of strangers and acquaintances, through the occasional advice and assistance provided by statutory and voluntary agencies, to the more regular support of family, friends and individual professionals. Choices are crucially affected by women's relative positions in society – as determined by combinations of class, race, disability, age, sexuality, whether or not we have children, where we live – as well as what support is available and when. Each woman must have the opportunity to choose what she – uniquely – wants. We need to be relentless in our struggle to preserve what small choice there is and to work to extend it.

Lessons

As a black mother of seven, a grandmother and a great-grandmother, Tessa feels it's important that she has been able to pass her strength on to her daughters.

I have noticed with my girls, they've seen what I've gone through. They've seen I've been a person who's fought my way through life, in one sense, and stuck by them. They're entirely different. My girls won't take that shit that I took, no way. They've said, 'Mum, we wouldn't take what you took.'

I'm very proud that they are like that. I always said to my girls, 'You don't take anything off a man that you don't want. As long as you can go to work and keep you and your kids, don't take it.'

Alabee is clear about the lessons she has learned in the years since she was sexually assaulted and viciously attacked with a cricket bat.

Once the initial shock had gone and the bruises were healed up, I can remember voicing all the time, 'This will never happen again. Ever, ever, ever. No one will ever hurt me like that again.'

I know that I also felt that there must have been something drastically wrong with me for it to have happened in the first place. I had low self-worth. I know I didn't think much of myself before that. But I do know one thing I was adamant on was that it would never, ever happen again to me. I would never put myself in that position where anybody could do it to me again.

For me, I think it is permanent. I think I try to be as careful as I can with partners that I choose. One reason that I would never like to get into a violent relationship that I didn't have the strength to get out of, is because I would never like my daughter to see that. I don't want her to ever experience that at first hand, being the one that looks on and can't do anything – really totally out of control, because she's not able to help or protect me. Because she has this protective streak for me.

Also, I feel that I have got to believe in myself, nobody else will do that for me. There's going to be moments I know that I'm going to perhaps feel a little bit unsure about my choice of a man. But if I am unsure to any degree, then I would get out of that relationship no matter how much I cared for him. I am not willing to stay in a relationship that I think is manipulative or dangerous to me in any way.

I see the abusive ex-boyfriend all the time now. The first time I saw him was about two years after he came out of prison. I was going to a party and he was coming out. I sort of froze. He said, 'I want to talk to you.' I went, 'We've got nothing to talk about.' My friends were with me and told him to piss off.

Then I saw him two years after that again. I was in a night club and he came over to me. He said, 'We really have to talk.' I said, 'What on earth about?' I didn't know it at that time, but he'd found out through other people that I was pregnant when he beat me up and that I had a miscarriage as a result. One of the reasons I'd gone round there that day was to make up with him because I was going to tell him I was pregnant. I didn't even bother on the day. I didn't, I don't know why, I didn't even use it to try and stop him doing it. This is the reason why he kept saying he wanted to talk to me.

Eventually I did talk to him. I did it in such a way that I said to him that I would meet him in a pub, just me and him. I had to do that. I had to show myself that I was no longer frightened. And I wasn't. I felt totally in control of the situation at the time.

Now when I see him, I just sort of, 'Hello, hi ya.' It makes me feel better doing it, because he's totally confused by the fact that I do it.

Getting her husband to leave, so that she could be in the house alone, was a formal symbol of separation for Samantha. But she had begun the process long before she and her husband split up.

My friends have changed radically, certainly since mid '86. Having met feminism and a women's group, I then went out and deliberately took the course of action whereby no intimate friend of mine was going to be a police officer.

I didn't want to be socialising with police officers, so I didn't go to social dos. I didn't go to the Christmas do. I didn't go to shifties [group of police officers' parties]. I didn't go to any dos or socialise at the police bar or anything like that.

I actually said, 'I'm going to make a conscious effort that all my friends will be outside the police force.' And I've retained that. I have one or two relatively close friends and my partner's a policeman, but otherwise, no.

The funny thing was, in 1986, I'd gone to this women's group to talk to them about the police, as part of my duty as an officer. I'd sat down next to this fifty-four-year-old lesbian woman who'd been raped by her lay preacher husband. She was a single mum, she was marvellous. She said, 'Are you a feminist?' I looked at her and said, 'Oh no, I'm not one of them.' She said, 'Have you read any feminist books?' She gave me *The Women's Room* and a couple of others. I went away and devoured these books, couldn't put them down.

At the next meeting, I sat next to her and talked to her. Bit by bit. She had two kids and was trying to get into an access course at university. She was doing a lot of radical stuff, but didn't have transport to her house, a couple of villages away from my town. So I used to drive her home.

It was on those very quiet drives through village roads, late at night, that little snippets would come out. I eventually started to open up and say to her what happened. She would talk about what I had as a person – who I was. She actually said, 'Who are you and what are you worth, tell me?' I said, 'I'm worth nothing.' She said, 'No, you're not. You're worth a lot.'

She was very validating and empowering and she nurtured me almost. Not to the point of smothering or mothering me. She gave me things she thought would help – books on domestic violence, et cetera. She questioned me all the time and really confronted me with stuff I was denying or lying about. All this crap about, 'I was beaten as a kid and it made me a fine, upstanding police officer.' What a load of shit. No child deserves to be beaten.

By challenging me on that, she got me on the adult bit about my husband. Because I couldn't turn around and say, 'No child deserves to be beaten, but a woman does.'

It was almost cyclical. There was this big, hard, super-hero woman at work. Then there was this very small person at home. When I was at work I had to be so big, strong, efficient and career-minded and all the rest of it. Whilst at work I would look back at myself at home and actually despise myself – really push down my self-esteem. That made it harder for me to go back home. I took to working later because I was happier being a police officer.

There was an issue around finances for me. I had my own salary and could have said to the bank manager, 'Right, I want a separate account, I don't want a joint bank account any more because of his alcohol habit and his lifestyle.' He was using up to £1000 worth of overdraft every month. So we were £1000 overdrawn. I was scrimping and saving and penny-pinching more and more.

I wasn't in the situation I've dealt with with some women who really are on their downers financially. That is the main reason they stay. For me, it was, 'What do I do about the overdraft? What if they make me pay it off? How can I afford that?' When we did separate, he cleaned out the bank account and I had to borrow some money till payday.

The greatest thing that stopped me going was the psychological pressures which were around. 'You have failed as a wife. You have failed as a potential mother. What the hell will your parents think? What will everybody else think?' There was that element in society that you are still seen as a failure if your marriage dissolves or breaks down.

The road to recovery is so long that you don't really realise how long it is 'cause you think you've actually managed to survive. You say, 'I'm a survivor.' Then something little and tiny and unimportant will happen and then you doubt your survivability.

I still have difficulty with people who I feel intimate with shouting at me. If a friend shouts at me or raises their voice, I go quite wobbly. Then I sit there afterwards thinking, 'Why did I ask him that? If I asked him that, am I really a survivor and am I healed?'

The answer is, 'Yes, I am.' It's just that sometimes you doubt yourself. Then you say, 'Hang on a minute, what are you worth?' That road to recovery is about learning about your own self-worth as well. That you're worth more than being a punch bag that doesn't fight back.

Fighting back is not necessarily about getting a knife out or putting bleach in his tea. Fighting back can be about making sure that you are looking after you – physically and emotionally. That you are getting support and eating healthily so that you are strong enough to be able to manage that first step of walking out.

A friend of mine once said of her own past, 'I had the wherewithal to get out, but not the wherewithin.'

Molly is still overwhelmed by her feelings of shame at caring for her abusive boyfriend.

I'm one of these people, I want everything done now. I want to get better. I want to get over it. I want to get my head together. I want to move away from here. Maybe one day, I'd like to meet someone else. I want it all now.

Then I look at other men in the street. I've started doing this more. Not looking at them as in, 'He's nice.' But every bloke I look at, it's like I think they've got potential to do that to me again.

It's an absolute mess. He's turned my life upside down. I've got no direction at the moment. I don't know whether to stay here or whether to move. I've been strongly urged to move. But will he hound me? Will he keep on?

Changes

Having stood up to her abusive boyfriend and the mental health establishment, Anita felt she was almost starting again.

> I haven't actually got that many close friends at the moment. I've discarded a lot of people. People that took advantage of me when I was down, to make themselves feel stronger and better about themselves. I began to see those things. But I'm feeling OK about that. I am gradually rebuilding a lot more carefully.
>
> My female friends now are able to give each other support, understanding and an awful lot of encouragement. Changes are going on with various of my friends, where they were in bad situations. Things are getting better.
>
> You've got to change yourself. I'm rebuilding my own life again.

With the support of Southall Black Sisters, Saroj is rebuilding her life too. Fighting against the Home Office's efforts to deport her, Saroj changed her friends for her mother's sake, as well as her own.

> The aunt and uncle who arranged my marriage, they didn't want to know me, because they thought it was all my fault. I stopped talking to them and I stopped relating what was happening in the house, because whatever I told my aunt, she told her sister in Fiji. Her sister then abuses and accuses my mother. I didn't want that to happen, so I stopped talking to her.

Sally did not want to destroy her husband's relationship with their daughter, but she is trying to reconcile how she feels now with who she was then.

> Part of me is still that person, obviously, but I just don't *feel* like that person any more. I feel like a different person. I see things differently. I see the world differently. I see myself differently.

I look back on that person and feel really sad for her. That somebody can be like that, can let somebody else treat her like that.

It is crucial to everyone who works with Candace in the Women's Aid refuge that each woman's perspective on her situation – especially in matters of personal safety – is respected. Though Candace is sceptical about statutory services like housing departments, and the law's ability to protect women, she is clear about the power of real support.

You can't give up. I think what you've got to do is give her support, give her that you're there. Remember, Women's Aid is here. We understand that women keep going back.

So you have to be supportive enough to say to women, 'Look, we understand. That's what the refuge network is all about. You can come back here, even if you go home.'

Other supporters shouldn't give up on women. That's what I tell them. Maybe family and friends need help, some sort of professional help – counselling, Victim Support or Women's Aid. I'd say to them, 'Let us – Women's Aid – deal with her. If she knocks on your door at two o'clock in the morning, take her in, but bring her round to us later in the morning. We'll deal with her. We'll listen to her problems, because that's what we're there for.'

What we do is show subtly that women can support themselves and that they can look after themselves. Like, for instance, we'll take women to the keep fit place. We'll show them how to live healthy and to love themselves. We show them independence, not having to depend on the man.

What happens to a lot of women is that they say, 'Oh, what am I going to do? He's gone, what am I going to do now?' We have to try to show them that they can look after themselves and give them self-respect back.

We also have these flats. When they're in one room in the refuge, it's communal. So what happens is the women all come together and they teach each other how to be a big, happy family. Then you get them in their single flats and they're still a nice family.

What we try to show women is that when they reach the flats, they can't ask us for a lot. They have to buy their own curtains, their own stuff. We will take her to the shops, if she wants to go, to help save money. We'll take her to the theatre, if she wants, to have a good time. We'll show her how to get kids into school; try to get her a job, an education.

We will show them where to go to college, we're very good at that, when it comes to college. We really think a woman should go to college.

Sally advises supporters about what she believes is and isn't helpful.

I think if you'd been in a similar situation yourself, then to share how you felt might be helpful. I think saying, 'I worry about you, I think you deserve better than this. I think you must be feeling really hurt,' or, 'I think you're in a frightening situation,' in a way helping me see the reality of the situation, I think these are helpful things to say.

What I don't think's helpful to say is, 'Yeah, he's a bastard.' I wouldn't think it's helpful either to say, 'This is really upsetting me.' Because that would make me feel like I couldn't tell you any more, I think. At some level you are finding it shocking. That could spiral into some kind of panic or feeling of even greater helplessness.

What I have now is an increasing sense of my own power, the sense that I can create my own life in the way I want. Which includes creating the kind of relationship that I want and that I've got the power to do that.

I'm not a powerless person who's just a victim of circumstances. The kind of relationship that I want might be possible. I think if I believe that, then that's what will happen.

Carmina survived her partner's attempts to starve her, after she persuaded the police to get him out. She also sees herself becoming more confident.

> I tend to tolerate a lot. I tend to let people punish me for things I haven't done. Now, at forty, I'm beginning to stop letting that be done to me. It's really hard, because I'm a very caring person.

> Out of not wanting aggravation, I would rather stay back than have aggravation. I'm trying hard not to do that now. But I don't want to change being me. I still want to be me, but I want to deal with things in a different way.

> Now I challenge conflict and will try to stand up for myself. But I still can't always. I find that in the male-dominated world the male will have the last word. Even if I try to explain that he's wrong, they always turn the blame back on to you, as a woman.

> There is also the constant male logic and lack of basic common sense. It is all in the everyday, unsaid things. So it is in *that* way that I fight, like at work and that. But they always seem to try to put you back down.

Mary was able to prevent her boyfriend from setting himself on fire. She also sought advice from a Romany woman. For Mary, the process of recovery is complex.

> There was no structure. The process I've been through is like a jigsaw puzzle without any picture on. You take all the pieces apart and you're re-arranging them. It's like you somehow have to go through that 'broken' period – I don't really like the words 'broken' and 'fixed', they don't make total sense to me – to re-sculpt.

> In your mind, you move to one place and then you go back and think, 'No, I haven't done something I meant to.' And you might move in another direction. Until you hold on to that fear and emotion and all that pain and go through that period, then, I think, the healing forms or starts.

I'd like to work to the point where I'm not in any relationship. How that will come about, will manifest, I don't know. I think I actually need time, now, because of the healing process.

I know that if anything changes with me, if there's any violence around me within the home, or if there's any kind of remark or anything, I get flashbacks. So that path has not yet been taped, healed. The scar tissue hasn't formed, so there's that I've got to address.

Supporters don't come every time without a judgement. Like the fifth time you've got to pick her up from the hospital and bring her home. It's hard to just go, 'OK, how are you?', without any of your shit put on that.

I think people need people to care for up to a point. But a lot of people cut off at that point. Instead of saying, 'This is really hurting me, to see you like this every time,' and not give that judgement stuff, they say, 'I can't come. I can't do any more.' Then that person is left without their supporter, even though something has happened to them.

The people from my original support network have moved on now. They've gone. The relationships broke down because as I got stronger and they could see that, that scared them. They needed me in that weak position for them to feel like they were getting something out of it.

People who are naturally good supporters have a strong sense of self. If they are then professional as well, you've got a very good quality of support. People who do it properly, every day, are the ones who don't feel the need to be dependent.

For me, I had to go through a long process of working with people to realise where I was dependent. And then to be clear about what my needs are and how I go about them. I'm still developing my strategy – how I deal with people. I feel like even though I've been working with people for a very, very long time, I'm just beginning.

I hope the women I work with get something from me. Whatever they want to take, as long as it doesn't cross the boundaries of my personal self. They should have a look at what I have to offer and put it back, throw it out the window, if they don't want it, if it's no good for them.

I really think, quite honestly, I don't have the desire for power over them.

Elsa saw getting a job as key to her gaining self-confidence and independence. As a result, she believes she was able to find and make use of an effective solicitor. For Elsa, recovery itself was physical and mental.

The first night he moved out of that house I went to bed and my body was so tired. I was so tired, I slept and I didn't want to get out of my bed.

The thing about it is, it took a long time to get over it. I was still talking about him. It took me a long time 'cause we'd been together for a long time.

What helped me, I think, was having my freedom. When I say that, I mean, I could walk out, I could do as I liked. I could do things that I couldn't do before and that helped. I didn't have to ask him for anything or wasn't dependent on him. I could do it on my own.

Elizabeth felt much better after she came out as a lesbian. One friend in particular has been supportive throughout.

She was completely accepting, understanding of what I'd been through and of my sexuality. I could talk to her about anything. I still can. She's still one of my closest friends.

When I was still with my partner, I used to come up to London and stay weekends with her. That became quite easy. I'd just say, 'I'm going to go and stay with her.' I'd do lots of baking, so it wasn't difficult for the kids or anything. All the pies would be in the freezer and off I'd go.

I still felt very confused about how I was going to leave. I hadn't got any money or anything. Then I got myself a job that was quite well paid, so I was able to save.

It was getting harder and harder to go back. Then she said that she'd just moved into a house with a room free and why didn't I move in, too? Just do it. And I said, 'Yes.' Just like that.

I came back and told my partner. By then we were both absolutely exhausted with each other. He said, 'Just go, just leave me. I don't want you around any more. I can't cope with it.'

I arranged for a friend to move my stuff. I'd gathered up quite a lot of bits and pieces around me over the years that were mine. I'd bought them with my money, almost like I was preparing for it. I got dishes and a settee that turned into a bed. It's like subconsciously I was planning this escape.

My youngest son came with me and stayed the weekend. It was hugely traumatic, leaving my sons, my house, my garden, my cats, my chickens, everything. I arrived in London on my own. She was there, but at work. I was very much thrown on my own resources. My son went back and I was alone for the first time in my life. I was absolutely terrified and cried constantly, all the stuff I'd pushed down.

I wept everywhere. On buses, in the Chinese take-away, in the launderette, walking down the street, I couldn't stop. I didn't even try, it was pouring out.

I went to the doctor, told her what had happened and said I needed counselling. She arranged for me to go for some free counselling, but that didn't work out. I tried another and that didn't work out either. Eventually I found the woman I still see.

I've been having counselling with her for three years and she's really pulled me through. I know I'd have got through it anyway, but I'm the person I am today because of her.

I was very, very lucky that I found her. Though I don't entirely think luck's got anything to do with it, I deserved to find her.

The process of healing is not this straight path. It's got all these cul de sacs, you appear to double back on yourself. You need to go back and haven't quite got enough out of it, you haven't learnt everything you need. So you go back and do it again.

Some of us never, ever stop. We keep going back. I don't know what you do for those women, except to say, 'Right. When you're prepared, when you need somewhere safe, here it is. We're not going to judge you or weigh you up or say terrible things like, "Why did you go back? It's your own fault."'

I think it's important not to think that you're ever finished with it. It's a constantly progressing programme of recovery.

The future

Daksha is now freed from the fear of her husband, even though he persistently threatened her in the street and at home. She has charted her future.

To tell the truth, I don't want any man now. I'm happy with my family. My kids and I can be very honest with each other. My son can even tell me when he talks with his father and that his father gives him money.

Before, my flat was undecorated, had no central heating, no fitted kitchen. I am doing everything slowly myself – central heating, fitted kitchen, bathroom. I am rebuilding my life.

I have been involved with Southall Black Sisters since 1987. When women come here I tell them that they have more strength than they know. I tell them that when I first came here, I didn't know how to deal with my life, because I was not strong enough. Now I fight back. I try to help women get the right advice so that they can live in the present and in the future.

Since Kiranjit was released from prison, she has dedicated herself to helping other women.

I do a lot of radio, press, TV interviews and attend meetings. I don't know how many times I have repeated my story. I never get a chance to forget my past. I can't forget, but on the other hand, I want to help.

I think the media campaign is what got me out. It put pressure on the law. I don't have any faith or respect for the law, but for my family, for my supporters – thousands and thousands of people.

I used to feel nothing, but now I feel something. I am a human being. The way I was treated before, nobody wanted to know me. Now people are proud of me. I've got more respect and love since I came out of prison. Before that, the world is not mine. I was just breathing in this world. Now every day I have something to accomplish.

There are so many things I want to do, to say to other women who have suffered violence. 'It's happening everywhere. I've seen so many women all over that it's happened to.' I've met all sorts of women with bruises, marks on their bodies, fractured bones and stitches they got from their husbands. I want say to all women – no matter whether they are Asian, white, African–Caribbean – I want to tell them that they shouldn't live with these men. They shouldn't stand for it.

If they can't leave, if they feel so helpless, they should go to a refuge, to a women's centre or to the police.

I used to think, 'It's all my fault.' Now I know I did nothing to deserve it. I tried to do everything my husband wanted. I wasn't living for myself, I was living for him.

Women shouldn't think like that. Women should think of their own and their children's happiness. They should get out and they shouldn't go back. Be positive.

The fairy tale is always meant to have a happy ending – man and woman heading off into the sunset, hand in hand, gazing adoringly into each other's eyes. What I have learned from writing this book is that there is another, better, kind of happy ending – that of women taking control and making better lives for themselves and everyone else. As Kiranjit says, 'Be positive.'

But, as Kiranjit also believes, it is not enough for individual women to be positive about our own lives. We all need to recognise that a large part of the struggle for independence from abuse takes place outside ourselves. We live in a world geared to controlling the abused (nearly always women and children), rather than targeting the abuser (overwhelmingly men). Until our energies are re-directed to the source of the problem, we are only tinkering with solutions. We are ignoring the reality of abuse – that abusers are usually serial and simultaneous. They rarely abuse only once and often abuse several women and children at the same time. We are also ignoring the natural dynamism of life. That if men are likely to be abusive, a woman may experience domestic violence again. This does not mean she is 'addicted' to abuse. We know that abusive men prey on women. There are any number of reasons why women might be particularly vulnerable – some may still be struggling to come to terms with past abuse. Though many women are able to avoid such men, even for those who aren't obvious targets it is not possible to be vigilant all the time. Nobody's perfect.

Finally, all forms of sexual violence will end only when women no longer fear or feel controlled by men. It is therefore of utmost importance not to close doors/shut out/drop/despair of women who don't leave abusive men. Abandoning her *feeds* on that fear (shame) and control (isolation). It denies the responsibility that a woman has already taken and therefore discourages her from trying to become more responsible. It also denies her knowledge of what she has already done. Knowing and understanding what has been accomplished and what women are capable of doing builds self-confidence and gives us opportunities to extend the responsibilities we have already assumed. Women are extraordinarily resilient and, with the help and support we need, most of us can and do survive remarkably well.

No one can give us our freedom from abusive men. Each woman must find her own way of knowing that it's not all her fault. But friends, family and professional supporters can help every woman to find a life of her own, finally making the world a safer place for everyone.

Notes

1. Kaufman and Zigler, 'The Intergenerational Transmission of Child Abuse', in *Child Maltreatment: Research on the Causes and Consequences of Child Abuse and Neglect*, Cichetti and Carlson (eds), Cambridge University Press, 1989.

2. Kelly, *Surviving Sexual Violence*, Polity Press, 1988.

3. Hotaling and Sugarman, 'An Analysis of Risk Markers in Husband to Wife Violence: the State of the Knowledge', in *Violence and Victims*, vol. 1, 101–24.

4. Star, Clark, Goetz and O'Malia, 'Psychological Aspects of Wife Beating', in *Women and Mental Health*, Howell and Bayes (eds), Basic Books, 1981; Gondolf (with Fisher), *Battered Women as Survivors*, Livingston, MA, 1988; Okun, *Abuse: Facts Replacing Myths*, State University of New York Press, 1986.

5. Okun, op. cit.; Dobash and Dobash, *Violence Against Wives*, Macmillan Distribution, 1979; Dobash, Dobash and Cavanagh, 'The Contact between Battered Women and Social and Medical Agencies', in *Private Violence and Public Policy*, Pahl (ed.), Routledge, 1985; Stark, Flitcroft and Frazier, 'Medicine and Patriarchal Violence: the Construction of the "private event"', in the *International Journal of Health Services*, vol. 9, 1979, 461–93.

6. Dobash and Dobash, *Women, Violence and Social Change*, Routledge, 1992.

7. Utting, Bright and Henricson, *Crime and the Family*, Family Policy Studies Centre, 1993.

8. Dobash and Dobash, *Women, Violence and Social Change*, Routledge, 1992.

9. As quoted in evidence by a chief constable, representing the Association of Chief Police Officers, to the House of Commons Home Affairs Committee on Domestic Violence in 1992, published in 1993.

Practical advice and supporters' guidelines

This practical advice is distilled from my own experience, as well as that of the participant interviewees and those who work on the frontline of domestic violence.

What to look out for if you think a woman is being abused

Single or repeated injuries with unlikely explanations.

Anxiety 'disorders' like sleeplessness.

Physical or mental problems that seem to go undiagnosed or untreated for no reason.

Apparent isolation from friends, colleagues, neighbours and family.

If in any relationship, but especially a new one, the man acts in an extremely jealous and possessive way or if he belittles her.

If a woman says she is to blame for a man's distress, annoyance or even anger.

Any other reasons that worry you.

What to do if you think a woman is being abused

If you've never discussed it with her, find a time when it is safe to talk with her. Your form of words will depend on you and on her, but be as direct (in a sensitive way), clear, calm and unjudgemental as possible, asking if she wants to talk about anything that's troubling her: 'Are things OK at home?' 'How are the two of you getting on?' 'I've noticed you're a bit tired and/or anxious.' 'He seems a bit touchy.' 'Is everything OK?' Then, slowly, try asking: 'Does he put you (your friends, family) down a lot or does he scare you?' 'How do you and your partner handle disagreements?' 'Are you safe at home?', 'Is he threatening you?' 'Are you frightened of him?' 'Is he hitting you?' If she does not respond, stop for the moment, but go back to it another time. If she persists in painting a rosy picture for a long time and you feel increased concern for her safety, you may have to consider more direct and specific questions about instances or injuries you have observed.

Remember that any evidence of abuse may be able to be used in the future. If you can, keep a good record of all the abuse you observe or that she reports: dates, times, injuries, any other damage. With her permission, take photographs of her injuries and any other damage the abuser has inflicted.

What everyone can do about domestic violence

Ring the police if you hear a woman or child scream, or if you see them being assaulted – anywhere, any time.

Ask yourself frequently (and at regular intervals) why you are being a supporter. Examine your own motivations closely. Do you have a need to control others? Are you trying to make up or compensate for your own experiences of abuse? Does someone else's unhappiness make you feel self-important? Does helping others make you feel morally superior? But don't feel guilty if you do recognise yourself in any of these descriptions. Just be aware that the desire to give support is not self-less. Acknowledge that there is an inherent power imbalance in relationships between supporters and supported and ask yourself: why are you doing this; what will you get out of it; who benefits?

Try to remember the following points.

• Some women found it helpful for supporters to tell them that the violence they were experiencing was unacceptable. It may also be possible, with a woman's permission, for supporters to confront the abuser directly.
• Men never have the right to abuse women or children.
• A man's home is not his castle.
• Neither a woman's submissive nor resistant response is a predictor of what will deter a man's abuse. Be clear that male violence is entirely the man's responsibility.
• One of the hardest things to do is to name what is happening. Women's silence about domestic violence is often about the fear of naming.
• Domestic violence is an issue of public concern, not a 'private' matter. Every business, organisation, agency, as well as educational, statutory, voluntary, medical and social institutions of whatever size should devise a strategy that offers everyone within its walls the fullest protection from abuse, and extends the maximum sanctions to abusers.

The single most important thing to remember is, NO MATTER WHAT, do not abandon her. Make her and the abuser aware that irrespective of the (apparent) rebuffs, rejections, hostility and even threats that you might get, you are never going to give up being there for her. That you are always watching out for what happens to her. That no matter what the abuser tries, he cannot isolate her from her supporters.

Finally, don't forget that nobody's perfect – least of all you. You will get it wrong occasionally and you shouldn't be overly critical of yourself when you do. It is highly unlikely that one mistake on your part will be devastating. After all, it's not your fault either.

How to support women who leave, go back and stay

Try to remember this advice.

• Though leaving, returning and staying are most often about a search for safety and security – a calculated strategy of self-protection (financial as well as physical) – be aware that leaving is also about emotional detachment. Returning is frequently a reaction to multiple pressures, such as personal threats and emotional pressure; threats of children being taken into care; concerns about disrupting children's home life, schooling, etc.; pressures from family, friends, community; nostalgia and the need for the security of one's own home, space, surroundings. Staying is often about what feels like the safest option for the woman and/or her children. It is also about the fear of being on one's own; believing that having made one's bed, one must lie in it – to fight or die; feeling a failure; and, of course, a myriad of social, economic and cultural constraints.

• Abusers and society in general punish lesbian women. Mothers who come out as lesbians often face custody battles and other homophobic harassment.

• The process of leaving is almost never a continual progression down a road – it is more like a pendulum or cycle. Leaving and going back are often about a gradual build-up of skills, strategies, confidence and security that will eventually enable a woman to make a safe, permanent escape.

• Returning and staying are not signs of failure. They are often done to manage safety as well as to build up to an ultimately safe and secure escape.

• Even after a woman separates from the man, the threats and abuse often continue. The most dangerous time for a woman – when she is most likely to be murdered by the abuser – is from just before the separation to about eighteen months or two years after the split. Try to remember that the overwhelming evidence is that these men don't change. Don't be fooled into listening to his promises or excuses. If he does really want to change, let him do it once the woman has found a safe and secure place for herself. Even if he gets into a men's programme, there is no evidence to suggest that it will do other than turn him into a more skilful abuser.

• Silence and pretending it hasn't happened can be the biggest enemy, reinforcing abusers' power. But try not to expect a woman to leave as soon as she is able to name herself as abused. Though some women can and do leave after the first time a man is abusive, many women believe they have a duty to stay.

• Blaming her and finding fault with her are negative responses. By helping her to assume responsibility for herself, you both enable and empower her to take greater control of her life. Tell her that you care, that she is worth worrying about and that you fear for her safety.

What professionals can do about domestic violence

Develop, enforce, monitor good practice *rules*, rather than *guidelines*, when dealing with all forms of sexual violence. It would be ideal both to develop and implement these with the independent and preferably active input of women who've experienced domestic violence (WED). Rules rather than guidelines are more susceptible to redress and enforcement by WED, Women's Aid Federations, etc. Work to integrate such rules/guidelines into all organisations and services, and back these by training and sanctions. Draw up the rules in a way that would allow for individual variation from woman to woman, but would also take into account racism, ageism, homophobia, ableisms, classism, etc. The best way for each organisation to begin is by having an independent audit, for example pay a local refuge or Women's Aid Federation to audit its services and to present recommendations that the organisation has guaranteed to implement within previously agreed parameters.

Make sure that domestic violence is not dealt with in isolation in your organisation, particularly if it's a large, bureaucratic structure. Issues about domestic violence should be thought about in the production of all guidelines/rules and in implementing delivery of service.

Ensure that official recognition is given to the following: that women are the experts in their own safety, yet receive no statutory protection from violent men and that therefore leaving/going back/staying is often the safest option; that all services need to be reorganised for the benefit of *users* rather than for the self-perpetuation of the institution, but that this can only be done by users having a real say. The actual nuts and bolts of this will vary (say from social services to housing departments) and will certainly need to be flexible enough to respond to domestic violence as a dynamic process rather than as a linear path with a beginning, middle and end.

Abusers very often never leave the woman alone, so it may be difficult to make contact with her safely. Persevere. Use your imagination. One doctor in America puts a pad of paper and a pen next to a list of basic questions on the wall in the toilet where women go to leave urine samples. They can then attach the paper to the specimen and hand it directly to the medical staff. This has also proved a good way for women who are embarrassed or ashamed to speak out in the first place.

You may feel more effective in dealing with domestic violence if you undertake some kind of group or formal preparation. This could include looking at attitudes – yours and others – about domestic violence: self-exploration, feminisation along with its social, cultural and economic contexts. Building up your knowledge includes being aware of and keeping up to date with all the resources available on political, social and cultural initiatives, research work and media coverage about domestic violence, including liaising with other individuals, organisations and agencies. Develop your skills: learn to listen, to share experiences and information. Work on yourself: be prepared to be self-aware and self-critical (whose needs are you really meeting?). Try to understand the importance of the support that *you* need, of the relevance of supervision in agencies and organisations. It is helpful to have clearly set boundaries of what you can and cannot do, what you as an individual professional and your organisation are and are not able to offer. These can be represented in your remit and in what you openly contract to provide, so that no one is in any doubt about where you and your organisation stand.

Know and acknowledge your limitations – whether these are personal or connected with an organisation/agency with which you work. Don't play God. You are not even partially, never mind solely, responsible for 'curing' situations of domestic violence. Be realistic. Don't make promises you can't keep. It is essential that you have open discussions with other supporters and colleagues and be clear about the boundaries and parameters of the support it is possible to offer. Supporters need support and a chance to reflect on what they are doing. As an individual you will then avoid being isolated and feeling that it's all down to you, and you will be of real value by extending the network of support to include other people. This will provide security within the organisation/agency of knowing what you and it are doing. Most importantly, the more people who are involved the more effective will be the support on offer – and the less each person will run the risk of feeling overwhelmed. Make sure you have a directory of different support organisations, refuges, helplines, etc., so that you can give information on where and how to get as much help as possible when a woman is ready for it. Recognise the importance of appropriate advice on her rights and the availability of social welfare benefits. It may take her days, weeks, months and, in all likelihood, years to use the information you offer. Don't ever give up.

Be aware of what many women describe as the fragile 'walking on eggshells' nature of their existence – of the potential danger that they face in even talking about abuse. Recognise that once it's revealed, it's named and can feel irrevocable.

Understand the associated feelings such as shame, a sense of failure, low self-esteem, fear of being alone, pride, concern for children. Recognise too the social and political isolation of being classified as a foreigner, of discrimination based on race, class, age, disability, sexuality, the culturally, socially and (sometimes) legally determined norms of women being considered property.

Retain a healthy scepticism about unitary theories that 'explain' domestic violence in terms of 'dysfunctional' families: 'cycles of abuse', 'learned helplessness', 'battered women's syndrome', women hooked on violence, female masochism and any others that reduce complex human behaviour into impossibly simplified shopping lists of symptoms. These either focus solely on women's conduct or on the predestined inevitability of violence. Understand that woman-blaming is a convenient tactic for abusers as well as for many political and social institutions that fear women's independence to run our own lives. Consider how these theories distort the reality of domestic violence and therefore the responses that individuals, organisations and agencies have to it. Remember that the overwhelming reasons why women don't leave are because of their knowledge of men's readiness and ability to use violence and threats of violence, as well as the superior economic and social status of men which allows them to stop women going and to hunt them down, often inflicting greater abuse when they do.

Understand that the power imbalances in society, especially those of gender, class, race, sexuality and disability, not only play a great part in the reasons that individual women don't leave, but have a profound influence in the construction of statutory as well as voluntary organisations that are meant to address all the issues connected with domestic violence. That the notions of mother-hood and fatherhood flow directly from the attitudes and values derived from these imbalances. Therefore the origins of what we each believe to be our own roles in society are predicated on our position within those inequalities. So that our assumptions about what families 'need' are often based not so much on adult experience, observation or scientific research, but on the distorted value systems within which we're brought up. Believing, for example, that families need fathers is a powerful article of faith that is used as a psychological, social and economic weapon to keep women from leaving abusers and for women taking the blame for the abuse.

Understand and explore your own position as a professional in the potential role of 'mother', as well as your own experiences of mothering – both as a child and as an adult parent. Think about how these relate to notions of good and bad mothering. This can also help you become the 'good enough' supporter.

Mothers of women experiencing domestic violence as well as those abused women who are mothers themselves need specific and positive support to counteract the universal tendency to blame mothers for all social ills. Help is required to recognise that being a mother is part of their lives but doesn't have to be their sole identity. They can be effective women, too. Mothers need to be supported to build up confidence to combat isolation, to build up/on expertise and strengths they already have. To do so is, in any case, cheaper and more effective than many of the harsh measures taken by social services and the legal system to punish women who don't fit statutory definitions of motherhood. Working with women to increase their own ability to run their lives is certainly better than transferring a woman's dependency from the abuser on to you. Find out what she thinks her particular obstacles are and recognise that these are real.

Work to recognise the individuality of each woman's experience as well as each woman's changing needs over time. Sometimes very specific, practical help will be most useful. At other times a woman will need emotional or even more general support.

Appreciate the benefits of mutual support groups of women who have had experience of domestic violence. Tell the woman that her experience is not uncommon, that she is not the only one, that it has happened before. At the same time, reassure her that though other women have experienced domestic violence, each woman's experience is unique.

In order to provide the best possible support, try to understand and be aware that women's apparent passivity is often an important defence mechanism and strategy for dealing with abuse: by 'invisibling' themselves many women – perhaps wrongly, perhaps rightly – hope this will reduce the threat and reality of violence; by psychologically 'blanking' many women keep from going completely crazy – this is called 'dissociation', and is a recognised reaction to many forms of personal violence. This does not mean that women are not feeling or experiencing pain or 'don't care' and have abnegated responsibility for themselves and their children. Such 'passivity' needs to be understood as normal behaviour in the circumstances in which many women find themselves. You should try to work with women to look at these aspects and to help them explore the meaning and effectiveness of such strategies. Only when women feel comfortable in owning the meaning of their actions, within the whole context of abusers' power and society's general lack of support and understanding, can change take place. This will enable each woman to decide who she is and what she wants. Only then can you help her achieve it.

The myths of common sense

That women ask for it/provoke it/must be doing something to make men abuse.

That because they are stuck in a 'cycle of abuse' women want/need/are addicted to/can't live without violence because of child-hood abuse and that men can't help it because they too are just victims of the 'cycle of abuse'.

That men abuse because of alcohol, drugs, poverty, unemployment, or racism.

That women are abused because they are bad wives or mothers.

That family therapy, mediation, couple counselling, marriage guidance is all that's needed.

That it's all the fault of the men's or women's mothers.

That if women really wanted to, they could just get up and leave.

That it only happens to women who are either too assertive or too submissive; too warm or too cold; too independent or too dependent.

That women fall victim to female masochism/'learned helpless-ness' and 'battered women's syndrome'.

That abuse only happens in dysfunctional, working-class families.

Summary of guidelines

Supportive	Unsupportive
Be quick to act	Slow to act
Believe her	Victim-blaming, believing in deserving and undeserving women
Respect her right to make decisions about her life	Judgemental, disempowering, demand proof of abuse
Accept/respect her choice to stay/leave/return	Tell her what to do
Respect confidentiality	Breach confidentiality
Provide safe accommodation, refuge or housing	Provide unsuitable, dangerous accommodation

Supportive	Unsupportive
Be responsive to hearing what she has gone through	Avoid talking about violence
See domestic violence as men's responsibility	Hold the view that domestic violence is women's responsibility and therefore collude with abusers and, by doing so, become abusive too
See each woman's experience as unique, personal and belonging to her	Assume you totally understand domestic violence and tell her 'I know just how you feel' – effectively colonising her experience
Be aware of all legal procedures and services, rules about housing, social services, health, educational, services, etc. Liaise regularly with local groups, people, agencies and organisations	Work in a vacuum
Ensure that you, your agency, organisation are/is informed and dependable. Set agenda around issues arising through consultation with women who've experienced domestic violence	Respond unpredictably and abusively by being inherently moralistic. Set agenda around preconceptions of deserving/ undeserving women
Question the meaning of the word 'victim'	Take a victim-blaming perspective
Be pro-active – that is create possibilities for women to make demands and ensure that the resources exist to fulfil them	Be reactive – that is do nothing unless forced into a corner and then respond grudgingly, defensively, making women wish they hadn't bothered

Campaigning for change

Campaigning doesn't just involve lobbying politicians and statutory agencies nationally and internationally. It can be done in our own communities working with local services, pressure groups, schools. But just as important are the daily encounters in pubs, shops, at work, over meals with friends, family and colleagues where we can challenge, discuss and try to make things better in our own lives.

Lobby for everyone to be educated and for the laws and social rules to be changed to challenge the notion that women and children are men's possessions. Work towards an end to privileging the nuclear family in all cultural, social and statutory aspects of life – recognising that the 'private' family is a recipe for abuse. Campaign to question the idea that a man's home is his castle and for everyone to live in more open structures which both ensure the emotional, psychological and material health/security of all members as well as giving each the space to develop their own identity.

Work to educate everyone to understand that there are no excuses for abuse. Devise a system to impose sanctions against all abuse and to privilege good behaviour. Campaign to develop an understanding that, though men's violence is primarily their responsibility, society has a very important secondary role in that it encourages men to be possessive and therefore abusive. Everyone has a responsibility to stop men and to support women.

Work to educate children to value parenting. Campaign to stop parents/schools/state valuing and turning out sexually violent, aggressive, individualistic, irresponsible boys. Lobby for all children to be educated to understand that girls' only and most important role is not necessarily to be mothers, but that, in any case, there is no mystique about mother- or fatherhood.

Work to encourage mothering and parenting to be simultaneously valued and redefined so that unrealistic expectations of children, women, men and society are not perpetuated. Campaign to stop blaming mothering for every social ill. Lobby to democratise initiatives to create political and social engineering of child-care and home-care to make it more equitably distributed. Work towards convincing everyone that economic and political parity is the key to all.

Campaign for systemic and endemic changes to be made to the way that statutory and professionalised voluntary agencies and institutions themselves are organised, flattening their hierarchies and opening up their rule-bound, self-preserving organisational structures. Work towards instituting a gender analysis within them, especially when dealing with sexual violence. Lobby to remove notions that see recipients as either deserving or un-deserving – depending on how well, for example, the recipients have learned to play the game – banishing the concepts of guilty and innocent victims.

Lobby for money to be spent/invested in new and refurbished, affordable long-term safe housing, as well as for money to be spent/invested in Women's Aid Federations of England, Wales, Scotland and Northern Ireland to expand/ update so they can accommodate short- and medium-term needs that are already provably there.

Lobby for immigration laws and the rules of statutory agencies that prevent women leaving to be scrapped.

Campaign for women to be able to have the social and financial independence to escape abuse.

Work for society to recognise that women are by far and away at greater risk from known men than from strangers. Campaign for this to be reflected in all legal, social, educational and political structures. Campaign for the legal system to be changed to focus not just on protecting women but also on preventing men from abusing. Society in general needs to re-focus its view that the worst thing is curtailing men's freedom to roam the world free to violate. We need to recognise the limitations of the law: that even if policemen didn't have a three times higher rate of sexual violence than men on average, they would still not be capable of protecting women and children from male violence; that even if the Crown Prosecution Service recognised that women withdraw criminal charges against abusers mainly out of fear, bringing men to court doesn't (like taking out injunctions/interdicts) afford women protection; that even if judges did not regularly deny women powers of arrest on injunctions, accuse victims of causing their abuse, allow men to get away with murdering women they (the judges) deem to be less than perfect, sending men to prison is most likely to make them worse when they (inevitably) get out.

Where to go for help

The Women's Aid Federations are a good starting point. They have information on refuge space, details of a wide variety of publications, and advice on the whole range of national and local services and organisations that deal with every aspect of domestic violence and related issues.

Women's Aid Federation of England helpline – (0117) 963 3542

Women's Aid Federation of Scotland – (0131) 221 0401

Women's Aid Federation of Wales – (01222) 390874

Women's Aid Federation of Northern Ireland – (01232) 249041

Women's Aid Dublin (Republic of Ireland) – (010 3531) 872 3122

Your local phonebook or directory enquiries should have numbers for Rape Crisis, Samaritans, police domestic violence units, Childline, Victim Support, local Women's Aid, etc. Remember you don't necessarily have to be the one experiencing domestic violence to get advice from these organisations – they are usually more than willing to help supporters. Most local councils keep lists of all kinds of nearby services for women and children experiencing domestic violence. Many also have excellent publications covering a whole range of advice for supporters – small and large things everyone can do that could be life-saving. Increasingly, local authorities are setting up their own initiatives as well. The best place to start is with the women's unit, or the equalities or equal opportunities officer. If the local police have a domestic violence unit or community liaison officer, they should also be able to put you in touch with local schemes and services.

Selected further reading

No book is complete. No book can tell the whole story. Here is a list of other sources of information – in addition to those referred to in the text which are annotated as footnotes. **General Reading** consists mainly of classic publications – some academic, some theoretical and others some of each, as well as polemical – that cover domestic violence, sexual violence or other aspects of women's lives in ways that give further insight into why women don't leave abusive men. Nearly all the books in this section have comprehensive bibliographies. **Specific Reading** covers single topic research and analysis, for example about areas like housing and injunctions. The last category is **Official Documents**. This is by no means a comprehensive list of all the research and literature published, sponsored or undertaken by the government. Though particular publications are cited, this section is intended more as an indication of where to look for particular kinds of additional information.

    Selected Further Reading is as subjective as the rest of this book. However, I have tried to recommend material that comes from as wide a range of perspectives as possible. So while I may not personally agree with every word in every publication listed – and, indeed, you will find in them viewpoints that diverge from those in this book – I believe that all the material listed in **Selected Further Reading** has something to offer.

General Reading

Bart, P. and Moran, E. (eds) (1993) *Violence Against Women – The Bloody Footprints*, Sage

Caputi, J. (1988), *The Age of the Sex Crime*, Women's Press

Dinnerstein, D. (1977) *The Mermaid and The Minotaur: sexual arrangements and human malaise*, Harper Colophon Books

Dobash and Dobash, (1992) *Women, Violence and Social Change*, Routledge

Dobash and Dobash, (1979) *Violence Against Wives*, Macmillan

Hague, G. and Malos, E. (1993) *Domestic Violence – action for change*, New Clarion Press

Hamner, J., Radford, J., Stanko, E. (eds) (1989) *Women, Policing and Men's Violence: international perspectives*, Routledge

Edwards, S. (1989) *Policing Domestic Violence*, Sage

Herman, J. (1993) *Trauma and Recovery*, Pandora

Jones, A. (1991) *Women Who Kill*, Gollancz

Jones, A. (1994) *Next Time She'll Be Dead*, Beacon, USA

Kelly, L. (1988) *Surviving Sexual Violence*, Polity Press

Martin, D. (1976, 1981), *Battered Wives*, Volcano Press

Pahl, J. (1985) *Private Violence and Public Policy*, Routledge

Radford, J. and Russell, D. (1992) *Femicide: The Politics of Killing Women*, Open University Press

Stanko, E. (1985) *Intimate Intrusions*, Unwin Hyman

Stanko, E. (1990) *Everyday Violence*, Pandora

Women's Aid Federation (England) (1989) *Breaking Through: Women Surviving Male Violence*, WAFE

Yllo, R. and Bogard, M. (eds) (1988) *Feminist Perspectives on Wife Abuse*, Sage

Specific Reading

Binney, V., Harkell, G., and Nixon, J. (1981) *Leaving Violent Men: A Study of Refuges and Housing for Battered Women*, WAFE

City of Aberdeen District Council Womens and Equal Opportunities Committee (1990) *Violent Marriages in the Aberdeen Area*

Malos, E. and Hague, G. (1993) *Domestic Violence and Housing*, WAFE and University of Bristol

Mama, A. (1989) *The Hidden Struggle: Statutory and Voluntary Sector Responses to Violence Against Black Women in the Home*, London Race and Housing Research Unit

North Eastern Legal Action Group-Women's Section and N.E. Women's Aid (1992) *It's Just A Domestic . . .' A Report on Domestic Violence Injunctions*, North Eastern Legal Action Group-Women's Section, c/o 195 Shields Road, Byker, Newcastle, NE6 1DP

Official Documents

Bull, J – Department of Environment (1993) *Housing Consequences of Relationship Breakdown*, London HMSO

Department of Environment (Homelessness Policy Divison), (1993), *Relationship Breakdown and Secure Local Authority Tenants*, DoE

Grace, S. (forthcoming) *Policing Domestic Violence in the 1990s*, Home Office Research Study 139, London HMSO

Law Commission (1992), *Family Law – Domestic Violence and Occupation of the Family Home*

McWilliams, M. and McKiernan J. (1993), *Bringing It Out In the Open*, Belfast HMSO

Morley, R. and Mullender, A. (1994) *Preventing Domestic Violence to Women*, Police Research Group, Crime Prevention Unit Series Paper 48, London: Home Office Police Department

Smith, Lorna (1989) *Domestic Violence: an overview of the literature*, Home Office Research Study 107, London HMSO

Victim Support (1992) *Domestic Violence – Report of a National Inter-Agency Working Party on Domestic Violence*

BULLYING AT WORK
How to confront and overcome it

By Andrea Adams

'It got to the stage where I felt too destroyed to go on fighting back. Going to work meant I'd be sick, I'd have diarrhoea, I'd start to shake and stammer' – *Student Nurse*

Bullying at work is only just beginning to be recognised as a significant factor contributing to workplace stress – and the costs of this can be great for both the individual and industry. Through devastating personal accounts this book explores the demoralising and often isolating experience facing countless women and men every day. The self-help sections offer important practical advice, organisational guidance and, ultimately, a way forward for all those who value the need for psychological well-being at work.

OUT IN THE OPEN
A Guide For Young People Who Have Been Sexually Abused

By Ouanié Bain and Maureen Sanders

'The most surprising thing for me was to find out that it wasn't some weird thing that happened just to me'

If you have ever experienced any kind of sexual abuse, this book is for you. Plain-speaking and sympathetic, it cuts through the silence and talks frankly about the range of feelings sexually abused young people experience. Including other people's stories and discussing honestly what can happen once the truth is told, it also offers practical advice and encouragement to young people on the road to recovery.

BY ALICE MILLER

THE DRAMA OF BEING A CHILD

A radically revised edition of her international bestseller.

Alice Miller has achieved worldwide recognition for her work on the causes and effects of childhood traumas – particularly with her bestselling *The Drama of Being a Child*. Now, fifteen years later, she returns to this book and radically rewrites much of it in the light of her moving beyond the framework of psychoanalysis. In this new edition she describes how we can use her discoveries to help free ourselves, resulting in a healthy new beginning for us and for our children.

PICTURES OF A CHILDHOOD

The first UK publication of the paintings central to Alice Miller's work

Having realised in the early seventies a lifelong desire to paint, Dr Miller found an unfamiliar world emerging from her paintings: not the 'nice' world of her childhood, to which she had always testified, but one of fear, despair and loneliness. Meditating on her spontaneously executed watercolours – sixty-six of which are reproduced here in full colour – and their implications, Dr Miller offers a profound analysis of the roots of creativity in the authentic self's struggle for survival.

THE UNTOUCHED KEY
Tracing Childhood Trauma in Creativity and Destructiveness

What did Picasso express in 'Guernica'? Why did Buster Keaton never smile? Why did Nietzsche lose his mind for eleven years? Why did Hitler become a mass murderer? In *The Untouched Key* Alice Miller explores with her usual insight and clarity the clues – so often overlooked in biography – connecting childhood trauma to adult creativity and destruction. Her conclusions reveal the roots and consequences of our timeless insistence on obeying oppressive parental figures that include psychiatrists and psychotherapists.